Sam Houston

A Study in Leadership

By Bill O'Neal
State Historian of Texas

EAKIN PRESS ᴠ**ᶠᴾ** Fort Worth, Texas
www.EakinPress.com

Copyright © 2016
By Bill O'Neal
Published By Eakin Press
An Imprint of Wild Horse Media Group
P.O. Box 331779
Fort Worth, Texas 76163
1-817-344-7036
www.EakinPress.com
ALL RIGHTS RESERVED
1 2 3 4 5 6 7 8 9
ISBN-10: 1-68179-037-4
ISBN-13: 978-1-68179-037-4

Cover Design by Flying Gorilla Studio
www.FlyingGorillaStudio.com

Dedicated to three history-minded individuals who have provided exceptional support during my tenure as Texas State Historian:

Mary Frances Payne Murphy, whose Texas roots trace back to the Lone Star Republic, and whose grandfather during boyhood occasionally shared his bed with a noted visitor from Huntsville—Sam Houston.

Foster Murphy, a World War II veteran and an accomplished businessman who, with his wife's approval, created the Murphy-Payne Foundation to establish a history lecture series at Panola College and to assist other history programs on campus—including activities of the State Historian.

Dr. Gregory Powell, whose presidency at Panola College truly has been a study in leadership—gifted, resourceful, visionary leadership.

Contents

Acknowledgments

Shortly after I was appointed State Historian of Texas in Austin in 2012, I was asked to deliver a lecture at the Bob Bullock Texas State Museum in Austin. My invitation came from museum director Joan Marshall, who requested that I provide a presentation on "Leadership Qualities of Sam Houston." I taught Texas history at Panola College for more than three decades, and every year I became more aware of the varied and powerful leadership roles played by Houston. Focusing on Houston as a leader was a captivating assignment, and audience response at the Bob Bullock Museum was most gratifying. After I was asked to deliver the program to other groups, I began to see the possibilities of developing the subject into a book, and Ron Chrisman, Director of the University of North Texas Press, offered excellent advice regarding the direction of the manuscript.

The focus of this book is to trace Sam Houston's evolution as a leader and to emphasize his leadership skills and gifts. Standard biographical information is relied upon, although I believe I added new dimensions to Houston's performance during the Regulator-Moderator War, having written a book on that conflict (*War in East Texas: Regulators vs. Moderators, 2006*). Therefore, footnoting is largely utilized for quotes from Houston or his contemporaries, as well as from Houston biographers and historians.

I traveled to the sites of Houston's life, even though I had visited most of these places—some of them many times—in past years. Accompanied by my wife Karon, I drove to Virginia and the "Sam Houston Wayside" adjacent to his birthplace and boyhood home. In eastern Tennessee I photographed and hiked across the homestead where the family relocated in 1806. Nearby we saw the churchyard where Houston's mother is buried, several miles south of Maryville. A few miles on the other side of town is the "Sam Houston Schoolhouse," a log structure where Houston taught as a young man. Nearby is a museum presided over by Bob and Mary Lynne Bell, who live on the grounds, and who were most helpful to us. At Lebanon, Tennessee, there is a replica structure which represents Sam Houston's first law office. Not far to the west is the Hermitage, Andrew Jackson's plantation home where Sam Houston was a frequent visitor. State museums in Nashville offer fine exhibits on Houston.

In Alabama we toured Horseshoe Bend National Battlefield Park. It was my first visit in nearly four decades, and there were many improvements. A couple of hours to the east is Marion, home town of Margaret Lea Houston. The director of the Chamber of Commerce, John L. Martin, guided us to the Lea home where Margaret wed Houston, to the college she attended, and to the boarding house he stayed in on trips to Marion. In Oklahoma we visited Fort Gibson and the grave of Tiana Rogers, along with Fort Towson, where Houston departed Indian Territory to cross the Red River into Texas.

In Texas, of course, there are a great many Houston sites. Among the most important are Nacogdoches and San Augustine, as well as the Halfway House Stagecoach Inn between them; Washington-on-the-Brazos, with its replica of Independence Hall, Anson Jones plantation complex, and the Star of Texas Museum; and of course the San Jacinto Battlefield and Monument. In Huntsville are Houston's favorite home, the house in which he died, his impressive gravesite, museums, and an enormous statue. Mac Woodward, director of Huntsville's Sam Houston Memorial Museum, answered my questions with patient command of all Houstonian matters. He explained to me that the museum staff regularly meets to discuss various aspects of Houston's personality or achievements or problems. He pointed out to me that Houston knew and had contact with fourteen United States presidents. We speculated on how this exposure and interaction with leaders at the highest level influenced Houston, and I explored this topic in Chapter Four. Sam Houston Regional Library near Liberty is a repository for more Houston images than in any other institution.

At every step on the trail of Houston I was enlightened in ways large and small. From museum and park officials I received information and printed materials and directions, and I am indebted to everyone who aided a fellow Houston enthusiast. My wife and I shot hundreds of photographs along the way, and here and there I sensed a few ghosts from Houston's past.

My office as State Historian is located on the campus of Panola College in Carthage, where I taught history and where my wife is a member of the math faculty. Sherri Baker, research librarian at Panola, applied her formidable detective skills in locating obscure sources for me through interlibrary loan service. I engaged Jessica Liles, a Panola student who performs secretarial work for my wife, to convert a major portion of my pencil and pad manuscript to electronic form, and she was conscientious and efficient.

Billy Huckaby, head of the Wild Horse Media Group, which now includes Eakin Press, graciously agreed to publish this book. Billy shared my vision of this approach to Sam Houston, and he and his staff produced a handsome volume with efficiency and dispatch. It was a pleasure to work with such a masterful group of professionals.

My wife Karon converted the balance of my manuscript to the requirements of the publisher. She shot a number of photographs, and because she traveled with me she was especially useful as a sounding board as this project developed. Karon provided perspective and advice, and my debt to her is deep and heartfelt.

What Historians Said About Sam Houston

One figure only stands like a colossus astride the middle decades of the 1800s: Sam Houston.

James L. Haley
Author of *Sam Houston* (p. xi)

He was one of the first truly remarkable public figures in America. From his first term as a congressman from Tennessee, beginning in 1823, until he was deposed from the governorship of Texas in 1861, he was constantly in the news. His protestations to the contrary, he clearly enjoyed the attention.

Marshall De Bruhl
Author of *Sword of San Jacinto, A Life of Sam Houston* (pp. xi – xii)

He was bold and intelligent, a finished master of guile and deception. He was always a diplomat and in crises he was much of a statesman and never a scoundrel. . . His tongue was mobile and persuasive and his pen facile and compelling in its logic, but his gift of silence – which often passed for consent – amounted to genius. He was all things to all men; Indian to Indians, frontiersman to frontiersmen, and spokesman of all people, general to soldiers, a political seer, and a talented actor who knew how and when to wear an Indian blanket, lion-skin coat, or a dress suit. Whether we like him or not in no way alters the fact that Sam Houston was no ordinary man.

Walter Prescott Webb
Author of *The Texas Rangers* (pp. 203-204)

Tragedies that would have overwhelmed lesser men had tempered [Houston's] strength. In each of his crises, his rugged courage prevailed. . . In countless numbers, his enemies had leveled every possible accusation at this gigantic target. But his record stands today, as it did then, a challenge to his critics.

M. K. Wisehart
Author of *Sam Houston, American Giant* (p. 649)

He was a difficult man for even his own age to understand; genius always is.

T. R. Fehrenbach
Author of *Lone Star, The Story of Texas and the Texans* (p. 349)

[F]ew men in American history have done more to widen their circle of political activity than [Houston], and within his circle he was singularly powerful in accomplishment and independent in thought. He branded his mark on Texas and left an indelible trace in our nation's history.

Llerena B. Friend
Author of *Sam Houston,*
The Great Designer, (p. 354)

Outside of his social circle on public occasions he drew the multitude to him by the power of his oratory. No man ever listened to him that was not desirous of hearing him again. The charm of his imposing presence and impressive manner drew people to him, and he knew well how to hold and entertain them.

Gov. Francis Lubbock
Author of *Six Decades in Texas* (pp. 73-74)

[Houston] would have been an impressive man in any company; here he rose to commander-in-chief of the Texas forces. But as he retreated steadily before Santa Anna, many soldiers and civilians alike had decided he was cowardly. When his Fabian tactics brought total victory in an 18-minute battle at San Jacinto, many others hailed Houston as a genius. His detractors regarded him as lucky.

Joe B. Frantz
Author of *Texas* (p. 75)

Had Texas and politics not intervened, Sam Houston could have been the Barrymore of the age. Nature had equipped him with a commanding physique, a powerful voice, and the mind of a perennial student. With a memory as broad as Texas, he developed an unusual mastery of words and a workable understanding of classic drama. These he accented by singular dress. But above all, he was astute in every means of moving men by his emotion.

Sue Flanagan
Author of *Sam Houston's Texas* (p. 133)

Houston expressed courage, not just the physical courage to lead men into battle but also the moral courage to stand for his beliefs regardless of the consequences. He had the kind of ambition and pride that leads men to excel. He liked to command; other men saw him as a commander, and in leadership positions, he would never do anything unworthy.

Randolph B. Campbell
Author of *Sam Houston and the*
American Southwest (p. 99)

Military and Public Service of Sam Houston

- U.S. Army: private, sergeant, ensign, lieutenant (1813-18)
- Adjutant general and colonel, Tennessee State Militia (1818)
- Prosecuting attorney of the District of Nashville (1819-20)
- Major general of the Tennessee State Militia (1821-23)
- U.S. congressman from Tennessee (1823-27)
- Governor of Tennessee (1827-29)
- Cherokee tribal emissary (1830-32)
- Delegate to Texas Convention of 1833 (April 1833)
- Delegate to Consultation of 1835 (October and November, 1835)
- Major general of Texas revolutionary army (1835-36)
- Delegate to Independence Convention at Washington-on-the-Brazos (March 1836)
- President of the Republic of Texas (1836-38)
- Congressman of the Republic of Texas (1839-41)
- President of the Republic of Texas (1841-44)
- U.S. Senator from Texas (1846-59)
- Governor of Texas (1859-61)

I could not be gotten into a schoolhouse until I was eight years old,
nor did I accomplish much after I started.

Sam Houston

Chapter One

The Making of a Leader

Sam Houston radiated leadership.

Physically imposing and a man of powerful convictions, Houston gravitated to leadership roles throughout his adventurous life. At twenty-one, Lieutenant Houston was wounded three times while leading charges at Horseshoe Bend. More than two decades later General Houston was badly wounded while leading the spectacular victory at San Jacinto. A prolific public life placed him in both the United States House of Representatives and the U.S. Senate, the governorship of both Tennessee and Texas, and the presidency of the Lone Star Republic—twice.

The leadership roles, the leadership qualities of Sam Houston are remarkable, historically significant, and worthy of examination.

• • • •

Samuel Houston was born on March 2, 1793, on the Timber Ridge plantation begun by John Houston, Sam's great-grandfather, in the mountainous frontier of western Virginia. Timber Ridge was located eight miles northeast of Lexington, the seat of Rockbridge County. Named after his father, Sam was the fifth son of Samuel and Elizabeth Houston. There would be another boy and three girls, so Sam was the middle of nine children. But there was nothing of the tranquil temperament of a typical middle child in his assertive, independent, ambitious Type A personality. Sam loved the forested hills that surrounded Timber Ridge, and he enjoyed boyhood adventures in the nearby wilderness.

Young Sam was strongly influenced by his father. As a young

man during the American Revolution, Samuel Houston enlisted in the patriotic cause, serving ably under fellow Virginian Daniel Morgan. Morgan had been a member of the Virginia Militia since the French and Indian War, and when the Revolution erupted he raised a company of nearly 100 men. Many of his backwoods soldiers were armed with hunting rifles, rather than military smooth-bore—and short range—muskets. Morgan instructed his sharpshooters to gun down British officers and their Native American scouts. He fought skillfully at Quebec and Saratoga and Cowpens, as a colonel commanding Morgan's Rifle Brigade. One of his company commanders was Captain Samuel Houston who, like Morgan before him, became an officer and inspector in the Virginia Militia after the war.

"A man of iron frame, commanding bearing, and fearless courage," Sam later wrote about his father, with obvious admiration. "He was known for only one position, and this was for a military life."[1]

By nature many boys take pride in the military exploits of their fathers, and Captain Houston had served in a legendary unit. Throughout his boyhood, Sam witnessed his father ride off, clad in military attire, to perform official duties. He must have seen militia company drills with his father at nearby Lexington. A deep military ardor developed in young Houston.

Sam's mother was a formidable woman who had to manage a great many children during her husband's military absences. "She was distinguished by a full, rather tall, and matronly form, a fine carriage and an impressive and dignified countenance," related Sam. "She was gifted with intellectual and moral qualities, which elevated her, in a still more striking manner, above most of her sex."[2]

Both of his parents had strong physiques. His father had a "powerful frame" and his mother was tall and stout. Little wonder that their son grew into a man of impressive size. Samuel and Elizabeth were intelligent and people of character. On a regular basis Captain Houston demonstrated leadership qualities through his military activities.

Young Sam was bright, but the energetic boy balked at the

The plantation home where Sam Houston was born stood on a hill above this marker. Fittingly, the marker is anchored by a 38,000-pound piece of Texas granite. *Photo by the author.*

prospect of confinement in school. "I could not be gotten into a schoolhouse until I was eight years old, nor did I accomplish much after I started."[3]

Frontier schools usually were one-room log buildings with no desks, just benches. Books and paper and chalk boards were rare, and often there were not even hand-held slates. Teachers, who frequently had little schooling themselves, had to rely upon short oral lessons to teach the 3-Rs: Readin', 'Ritin', and `Rithmetic. School children would recite the teacher's lessons aloud, repeating it until memorized. Pupils were expected to recite loudly and often in chorus. These "ABC schools" or "vocal schools" or "blab schools" sometimes were entertaining to the students. But little Sam Houston was not entertained, later estimating that he barely attended school for a total of six months near his home.

"I learned to read and write, and gained some idea of imperfect ciphering."[4] Having learned to read, however, Sam opened the door to self-education. Like another backwoods boy fourteen years his junior, Abraham Lincoln, Sam had only a skimpy education but became an avid reader.

Sam and Abe also shared a dislike of the drudgery of farm work. Despite his disdain for school, Sam later complained that he "was compelled to devote more of his time to farm-work than to school . . ."[5] If he disliked school, he despised working in the fields.

Major Houston—promoted by the Virginia Militia in 1803—may have passed on this trait to his namesake sons, preferring to spend time on inspection trips rather than in his own fields. His older son tried to shoulder greater responsibilities on the plantation, but debts accumulated. Now in his fifties with growing health problems, Major Houston acquired cheap land in eastern Tennessee, where there were relatives.

He bought a large wagon and team, to go with a smaller conveyance already on the plantation. Having already sold parcels of his land for needed cash, he now arranged the sale of the remainder of his property. The Timber Ridge plantation would sell for one thousand pounds.

In the midst of these preparations, Major Houston died—perhaps fittingly—while on a militia inspection trip. Young Sam was only thirteen. Houston left his widow with six sons and three daughters and considerable debt. But fifty-two-year-old Elizabeth Paxton Houston went to work closing out the Virginia property, paying off family creditors, and packing up for the long, rugged trip to a new frontier home.

Sam, at thirteen, was excited by the prospect of a pioneer journey. Sam's admiration of his mother soared: "she was not a woman to succumb to misfortune" he reflected, also extolling her "heroism" and "her usual determination of spirit."[6]

The Houston patriarch was dead, but Sam witnessed the family leadership vacuum courageously filled by his stalwart mother. The Houston family would be led to a new frontier home by a resolute and authoritarian matriarch.

Family belongings were packed into the two wagons and the Houstons set out across the Allegheny Mountains. The journey was about 300 miles cross-country, but it was much farther when traversing precipitous and winding mountain trails. Houston later spoke of "severe hardships" as the family trekked through "unpeopled regions."[7]

But at thirteen Sam had never traveled far from home. He had a restless, adventurous nature, and the first major journey of his life featured magnificent scenery, countless new experiences, and the classic American anticipation of a fresh start on a new frontier. Despite the hardships of wilderness travel, the overland trek of 1807 unleashed the boy's nomadic instincts.

As an adult he became a compulsive traveler, undeterred by distance or hardship or lack of accommodations in a slow-moving age. The exhilaration of journeying to new places, of seeing new people or old friends, made the roving lifestyle of a wayfarer irresistible to Sam Houston.

At last the Houstons arrived at the log cabin village of Maryville, about twenty-five miles southeast of Knoxville. Major Houston had negotiated for more than 400 acres of land on a branch in Baker's Creek Valley, about eight miles south of Maryville.

Elizabeth Houston patented the hilly property, with the Great Smoky Mountains looming just to the west. The family erected a hillside cabin, and began clearing the land.

Among the belongings the Houstons brought from Timber Ridge was Major Houston's modest library. Young Sam already had dipped into these books, being far more interested in reading than in the instruction of a frontier schoolhouse. Sam was especially captivated by Alexander Pope's famous translation of *The Iliad,* the Greek epic poem set in the

The East Tennessee farm pioneered by the Houston family is designated by a roadside historical marker and, at the home site, by a trio of flagpoles, for the banners of the United States, Tennessee, and Texas. *Photo by the author.*

Trojan War. The siege of Troy, the heroic exploits of Achilles, the drama involving Agamemnon, King Priam, Hector, Paris, and the beautiful Helen—the entire tale called out to young Sam. He read and re-read *The Iliad*, and in Tennessee he far preferred reading to the grueling work of building a farm.

Sam's mother sent him to the Maryville Academy, which he later described as "a rude frontier school."[8] Sam took little interest in his lessons, but he could not put down *The Iliad*, "which I read so constantly that I could repeat it almost entire from beginning to end."[9]

His mother was a devout Presbyterian, and she had brought Sam and the other children with her to the rock church close to their Timber Ridge house. In Tennessee she attended a Presbyterian church a couple of miles east of her home, and she is buried there in the church yard. As a boy, Sam attended church with his mother, and he read the Bible in the King James Version, with its stately, well-constructed grammar. He memorized Biblical passages, and he memorized Shakespeare. Later he quoted impressive passages in public addresses, a practice he cultivated and eventually recommended to his older son.

While Sam was wandering in the woods to pursue his reading program, his mother and brothers were toiling to improve the family fortunes. As their farm developed, the Houstons acquired an interest in a general store in Maryville. It was decided that since Sam was of little use around the farm, he should work at the store, and he was installed at the Maryville mercantile.

By now Sam was fifteen. He stood nearly six feet tall and he resented the bossiness of his older brothers. He took an instant dislike to clerking. Writing in the third person years later, Houston unhappily recalled that "standing behind a counter was not a life to please a mind of his caste, and he disappeared." Meaningfully, Houston added "that the wild liberty of the red man suited his nature far better than the restraints of the white settlements."[10]

Cherokee country was just to the west of the region where the Houstons settled. A peaceful, agricultural people, the Cherokee nation was the most advanced of "Five Civilized Tribes" of the American southeast. There was trade and other interaction between whites and the Cherokee. During his first couple of years in Tennessee, including whatever time he spent in the store, young Houston doubtless had contact with Cherokee people. At some point the notion of living with the Cherokee occurred to him, igniting his imagination and sense of adventure.

Most Cherokee settlements were built alongside rivers, which were wilderness highways. Houston learned of a sizable village about fifty miles —as the crow flies—southwest of his family home. Home to perhaps 300 people, Cayuga town was on an island in the Hiwassee River not far from its confluence with the Tennessee River. The headman of Cayuga town was an impressive leader named Oolooteka. Oolooteka was a prosperous merchant and planter known to whites as John Jolly, and he would rise to prominence among the Cherokee.

Sam Houston had the gift of making friends, and when he arrived in Cayuga town he quickly became well-liked. The bright lad learned the Cherokee language, and he embraced his new lifestyle. Oolooteka, who spoke no English, was impressed by the strapping youngster. Oolooteka adopted Sam and renamed him "Colonneh," which meant the Raven, a Cherokee symbol of good fortune.

Cherokee towns featured wattle and daub houses, made by weaving river cane, vines, and wood into a frame, which was coated with plaster. Roofs were either thatched with grass or shingled with bark. These Cherokee houses were roughly as stable and as snug in the winter as most pioneer log cabins. Cherokee towns featured a multi-sided structure for ceremonial occasions, as well as a ball field with benches for spectators. A stickball game resembling lacrosse was popular, and it is easy to imagine the tall, rangy, white teenager loping across the ball field with his youthful friends.

On the field of play, Cherokee children enjoyed trying to throw darts through a rolling hoop, and the Raven surely tried his luck at this game. Children had dolls and toys, but they also were assigned chores. Cherokee adults took turns at storytelling with the children, and teaching the traditional music and crafts.

Cherokee men hunted deer, wild turkey, and small game with

bows and arrows. They also employed blowguns, a new device for the Raven. Men also fished, with poles and spears, often from long hollowed-out log canoes.

Cherokee diets also were supplemented by pigs and cattle. Women cultivated fields of corn, beans, squash, pumpkins, and sweet potatoes, while gathering strawberries, nuts, plums, and wild apples. Cherokee women cooked cornbread, stews, and soups. At Cayuga town the diet was varied and substantial.

Since the 1700s Cherokee attire had been influenced by English and American styles. Women wore cotton blouses, or poncho-style blouses of woven fibers. They wore wraparound skirts, often decorated with ribbon appliqués. They adorned themselves with bead necklaces and copper armbands. Women wore their hair long, but men usually shaved their hair, except for a scalp lock. Everyone wore moccasins, and men usually added leggings as well as breechcloths. Many men were fond of feathered turbans. Oolooteka, who disdained to speak English, dressed in buckskin, with a hunting shirt, leggings, and moccasins.

This all seemed exotic and fascinating to the Raven, who always enjoyed donning a feathered turban or hunting shirt or an Indian blanket. He hunted and fished and played stickball with his new companions. Tall and handsome, he dallied with Cherokee maidens. In a Cherokee town men did not work in the fields, which certainly suited the Raven. Indeed, the Raven reveled in the Cherokee lifestyle, commenting that "this mode of living initiated him into all the secrets of Indian life . . . " It was a way of life he embraced.[11]

After several weeks the Houston family heard where Sam had disappeared to, and a couple of brothers were dispatched to bring him home. But since "he was living greatly to his own satisfaction," the Raven refused to leave Cayuga town.[12]

"When they asked me why I left home," related Houston frankly, "I replied that I preferred measuring deer tracks to tape, and that I liked the wild liberty of the Red men better than the tyranny of my own brothers. I told them to go home and leave me in peace."[13]

The Houston family thought "that this was a freak from

which I would soon recover, when I got tired of the Indians . . ." The Raven did not tire of the Indians, but his clothing became threadbare. After several months he came home to refit himself. "I was kindly received by my mother, and for awhile my brothers treated me with due propriety. But the first act of `tyranny' they showed, drove me to the woods again . . ."[14]

The pattern of the next three years was set. Once or twice a year Sam would come home to see his mother and younger siblings. He renewed his wardrobe and bought small gifts for his Cherokee friends, apparently on credit terms with the family store. Then he returned to Cayuga town, "where I passed months with my Indian mates, chasing the deer through the forest with a fleetness little short of their own—engaging in all those gay sports of the happy Indian boys, and wandering along the banks of some streams by the side of some Indian maiden . . ." In the woods he also read from his ever-present copy of *The Iliad*. "It was the molding period of life," he realized, adding conclusively: "Certain it is that my early life among the Indians was a necessary portion of the wonderful training that fitted me for my destiny."[15]

By the time Houston was eighteen, "I had incurred a debt which I was bound in honor to pay."[16] The visits to the store for clothing and gifts had added up, and now it was time to settle accounts. Throughout his adult life Houston often made purchases on credit and borrowed sums of cash from his friends. But he faithfully paid his debts, and in turn he was willing to make loans to his friends.

So in 1811 he left Cayuga town with a scheme to raise money to satisfy his creditors. Of course he had no intention of returning to the family farm or store. His unlikely course was to open a school. As a young scholar Sam had spent six months or so in the little school near Timber Ridge, along with another brief tenure at the Academy in Maryville.

Although he had no academic credentials, he was an accomplished reader, which was the basic qualification for teachers of frontier blab schools. But having squirmed his way through such lessons as a pupil, eighteen-year-old Houston felt certain that he could offer better instruction. By this point he had read the *Odys-*

sey, Homer's epic Greek poem about the adventures of the great warrior Odysseus as he tried to return home after the Trojan War. And to explore the truth behind the legendary exploits depicted in *The Iliad* and *Odyssey,* he read an English translation of *Ancient History* by the French historian Charles Rollin. The Rev. Jedidiah Morse, known as the "father of American geography" (and as the father of Samuel F. B. Morse), wrote highly popular geography books. Houston devoured *American Geography,* returning to it repeatedly and mastering geographical details that he utilized throughout his career.

As a teacher Houston was capable of enlivening his classroom with tales of ancient heroism and drama, of history and geography, of Cherokees and the wilderness. As an "Indian professor" he knew he could captivate his students with details of the Cherokee way of life.[17]

He secured a school building, a log structure erected in 1794 outside Maryville. Today known as the "Sam Houston Schoolhouse," the one-room school boasted a unique feature. Along the

In 1812 Sam Houston taught a term of school at this log structure built in 1794. Located three miles north of Marysville, Tennessee, the "Sam Houston Schoolhouse" is operated as a museum. *Photo by the author.*

walls there was a long, narrow window. The two long shutters were hinged at the bottom from the inside, and could be utilized as a writing platform, where older students could stand and compose or cipher.

Professor Houston was so confident in the superior offerings of his school that "I charged what was considered an exorbitant price." No previous schoolmaster in the area had charged more than $6 per term. "I thought that one who had graduated at an Indian university ought to hold his lore at a dearer rate and raised the price to $8 . . ." He asked for one-third of the tuition in cash; one-third in corn delivered at the mill; and one-third in domestic cotton cloth, of variegated colors, in which their `Indian professor' was dressed."[18]

Houston crafted an Indian professor baton from a sour wood stick, whittled into circular spirals. One half was placed in a fire, turning it blue. "With this emblem of authority in my hand," he reminisced nostalgically, "dressed in a hunting-shirt of flowered calico, a long queue down my back, and the sense of authority over my pupils, I experienced a higher feeling of dignity and self-satisfaction than from any office or honor which I later held."[19]

His exotic appearance and approach to instruction worked. Despite his elevated tuition rate, Houston's one-room school filled with students, and soon he had to turn away applicants. But when he made enough money to pay his debts, he shut down the school. Perhaps thoughts of his success in the classroom inclined him to seek a higher educational level, and he again enrolled in the Academy at Maryville. The professor must have remembered Houston's weakness in math, as well as his interest in Greek classics, and he thrust into Sam's hands a copy of Euclid's *Geometry*.

"I carried that ugly, unromantic book back and forth to and from the school a few days, without trying to solve even so much as the first problem, and then came to the very sensible conclusion that I would never be a scholar!"[20]

Houston quit the Academy—again—early in 1818. He was nineteen, soon to be twenty, and he stood two inches over six feet. Despite his love of reading, a life of action called out to him. At this point the United States had been involved for several months in another war with England, and a U. S. Army recruiting party marched into Maryville to enlist soldiers.

It was the darkest night of my life.
Lt. Sam Houston

Chapter Two

Combat Leader

In March 1813 a recruiting detail of the United States Army regulars marched into Maryville. Their blue uniform coats and shakos contrasted impressively with white waistcoats and breeches. A flag fluttered bravely, there was a drum roll, and the sergeant in charge spoke of the War with England and the need for men of courage and patriotism. Silver dollars were spread on a drumhead and men were invited to enlist.[1]

Sam Houston promptly stepped forward and picked up a silver dollar, signifying his willingness to serve. With a war on against the British, Sam was inclined to emulate his father's example during the Revolution. The inspiring presence of the sharply-dressed regulars—as opposed to the ill-matched militia men Sam had seen all of his life—triggered his military impulse. But friends who knew that his father had been an officer taunted that he could not be a common soldier, a mere ranker.

"And what have your craven souls to say about the ranks?" retorted the patriotic new recruit. After a few more cutting remarks, he vowed with vehement resolve: "You don't know me now, but you shall hear of me."[2]

Houston had just turned twenty. Any recruit under twenty-one had to have parental approval. Elizabeth Paxton Houston gave her signature, and presented her son a gold ring with the word "Honor" engraved on the inside. Houston wore the ring all of his life, and remembered her parting challenge "that while the door to my cottage is open to brave men, it is eternally shut against cowards."[3] When Houston returned to her door months later, he was a wounded hero and barely recognizable to his own mother.

The official date of Sam Houston's enlistment in the Seventh U. S. Infantry Regiment was March 24, 1813. Private Houston soon was promoted to sergeant "because of his skill as a drill-master . . . "[4] Tall and with the military bearing of a natural soldier, Houston impressed Lt. Col. Thomas Hart Benton and was elevated in rank from private to sergeant. Sergeant Houston was no stranger to close-order drills, and his experience as a teacher during the past year equipped him to instruct raw recruits.

On July 29, barely three months after joining the army as a private, he was promoted to ensign and transferred to the newly-organized Thirty-ninth Infantry Regiment. By now an accomplished drill instructor, he boasted that he "was prominent in organizing and drilling the eastern battalion of the 39th regiment of infantry." He was prominent enough to earn promotion to third lieutenant on the last day of 1813. Within three months Lieutenant Houston would lead a platoon into hand-to-hand combat.[5]

Instead of doing battle against British soldiers, his father's foes during the Revolution, Lieutenant Houston found himself marching against Creek "Red Stick" warriors. Since colonial times English traders had engaged in commerce with the Creek and numerous other tribes.

In the American northwest the gifted Shawnee leader, Tecumseh, was commissioned a brigadier general by the British, who promised to provide arms to his warriors. Dreaming of a powerful confederacy of Native American tribes, Tecumseh spent six months in 1811 visiting tribes in the South. Many Creeks responded to Tecumseh's plan for a military confederacy against white settlers, and they readied their crimson war clubs—"Red Sticks."

Before the year was out Tecumseh was leading northern warriors against American intruders. For two years Gen. William Henry Harrison conducted a campaign which climaxed in victory at the 1813 Battle of the Thames in Canada. Tecumseh was slain and the northwest lay open to settlers.

By 1813 Red Sticks, led by a half-blood war chief known as Menawa or Bill Weathersford, went on a rampage in what would become Alabama. Settlers forted up in stockades, but at Fort

General Andrew Jackson commanded U.S. Army regulars and militia volunteers at the Battle of Horseshoe Bend. *Author's collection.*

Mims, forty miles north of Mobile, 400 men, women, and children were slain and scalped. The Fort Mims Massacre became a rallying point for angry Americans, and General Andrew Jackson marched south at the head of the Tennessee Militia.

In 1802 Jackson had been elected major general of the Tennessee Militia (a position he one day would help Sam Houston attain). Jackson's force was supplemented by Cherokee allies and friendly Creek warriors. With 2,500 men, General Jackson was victorious in battle at the Creek villages of Tallushatchee and Talladega. But the momentum of the campaign was slowed by supply delays and enlistment expirations and mutinous behavior by militia men, who bridled at military authority. After wintering at Fort Strother, where he was resupplied and reinforced, Jackson resumed his advance in January 1814. But there were bloody clashes at Enitachopco and Emuckfau creeks, and Jackson again fell back to Fort Strother.

Once more he was forced to deal with disobedient frontier militia men, who continued to flirt with mutiny. To stabilize his command, Jackson had requested Army Regulars, and now he learned that the Thirty-ninth Infantry Regiment was marching to reinforce his campaign. Striding at the head of his platoon was Third Lieutenant Sam Houston.

The Thirty-ninth, with a strength of more than 350 regulars, reached Fort Strother on February 13, 1814. General Jackson now could put more than 3,000 men into the field. He planned an assault on the fortified refugee village of Tohopeka at a horse-shoe-shaped bend of the Tallapoosa River.

During the winter of 1813-14, while Jackson was dealing with supply and discipline problems, the Creeks also were regrouping. While battling Jackson's militia during the fall, Red Stick losses were heavy, and during the winter it was increasingly difficult to feed everyone. Warriors from decimated bands drifted to Tohopeka, until upwards of 1,000 Red Sticks were preparing to make a stand under Menawa/Weathersford. While warriors erected a stout barricade of logs and earth across the neck of the peninsula, log huts were fashioned at the bottom, or south end, of Horseshoe Bend peninsula. A number of dependent women and children were housed in the huts, along with the warriors.

The barricade featured a double row of logs with packed earth between. Five to eight feet tall, the barricade was loopholed, and soldiers attempting to scale the wall at almost any point were subject to enfilade. Past the barricade the forested, broken ground rose before angling down to the river, where Menawa established a fall-back position, building a heavy log roof across a ravine.

During the 1960s the National Park Service erected a replica section of the barricade that stretched across the neck of the Horseshoe Bend peninsula. *Photo by the author.*

This redoubt was loopholed and difficult to approach.

From Fort Strother on the Coosa River to Tohopeka on Tallapoosa was a distance of fifty-five miles southeastward through thick forests. As Jackson's army advanced, he sent Cherokee and Creek scouts to reconnoiter Tohopeka. After a ten-day march, the American force approached the Creek stronghold. General Jackson sent Col. John Coffee—his devoted friend, business partner, and nephew by marriage—with a large force of militia sharpshooters and Indian allies below the river. Riflemen were positioned across from the peninsula to prevent the Red Sticks from escaping. Indian scouts swam across the river and brought back a great many of the canoes.

On the next morning, March 27, Jackson led his assault and reserve forces of 2,000 men into position. The Thirty-ninth Infantry Regiment was part of the attack unit. Jackson had hauled through the wilderness two field guns, a six-pounder and a three-pounder. This little artillery battery was wheeled into a place on "Gun Hill," an elevated site overlooking the barricade. The two light field guns bombarded the barricade from 10:30 a.m. until one in the afternoon, but the solid shot did little damage.

As both sides prepared for battle at the barricade, action suddenly erupted in the rear. According to Houston's account, the Cherokee allies "crossed the river in the canoes, set fire to a cluster of wigwams, and, under cover of the smoke, rushed upon the rear of the enemy," who were manning the barricade.[6] But before unleashing his attack, General Jackson chivalrously allowed more than 300 women and children to leave the peninsula.

The Thirty-ninth Infantry and the East Tennessee Militia Brigade then advanced on the log breastworks. The first man to clamber over the barricade was Major Lemuel Montgomery, who was immediately killed. Almost simultaneously Lieutenant Houston, leading the extreme right of the Thirty-ninth, scaled the barricade wielding his saber. Although struck by an arrow in his upper thigh, he stayed on his feet and fought off nearby Red Sticks, handling his saber with a strength in his right arm that never again would be as great.[7]

When his platoon arrived beside him, Houston insisted that

one of his comrades pull out the arrow so that he could return to the fight. When the man failed twice, Houston threatened him with his sword. The arrow was jerked out, but the barbed arrowhead brought a hunk of bloody tissue with it. Bleeding badly, Houston limped back to a medical station to have his wound bandaged. General Jackson rode by and ordered the wounded officer not to return to battle.[8]

Meanwhile, the barricade was stormed and the surviving warriors retreated into the eighty wooded acres of the peninsula. Houston, "determined to win a warrior's fame," arose and hobbled past the barricade and toward the action. A large number of Red Sticks retreated to the ravine redoubt. Artillery could not be hauled to this difficult position, so Jackson called for a charge. Lieutenant Houston limped forward, seized a musket, and headed for the redoubt himself.[9]

No one followed. Five yards from the redoubt Houston stopped and leveled his musket. But gunfire from the loopholes wounded him twice more: in the right arm and right shoulder. His bleeding arm hung useless at his side as he staggered away. Out of range, he collapsed to the earth. "No quarter was given or taken, and the work of slaughter was continued," reported Houston. The redoubt was never stormed, but it was set ablaze.[10]

The Red Sticks were crushed. Dead warriors lay at the barricade and across the peninsula. Many tried to swim the river, but their bodies now floated in the water. A few made it to the other side, only to be killed. On the ground there were 557 Red Stick corpses, while another two to three hundred were lost in the river. Perhaps 800 or more warriors died that day, but General Jackson spared Menawa and compelled him to sign the Treaty of Fort Jackson, by which the Creek tribes coded twenty million acres of land to settlement. It was a lesson that Houston could recall two decades later at San Jacinto.

Jackson lost only forty-nine dead and 154 wounded, including several who were expected to die. Thrice wounded, Lieutenant Houston was in the latter category. "One ball was extracted," reported Houston, "but no attempt was made to extract the other, for the surgeon said it was unnecessary to torture me, since

I could not survive until the next morning."[11]

The second ball was buried deep in Houston's shoulder, which is a complex and sensitive physiological mechanism. No anesthesia had yet been developed, so the remark about torture was accurate. But the surgeon's bedside manner was cruel, tactlessly telling the wounded man that he would die before morning.

"Comforts were out of the question for any," pointed out Houston, "but I received less attention than the others, for everybody looked on me as a dying man, and what could be done for any, they felt should be done for those who were likely to live. It was the darkest night of my life."[12]

There was nothing to relieve the pain of three wounds. There were no transfusions, of course, to replace the blood he had lost. With no "comforts," there was little liquid intake to rebuild his internal blood supply. There was no encouragement from doctors who fully expected him to die. But Houston survived that long, painful, miserable night.

The next day a group of wounded men set out for Fort Williams, more than sixty miles distant. Houston was placed on a litter borne by horses. "Here I remained, suspended between life and death, for a long time, neglected and exposed."[13]

Houston made little progress toward recovery, and finally discharged militia men from Tennessee brought the lieutenant with them. It was another torturous journey, one he could not forget. "I was not only helpless but suffering the extremist agony. My diet was of the coarsest description, and most of the time I was not only deprived of medical aid, but even of the simple remedies which would, at least, have alleviated any sufferings. Our toilsome way was through the forests where we were obliged to camp out and often without shelter. No one around me expected me to recover."[14]

Delivered first to the home of a cousin, Houston finally was taken to his mother in the latter part of May, almost two months after the battle. A severe weight loss rendered him gaunt and skeletal, and Mrs. Houston declared that she would never have known him except for his eyes. His mother and younger sisters provided food and care, and soon he was able to ride into Maryville to seek medical aid from a local doctor. But the doctor had little training and Houston's condition noticeably declined. Next he tried an army surgeon in Knoxville, but Houston's condition seemed so fragile that the doctor feared the worst and did not want to risk extracting the ball in his shoulder.

Always restless, Lieutenant Houston soon felt strong enough to ride horseback "by short journeys" to Washington D.C. He arrived not long after the Capitol and Executive Mansion were burned by invading British troops. The young officer was incensed: "my blood boiled when I saw the ruin," and he agonized "that my right arm should be disabled . . . while the foe was still prowling through the country." But his wounds were "still festering," and with winter approaching he rode over the mountains to Lexington, where he enjoyed the company of relatives and old friends until early spring.[15]

Feeling "sufficiently recovered to be able to do my duty as a soldier in some situation," Houston rode across the mountains to Knoxville. There "I heard the glorious news of the Battle of New Orleans," of the triumph of General Jackson. But he realized that the end of war would bring a reduction in the United States Army.

On March 1, 1815, Houston wrote to Secretary of War James Monroe. Pointing out that he had "quit the peaceful walks of scholastic life" (as though he had intended to remain a scholar or teacher) and that he had "fought & bled for my country," he asked to "remain in the service if consistent with your pleasure." Lieutenant Houston wrote a similar letter to his congressman, John Rhea.[16]

At this time the army surgeon in Knoxville found Houston remarkably improved. Feeling that the young officer might recover if the ball in his shoulder could be removed, the doctor recommended an army surgeon stationed with the First Infantry Regiment in New Orleans. Apparently Secretary of War Monroe recommended Houston to his friend, President James Madison, because on April 20, 1815, the president promoted the young hero to second lieutenant, "to rank as such from the 20th of May,

1814." His commission would be in the First Infantry, because Lieutenant Houston was transferred from the Thirty-ninth on May 17, 1815. With the nation at peace, the army was reduced and the Thirty-ninth was disbanded.[17]

For the trip to New Orleans, Houston assembled "a choice but small library," which included Pope's *Iliad*, of course, along with a volume of Shakespeare, *Robinson Crusoe*, *Pilgrim's Progress*, the poetry of Dr. Mark Akenside, the copy of the Bible that his mother had given him, and a few other books from his father's collection. Houston and a couple of companions—including Edward White, future congressman and governor of Louisiana—embarked on a skiff down the Cumberland, Ohio, and Mississippi rivers. As they neared Natchez, "we saw a vessel coming up the tram without sails, sending up a heavy column of smoke. Instead of being a vessel on fire, as we first supposed, it turned out to be the first steamboat that ever went up the Mississippi River."[18]

The travelers sold their skiff and purchased steamboat passage to New Orleans. After reporting for duty, Lieutenant Houston submitted to another painful surgery. The ball had shattered his upper arm just below the joint, then "passed round and lodged near the shoulder blade." The operation produced excruciating pain and copious bleeding, and "well-nigh proved fatal," according to the agonized patient. Following a winter of extreme suffering," in April 1816 he was sent to sea for medical attention in New York City. It was Houston's first visit to this impressive, enterprising city, and he stayed for several weeks.[19]

Although his health improved somewhat, the shoulder wound continued to drain. Indeed, the bandage needed to be changed every day for the remainder of his life. The wound never healed, movement in his right shoulder was permanently impaired, and his arm remained weakened. Lieutenant Houston paid a permanent price for his valor at Horseshoe Bend.

After leaving New York, the injured lieutenant visited in Washington en route to Tennessee. Back in Maryville he saw friends and enjoyed a brief romance with the "Princess of E. T." (East Tennessee). His next posting was at Nashville, where he was assigned to the office of adjutant general of the Southern Division of the U. S. Army. The division commander was Major General Andrew Jackson, who was transferred to the Regular Army after his triumph at Horseshoe Bend. Lieutenant Houston would have the opportunity to improve his friendship with General Jackson, while his clerical duties in the adjutant general's office were light and hopefully helpful to his continuing recovery. A gregarious and convivial man who made friends easily, Lieutenant Houston enjoyed a pleasant life, and he joined a prominent fraternal order, becoming a Freemason.

Houston's Nashville sojourn ended in 1817, with a new assignment from General Jackson. Problems with the Seminoles provided Jackson a pretext to seize Spanish Florida, but there was an unexpected distraction from the Cherokee. The previous year a group of Cherokee chiefs had signed the Treaty of 1816, ceding 1.3 million acres of traditional tribal lands to the federal government in exchange for lands west of the Mississippi River and promises of generous subsistence.

These chiefs probably had been bribed, because the Cherokee people loved their homeland and felt deep suspicion of the West, where the sun daily set into darkness. Many Cherokee chiefs and tribesman had not been consulted about the treaty and became restless and rebellious. Andrew Jackson needed someone who could calm the Cherokee, persuade them to accept the troublesome treaty. He needed someone who spoke the Cherokee tongue, someone who understood their customs. The choice seemed clear-cut. Lieutenant Houston agreed to Jackson's request to serve as sub-agent to the Cherokee, and his appointment was dated October 21, 1817.

When the Raven returned to the Cherokee, he no longer was the gangly teenager of 1808-1811. Six years had passed, and he now was twenty-four, an officer In the United States Army and a government representative to the Cherokee. Tall and impressive in appearance, he was confident that he could help his old friends. With winter arriving, the new sub-agent obtained blankets and cooking kettles and steel traps. After distributing these items, Houston began negotiations. Oolooteka, who had signed the treaty, agreed to leave his comfortable home. His people boarded boats full of supplies, and each of more than 100 war-riors proudly held a new rifle. This impressive departure certain-ly helped to convince others to move to Indian Territory.

But Tahlhontusky, an older brother of Oolooteka, had led his band west a decade earlier, and now he was back with reports of inferior land in Indian Territory, warlike neighbors, and unkept promises by the government. Sub-agent Houston agreed to escort his foster uncle and a Cherokee delegation to Washington, D.C. For a meeting with Secretary of War John C. Calhoun, Houston wore Cherokee attire instead of his army uniform. When the del-egation exited Calhoun's office, the Secretary asked Houston to stay. Secretary Calhoun angrily dressed down Lieutenant Hous-ton for being out of uniform at an official meeting. Houston never forgot Calhoun's words or tone. As president, Andrew Jackson despised Calhoun, but first the South Carolinian was the enemy of Sam Houston.[20]

Lieutenant Houston experienced considerable difficulty with Sec-retary of War John C. Calhoun. These two strong-minded men resumed their uneasy acquain-tance in the U.S. Senate, from 1846 until Calhoun's death in 1850. *Courtesy National Archives.*

Within days Secretary of War Calhoun summoned Lieutenant Houston and delivered an accusa-tion of slave smuggling. While with the Cherokee Houston had halted slave smugglers, but they succeed-ed in having him charged. There were also allegations of impropri-ety with government funds. Hous-ton had kept records which proved his innocence, and throughout his career he would maintain a reputa-tion for financial integrity. Further-more, President Monroe, who had dealt with Houston while serving as Secretary of War, demonstrated his confidence in the young officer by promoting him to first lieutenant in the First Infantry on March 5, 1818, "to rank as such from the 1st of May, 1817."[21]

But Houston had been insulted, both professionally and personally, and he especially resented his maltreatment at the hands of Secretary of War Calhoun. Feeling "slighted," Houston submitted a letter of resignation from the army, requesting that his commission be mailed to him. He accompanied the Cherokee delegation back to the Hiwassee River, then continued his wilderness ride toward Nashville.[22]

Houston served in the U.S. Army for five years, from just past his twentieth birthday to his twenty-fifth. During his first year as a soldier he won rapid promotion and distinguished himself in combat. Houston demonstrated reckless courage under fire, and he matured impressively as a leader of men. While in the army he attracted the favorable attention of such eminent men as future president Andrew Jackson, President James Monroe, Thomas Hart Benton, future Louisiana statesman Edward White, and Tennessee Governor Joseph McMinn. As an enlisted man and a junior officer, Houston excelled at the profession of arms. He shed blood for his country, nearly dying in battle. And in the army he first achieved notoriety. Houston learned that his battlefield exploits "excited the admiration of the whole army" and generated "the lasting regard" of General Andrew Jackson, who became his friend and champion.[23]

He enjoyed unbounded popularity among men and
he was a great favorite with the ladies.
Judge J. C. Guild

Chapter Three

Rise of a Political Leader

When Lieutenant Houston resigned his commission in the spring of 1818, he faced an unpleasant financial reality: "my pay in the army had been inadequate for any necessities, and I found myself burdened down by a load of debt." It was a problem he would face throughout his life, but always he found a way to pay his creditors. "I sold the last piece of real property I possessed," stated Houston, apparently referring to his share of the family farm, which he probably sold to an older brother. But even after applying "the last farthing" of the sale price to his debts, Houston still owed several hundred dollars.[1]

For years Houston had realized that he would have "to pursue some course for a livelihood which will not be laborious as my wounds are not near well."[2] Of course, healed or unhealed, Houston never would have followed a "laborious" livelihood—specifically tilling the soil. The agricultural pursuits which occupied a majority of American men early in the nineteenth century held no appeal for Houston.

Instead he intended to take up the legal profession, and he rode to Nashville, where he had made friends and contacts—including Andrew Jackson—during his military posting in 1816-17. Houston contracted to read law in the Nashville office of Judge James Trimble, an old friend of the Houston family in Virginia. Judge Trimble prescribed an eighteen-month course of study before his pupil would apply for admission to the bar.

Houston had no intention of taking a year and a half. "I read a few of the standard works prescribed in a course of law studies, and read them thoroughly. I grasped the great principles of the science, and they were fixed in my mind forever."[3]

Houston had trained himself since boyhood to memorize long passages from books. He had the actor's gift of learning lines—indeed, he essayed several roles in the Nashville Dramatic Club during this period. Houston applied his powers of reading and memorization to Judge Trimble's law books. It certainly was not a broad legal education, but Houston committed to memory enough basic principles to pass the bar exam. He would practice as a country lawyer off and on during the rest of his life. He was a capable attorney with exceptional oratorical ability, but lawyers in a frontier society had difficulty in collecting fees. Probably Houston's understanding of the law was most helpful when he was in the U.S. Congress, governor of two states, and president of the Republic of Texas.

The new lawyer was offered an office for one dollar per month by Isaac Galladay, postmaster of Lebanon, a little town thirty miles east of Nashville. Houston acquired a small law library on credit and brought it to his log cabin office. As postmaster Galladay gave Houston postage on credit. As store owner Galladay extended credit for Houston to indulge his flair for eye-catching garb. He wore tight breeches, fancy waistcoats beneath a plum-colored coat, and a bell-crowned beaver hat. Houston's flashy attire and tall, handsome figure attracted notice as well as clients.[4]

He rode into Nashville as often as possible, maintaining his friendships in the larger town. When Andrew Jackson was at home, Houston stopped at The Hermitage, a few miles east of Nashville. Houston and Jackson grew closer, and at the Hermitage, Houston found himself in company with such prominent men as Governor Joseph McMinn. Governor McMinn, impressed by Houston and probably influenced by Jackson, appointed Sam as adjutant general of the Tennessee State Militia with the rank of colonel.[5]

Soon Colonel Houston enlisted the aid of Governor McMinn in running for the office of prosecuting attorney of the Nashville District. During the same period, Houston was asked by Chief Oolooteka to become Indian agent to the Cherokee. Houston asked the advice of General Jackson, who wrote to Secretary of War Calhoun to request the appointment of Houston as agent to the Cherokee: "I have no hesitation in saying that Col. Sam Houston is better qualified for this station than any other man of his age I am acquainted with; he is honourable, honest and brave . . . "[6] Jackson lobbied successfully. Houston received the appointment, but declined because he won the race for prosecuting attorney in October 1819.

Houston's victory necessitated a move to Nashville after less than a year in Lebanon. Before commencing the two-year term, Houston addressed a large crowd from the steps of the courthouse in Lebanon. "The time has come when I must confess that it is with feelings of sincere regret that I leave you. I shall ever remember with emotions of gratitude the kindness which I have received at your hands." These words must have been directed in strong part to Isaac Galladay. Then Houston began to quote the Bible, Matthew 25:35-36. "I came among you poor and a stranger, and you extended the hand of welcome, and received me kindly. I was naked, and ye clothed me; I was hungry, and ye fed me."[7]

The Tennessee state capital had first been located in Knoxville, from 1796 until 1812, when it was moved to Nashville. In 1817 it returned to Knoxville for a year before being transferred to Murfreesboro. In 1826 the capital found a permanent home in Nashville. When Houston moved back, Nashville was the governmental seat of only Davidson County. But General Andrew Jackson lived nearby, and there was a sense of upward mobility in the growing town of 5,000. The Nashville Dramatic Society had disbanded, but Houston joined the Tennessee Antiquarian Society. He was friends with attorneys and militia officers and other leading citizens. "Brought into collision with the most eminent legal talent of the state" because of his new position, he improved his legal skills. But a year "of the unceasing duties of his new office" brought him little profit, so he resigned and entered private practice in Nashvlle.[8]

Houston was a sociable man about town, but he also spent considerable time in Murfreesboro, headquarters of the Tennessee Militia. Popular among his fellow militia officers, Houston found himself talked about as their major general. Houston commanded immediate respect among the militia as a former regular army officer and a combat hero, and he was a close associate of General Andrew Jackson. In 1821 the militia officers elected Houston major general and commander of militia.

Major General Houston was only twenty-eight, and he must have yearned for his father's approval. In a division order dated January 21, 1822, Major General Houston expressed gratitude for "the distinction conferred upon me" and confidence in the ability "of all its officers, faithfully to discharge their duty." But Houston had campaigned as a regular army officer alongside militia, and he had heard Andrew Jackson expound on the constant disciplinary problems posed by militia volunteers (problems which Houston would have to face in Texas in 1835 and 1836).

"Order and subordination are indispensably necessary, and are strictly enjoined," Houston stated in his division order. "No exertion on my part shall ever be wanting to improve the discipline . . . "[9] Houston would always bear these sentiments in mind.

Major General Houston now pressed unfinished business that Lieutenant Houston had taken up with Secretary of War Calhoun. As sub-agent to the Cherokee, Lieutenant Houston had incurred travel expenses totaling $170.09. Houston submitted proper documentation, but encountered a bureaucratic runaround that resulted in several exchanges of correspondence but no payment from the government. On June 24, 1822, an exasperated Major General Houston fired off a letter of complaint to Secretary Calhoun, detailing the latest technicality from an assistant auditor in the Treasury Department. "Perhaps this is a rule established at [Washington] City, but it won't meet our Backwoods notion of Justice."[10]

A month later Houston received a draft for $170.09, payable at a Nashville bank—at a twenty-seven per cent discount. Houston promptly returned the draft with a request for proper payment, and he sent another angry letter to Calhoun. "I can see no reason for this course of conduct pursued by you, towards me; unless it be that I am the same man against whom you conceived so strong a prejudice in 1818, when I was assist. Indian agent."

Houston was just getting warmed up. "Sir, I could have forgotten the unprovoked injuries inflicted upon me, if you were not disposed to continue them. But your reiteration shall not be unregarded. I will remember your personal bad treatment . . . All this I will remember as a man."[11]

In view of Houston's successful participation in an 1826 duel and in a brawl with a congressman in Washington six years later, Calhoun probably was fortunate that this livid man of action was nearly 700 miles distant in 1822. Two years later Houston received what was intended to be a "final" expense settlement, but again he was shorted thirty-six dollars. Houston's complaint to Calhoun this time was more controlled. "There was no such thing known in the army as bearing the expenses of an officer and docking his transportation," he pointed out.[12] And at last he received the thirty-six dollars.

Soon after becoming major general of militia, Houston seized an opportunity to continue his remarkable rise. Houston was ambitious and intended to capitalize on his momentum. In 1818-1821 he was appointed adjutant general of Tennessee Militia, won election as prosecuting attorney of the Nashville District, and was elected by his fellow militia officers as major general. With growing confidence and the support of powerful men, Houston ran for Congress in 1823.

Rapid population growth in Tennessee (from 261,727 in 1810 to 422,823 in 1820) resulted in an increase in congressional seats, from six in the Census year of 1820 to nine in 1822. The Ninth Tennessee Congressional District included Nashville, and Major General Houston offered himself for election. His mentors, Governor Joseph McMinn and General Andrew Jackson, maneuvered behind the scenes to insure that he had no opposition.

In February 1823 he wrote a letter of gratitude to Governor McMinn, reflecting that: "Five years since I came to this place, without education more than ordinary —without friends—without cash—and almost without acquaintances—consequently without credit." In a similar letter six weeks later, he remarked upon how much his friends—like McMinn—meant to him. "I dearly love my friends because they have been everything to me.

I part with them as a Miser does his treasure with anguish and regret."[13] Sadly, he soon had to part from McMinn, who died at sixty-six on October 17, 1824.

By that time Houston was a member of Congress. Unopposed, he won election by unanimous vote in September 1823 and took office in December. Congressman Houston's return to Washington was one of personal triumph. Ever the clothes horse, Houston enlisted a friend to take him from one hat shop to another, finally selecting one with just the right width of brim. The two men next walked to the Capitol and entered the House of Representatives. "Now, I am a member of Congress," he said, adding with relish, "I will show Mr. Calhoun that I have not forgotten his insult to a poor lieutenant."[14]

Houston was joined in Washington by Andrew Jackson, who had been elected to the U.S. Senate by the Tennessee State Legislature. Jackson had been sent to the Senate in 1797, but he resigned after five months because of impatience with the sluggish pace of Congress. Jackson returned to the Senate in 1823 with growing support from the American people for the nation's highest office. Since at least 1822, Houston had urged his mentor and friend to run for the presidency. Writing from the state capital at Murfreesboro, Houston informed Jackson: "On this day a resolution has passed the Senate (unanimously) recommending you as a person most worthy & suitable to be the next President of our Union . . . You are now before the eyes of the nation. You have nothing to fear, but everything to expect . . . The next President will be the `People's Choice.'"[15]

Congressman Houston campaigned actively for Jackson during the Presidential Election of 1824. There was a four-way race between Jackson, Secretary of State John Quincy Adams, Secretary of Treasury William H. Crawford, and Henry Clay, personable Speaker of the House. Although Jackson won the most popular and electoral votes, there was no majority, so according to the Twelfth Amendment the election would be determined by vote of the House of Representatives among the top three candidates. Clay finished fourth, so he was out, but as Speaker he would almost certainly determine the outcome of the House election. Crawford suffered a paralytic stroke, which meant that the House vote would be between Jackson and Adams. With the support of Speaker Clay, Adams won the presidency. Adams became the fourth consecutive Secretary of State to be elected president, and when he appointed Henry Clay as the next Secretary of State, Jackson and his supporters cried, "Bargain and Corruption."

The new vice president would be John C. Calhoun. Calhoun had intended to enter the presidential race of 1824, but soon decided he could not win. Instead he ran for vice president, winning overwhelmingly. Andrew Jackson, although chairman of the Senate Committee on Military Affairs, soon resigned his senate seat and returned to Tennessee to prepare a presidential campaign for 1828. A few months after President Adams was inaugurated, the Tennessee State Legislature nominated Jackson for president, thus setting the stage for a rematch in 1828 between Jackson and Adams.

As Jackson built a political machine of unprecedented organization and size, Representative Houston, Senator John Eaton, and Judge Jacob Isaaks began to write articles and letters to advance Jackson's candidacy to the public. Houston apparently was the author of a campaign biography, *A Civil and Military History of Andrew Jackson by an American Army Officer*. An appreciative—and demanding—Jackson called this trio of political writers his "Literary Bureau."

Meanwhile, Houston participated in the daily activities of the House of Representatives. He learned to deal with constituents seeking office or patronage, a craft he would employ throughout a career spent in important political positions. As a novice in Congress he heard the debating and oratorical skills of Daniel Webster and Henry Clay, who not yet had moved from the House to the Senate. He learned intricacies of political maneuver from the most skilled politicians in America, and he watched debate over great issues of the day. One of the most important issues for a congressman from a western state was internal improvements—government funding of roads and bridges and canals. Congressman Houston supported bills needed to provide infrastructural improvements on the frontier.

In Washington Houston lodged at a boarding house, but in the evenings he enjoyed socializing with a growing circle of friends. Tall, handsome and well-dressed, Houston acquired polish in Washington social circles. When he first arrived as a freshman congressman, he closely observed Senator Andrew Jackson. "The General is calm, dignified, and makes as polished a bow as any man I have seen at court," he wrote to a friend. Houston also remarked on how the famous general had not yet deigned to enter the House, instead allowing the representatives to seek his company. "He is much courted by the Great," remarked Houston with admiration.[16]

A social and historical highlight began at the start of the second session of the Eighth Congress, in December 1824. The Marquis de Lafayette, patriotic young French nobleman who fought alongside American soldiers during the Revolution, returned to the United States to great acclaim in 1824. Now sixty-seven, the Marquis was enthusiastically welcomed to the capital of the nation he had helped to establish. Sam Houston was a member of the party which escorted the old hero into the House Chamber. Lafayette resided in O'Neill's Tavern, where Andrew Jackson—still in the Senate—also stayed. Houston had the opportunity to socialize with Lafayette and Jackson at O'Neill's and, later in the Frenchman's grand tour, at The Hermitage.

In 1825 Houston ran for re-election to Congress, and again he faced no serious opposition. During his second term he remained busy as a member of Jackson's Literary Bureau and in making campaign speeches. Houston's first speech in the House of Representatives came early in his first term, on January 22, 1824. He spoke intensely on the subject of Greek independence, while the descendants of his *Iliad* heroes battled for freedom from the Ottoman Empire. By the time Houston reached his second term he did not hesitate to rise before his colleagues, holding forth with eloquence and passion in a deep, ringing voice.

Between congressional terms Houston returned to Tennessee, staying at the popular Nashville Inn and practicing law. But prior to his second session of the Nineteenth Congress, Houston's sense of honor and the *code duello* cornered him into fighting a duel. In fact, early in 1825 a duel was anticipated between Houston and a Tennessean named Gibbs. Both men were Masons, and fellow lodge members worked to avoid a conflict on the field of honor. Indeed, as soon as a perceived affront produced a challenge, friends and relatives and seconds tried every possible recourse to satisfy the conventions of honor without resorting to violence. As a result, most expected duels failed to materialize, including the one between Houston and Gibbs.

But just as Houston evaded one duel, another clash of honor developed. In 1826 the postmaster of Nashville resigned, and the Adams administration supported John P. Erwin, a Nashville newspaper editor—and a relative by marriage to Secretary of State Henry Clay.

Jackson instructed Houston to "Attend to this business." Houston accordingly attempted to block the appointment. He wrote a lengthy letter to President John Quincy Adams: "It is with respect and delicacy that I address you on the present occasion . . ." Houston pointed out that Nashville citizens had indicated their preference for the interim postmaster to Erwin. "Mr. Erwin is not a man of fair and upright moral character," stated Houston. "He does not pay his debts, tho' all believe him able to do so . . . " Houston related that Erwin had been seen eavesdropping late at night at the window of a political opponent. "He would not command public confidence, because these fact are known in the society of Nashville!"[17]

Houston's confidential remarks to President Adams somehow reached Erwin, who demanded a retraction from the congressman. Houston refused, and the affronted Erwin determined to issue a challenge. But in Nashville no one could be found who would stand as Erwin's second and deliver the challenge to the popular Houston. General William A. White, a lawyer from Gallatin, was approached, but he felt no animosity toward Houston and would not participate. A professional duelist, who called himself John T. Smith, was imported from Missouri to Nashville to deliver the challenge.

As soon as Smith stepped off the stagecoach in Nashville, he confronted Houston's second, a Colonel McGregor. McGregor would not accept the note, on the grounds that Smith was not a Tennessee citizen. Smith then marched to the Nashville Inn, as crowds of onlookers followed the drama. General White stood with Smith as a witness, and when Houston, too, declined, White unwisely sneered a taunt. Houston reiterated that he had not accepted the note from Smith. "But I will receive one from you, General White, with pleasure:"

"I will receive one from you, General Houston."

"The saddle is on the other horse, General," pushed Houston, "and that is enough to be understood between gentlemen."

"If I call you there will be no shuffling, I suppose," replied White.

"Try me, sir."[18]

Erwin did not follow through, and Smith left town. Finally White, as a point of honor, issued a challenge, which Houston accepted. General White was known to be a poor pistol shot, and Houston sportingly chose pistols at almost point blank fifteen feet. Practicing on the grounds of The Hermitage, Houston was advised by General Jackson—a famously experienced duelist—to bite a bullet as he squeezed the trigger. The dueling ground was just across the Tennessee state line, in Simpson County, Kentucky. At dawn on September 23, 1826, two parties of men solemnly met and the principals selected weapons. Standing fifteen feet apart, Houston and White gripped their pistols and listened for the order to fire. General White collapsed with a ball in his groin. Thinking that he would die, White forgave Houston.

But White survived, following four months in bed. The next year Houston was indicted by a Simpson County grand jury, but Tennessee officials ignored the extradition request. Houston, meanwhile, refused to accept compliments for his performance on the field of honor, and he was instrumental in keeping Jackson —a presidential candidate—from delivering a challenge when an opponent criticized his leadership at the Battle of New Orleans. Despite whatever regrets Houston may have over nearly killing a man with whom he had no quarrel, in many quarters the duel with General White added to the growing respect for the rugged soldier/politician.

Houston began to be talked of for governor. The current governor was William Carroll, a longtime friend of Jackson who had fought at the Battle of New Orleans and who had served as major general of Tennessee Militia. But in 1827 Carroll was concluding his third consecutive term as governor, and the state constitution required him to step aside. (Later Carroll would return to the governorship for three more consecutive terms.) For 1827 Andrew Jackson intended to keep the governor's office in friendly hands. Both Jackson and Carroll supported Houston, who eagerly grasped the next opportunity.

Houston had conducted two successful congressional campaigns, along with a winning campaign for prosecuting attorney of the Nashville District. He was a natural campaigner, with his love of travel, of socializing with men and women, and of giving speeches to receptive crowds. Everywhere he went he was the center of attention, and confidently he rode into towns astride a handsome mount, dressed in clothing meant to attract notice.

"Houston stood six feet six inches in his socks, was of fine contour, a remarkably well proportioned man, and of commanding and gallant bearing," described Judge J. C. Guild, a friend and admirer who was one of many who assumed the big man was taller than his actual measurement. [Houston] had a large, long head and face and his fine features were lit up by large eagle-looking eyes; possessed of a wonderful recollection of persons and names, a fine address and courtly manners and a magnetism approaching General Andrew Jackson. He enjoyed unbounded popularity among men and was a great favorite with the ladies."[19]

As he entered his thirties, Sam Houston enjoyed exceptional good looks: handsome features, curly reddish hair, a cleft chin, and an imposing physique. Courtesy Tennessee State Museum.

On election day Houston rode to each polling place in Nashville "mounted on a superb dapple-gray horse." He was resplendent in a ruffled shirt with a standing collar and military stock. He wore black trousers and a black satin vest, and his outfit was topped with a bell-crowned black beaver hat. His feet were encased in embroidered silk stockings and black pumps adorned with silver buckles. This flashy ensemble featured an exotic touch: draped across his shoulders, in place of a coat, was a handsome Cherokee hunting shirt, gathered at the waist by a beaded red sash fastened with a polished metal clasp.[20]

Houston won by more than 11,000 votes, 44,426 votes to 33,410 for Whig candidate Newton Cannon. The new governor delivered an uncharacteristically brief acceptance speech at his inauguration, held on October 1, 1827, at the First Baptist Church of Nashville. He was thirty-four, just nine years removed from the U.S. Army. At every step of his rapid ascent to high office Houston donned the mantle of leadership readily and confidently. Handsome and self-assured, he moved easily in high circles.

Governor Houston rode to Knoxville to thank his friends in east Tennessee for their support in the election. He was feted at a banquet, which climaxed with nearly sixty toasts. He championed a program of internal improvements and of education for Tennessee, while continuing to work on Jackson's "literary bureau." Late in December and into January, he was a member of a party which traveled to New Orleans aboard the steamboat *Pocahontas*. There was an annual celebration on the anniversary of the Battle of New Orleans, and General Jackson himself would be present in January 1828—an event which would remind the nation of his war record.

Governor Houston was one of the hosts for General Jackson and his wife Rachel for a Christmas Eve banquet at the Nashville Inn. Three days later Houston was a prominent member of the party that joined General and Mrs. Jackson on the *Pocahontas*. The *Pocahontas* made its way northwest down the Cumberland River to the Ohio and a short connection to the Mississippi. Jackson, of course, was not only a revered military hero—he was the popular choice to win the presidency the following November.

At river towns and wood stops and even along river banks

people gathered to cheer and fire guns in the air. In New Orleans a crowd of thousands was on hand to greet General Jackson, who accepted the accolades standing at the stern rail, hat in hand. There was a grand dinner, and during the endless speeches Houston slipped out with another bachelor—a son of Alexander Hamilton—to seek other entertainment.

When Houston first visited New Orleans in 1816, undergoing difficult surgery on his shoulder, the young officer sampled as many of the delights of New Orleans as his condition permitted. Still a bachelor at thirty-four, Houston had a long reputation as a hard drinker and carouser, and he may have recalled some of his New Orleans haunts from 1816.

During the rest of 1816 Governor Houston was engaged with the business of Tennessee and the presidential campaign of Jackson. The campaign of 1828 was harsh and scurrilous. Jackson's supporters constantly reminded the nation of the "corrupt bargain" that had placed John Quincy Adams in the presidency, and virtually all of his policies were criticized. Opponents of Jackson accused him of murder, as a duelist and for executing soldiers during the War of 1812. As a potential first lady Rachel was excoriated as a dowdy, pipe-smoking woman of the backwoods—and as an adulteress. When Andrew and Rachel were "married" in 1791, they did not realize that her divorce from her abusive first husband was not yet legal (even though Jackson, as an attorney, should have made himself aware). Although legally remarried in 1794, Andrew and Rachel periodically were subject to slander, a factor in Jackson's dueling career. By 1826 the Adams campaign had taken up the old issue, and by 1827 the mudslinging was vicious.

In November 1827 Jackson won a decisive victory, and politically Tennessee became the most important state in the Union. Sadly, Rachel Jackson died suddenly at The Hermitage on December 22, 1828. Although Rachel had been in ill health, her husband was convinced that the calumny she suffered had triggered her death. Over her grave Jackson bitterly vowed: "In the presence of this dear saint, I can and do forgive all my enemies. But those vile wretches who have slandered her must look to God for

Andrew Jackson bought 625 acres of land twelve miles east of Nashville in 1804. The first substantial residence was erected in 1819, about the time young Sam Houston began to visit the Jackson home. In 1831 President Jackson extensively remodeled the Heritage. Although the mansion was badly damaged by fire three years later, it was rebuilt utilizing the foundation and original walls. A grieving Houston arrived here in 1845, just hours after Andrew Jackson died. *Courtesy The Hermitage National Historic Site.*

forgiveness."

The Christmas Eve funeral was held at The Hermitage, and a throng estimated at 10,000 gathered o the grounds. Burial followed in Rachel's garden, and Sam Houston led the cortège to the grave. In ensuing weeks Houston frequently was at the side of the grief-stricken president-elect. Speculation grew that one day Houston would follow his friend and mentor into the presidency. Meanwhile, Governor Houston decided to run for a second term in 1829, and he had every expectation of re-election. His future seemed limitless.

*To you, General [Jackson], I find myself vastly
indebted for many principles which I
never abandoned through life.*
Senator Houston

Chapter Four
Influence of Prominent Leaders on Sam Houston

From the time he was a young man, Sam Houston observed and interacted with, worked alongside and sparred against, conversed with and corresponded with, laughed with and imbibed with the most prominent men of the age. He watched them, noted what they wore, listened to their public speeches, learned from them. He knew every president from Thomas Jefferson to Abraham Lincoln, fourteen in all, plus the president of the Confederacy, Jefferson Davis. In addition Houston knew such notable leaders as Henry Clay, Thomas Hart Benton, Daniel Webster, and John C. Calhoun, although Houston's long relationship with Calhoun was abrasive. And of course, Houston enjoyed a spectacular relationship with the most powerful politician of the age, Andrew Jackson.

During Houston's boyhood his father provided an image of military leadership. Major Houston manifested a "commanding bearing, and fearless courage," qualities Sam felt were passed from father to son.[1] At thirteen Sam lost his father, but within a couple of years he went to live with the Cherokee, and was adopted by Oolooteka, chief of his village—and another image of authority. "He had the most courtly carriage in the world, and never prince sat on a throne with more peerless grace than he presided at the council of his people."[2]

At twenty Houston enlisted in the U.S. Army. Lt. Col. Thomas Hart Benton was immediately impressed by the tall, self-assured private, who was promoted to sergeant within days. Sergeant

Houston became an excellent drillmaster and again won promotion, to ensign and then to lieutenant. Houston proved worthy of the confidence and support of Benton, who was the first important American leader to recognize his "soldierly and gentlemanly qualities . . . " Benton found Houston "frank, generous, brave . . . and always ready to answer the call," and he pointed out the young soldier to General Jackson.[3]

Thomas Hart Benton was eleven years older than Houston, and as a young lawyer in Tennessee he was mentored by Andrew Jackson. The hot-tempered Benton was involved in duels, and during a brawl in Nashville he angrily shot Jackson, then was wounded five times by Jackson's friends. Benton moved to Missouri, although he and Jackson were reconciled several years later. When Missouri achieved statehood in 1821, Benton was selected as one of two charter senators from the new state. During

the next three decades. Senator Benton was an eloquent champion for westward expansion. He contacted Governor Houston in 1829, and in 1846 the two statesmen were reunited in the U.S. Senate.

Upon recommendation of Benton, General Andrew Jackson was the next prominent leader to take notice of Houston, and he witnessed the raw courage of the lieutenant at Horseshoe Bend. Jackson's father died before Andrew was born, and he was fourteen when his mother died. During the American Revolution a British officer slashed young Jackson with his saber, and he bore the scars throughout his life. As a young man he made his way as a backwoods lawyer and as a planter. For many years his Hermitage plantation headquartered in a collection

Lt. Col. Thomas Hart Benton was the first man of prominence to aid Sam Houston, helping the recruit to rise immediately from private to sergeant. Benton and Houston reunited in the U.S. Senate in 1846. *Courtesy National Archives.*

of log cabins, before Jackson built a mansion with white pillars and wide verandas and a beautiful curved stairway. Jackson rose to prominence as a military and political leader. As the nation's seventh president, he was regarded as the first chief executive with common origins, as the strongest president America had yet experienced, and as a leader of such force that he provided iden- tification to his era—the Age of Jackson.

Andrew and Rachel Jackson had no children, although they adopted one of Rachel's nephews and named him Andrew Jack- son, Jr. Through the years Jackson mentored a number of prom- ising young men. One favorite was Major Lemuel Montgomery, and Jackson wept over his body at Horseshoe Bend. James K. Polk, a contemporary of Sam Houston, was a protégé of Jack- son, so devoted to "Old Hickory" and his policies that he became known as "Young Hickory."

None of Jackson's protégés had more of his attention or sup- port or loyalty than Sam Houston. Jackson, who had no son, and Houston, fatherless since the age of thirteen, responded strongly to each other. Jackson promoted Houston's career with decisive influence, from militia commander to congressman to governor, as well as in countless small ways. Houston became part of Jack- son's inner circle, a frequent visitor at the Hermitage, making valuable acquaintances while developing genuine affection for the "Old Chief" and for Rachel. An intimate of Jackson's while the Old Chief became the most powerful and popular man in America, Houston emulated his mentor—even to the technique of a bow—and he assisted the great man in any way possible. And always he remembered "the principles of that Democracy that was taught at The Hermitage, and treasured up by us."[4]

In a lengthy letter to Jackson, his "venerated friend," Sam Houston, now forty-nine, detailed his mature reflections on gov- ernment and government officials. "To you, General," he con- cluded, "I find myself vastly indebted for many principles which I never abandoned through life. One is a holy love of country and a willingness to make every sacrifice to its honor and safety, next a sacred regard for its constitution and laws . . . "[5] Of all of the prominent leaders who influenced and advised and promoted Sam Houston, Andrew Jackson was the most prominent and influential.

Tennessee Governor Joseph McMinn was of great aid to Houston early in his political career. "Governor you can help me up the rugged hill of life," wrote Houston.[6] Governor McMinn was receptive to the impressive young man. Like Andrew Jackson, Governor McMinn had no sons (and his only daughter died in 1815). McMinn readily mentored Houston, aiding his election as prosecuting attorney of the Nashville District, appointing him adjutant general of state militia, and helping him run for Congress unopposed. Houston solicited McMinn's assistance, understood that the governor was key to his early advancement, and expressed heartfelt gratitude.

When newly-elected congressman Sam Houston rode to Washington, D.C., in the fall of 1823, he carried a letter of introduction to Thomas Jefferson. Houston was eager to meet the author of the Declaration of Independence, the Founding Father who had served as president for eight years during his boyhood. Andrew Jackson agreed to provide an introduction, and Houston rode up a mountain road to Monticello. Jefferson's unique mansion featured—among other things—a large, airy reception hall which served as a museum of his myriad interests and long career. Jefferson was eighty when he met the new congressman, who was thirty. It is not known what the two men discussed; perhaps their meeting was merely polite and brief. But just being in the presence of Thomas Jefferson, shaking his hand and hearing his voice and seeing the house that was such an authentic reflection of the man—this connection with the independence movement and the formative years of the republic was more than enough.

Jefferson's successor as president, James Madison, served from 1809 until 1817. The diminutive Madison, known as the "Father of the Constitution," signed Sam Houston's promotion to second lieutenant in 1815. Madison's wife Dolley was a legendary First Lady, delightful in demeanor and exotic in dress (Houston probably would have worn one of her turbans). In February 1849, when President James K. Polk was about to leave office, the White House was opened for one of his final receptions. The guest of honor was Dolley Madison, now an eighty-one-year-old widow with only a few months left to live. President and Mrs. Polk paired Senator Sam Houston with Dolley, and one last time Mrs. Madison—on the arm of Houston—was a central figure in a White House social event.

James Monroe was Secretary of War for President Madison when, in 1815, he received a respectful letter from Third Lieutenant Sam Houston. Houston asked to remain in the peacetime army, which was being down-sized. Secretary Monroe transferred Houston to a permanent regiment and issued a promotion to second lieutenant, a document signed by President Madison. By 1818 Monroe was president, and he signed another promotion for

At the final presidential reception of Houston's friend James K. Polk, the senator from Texas was paired with former First Lady Dolley Madison during her final White House social event. *Courtesy National Archives.*

Houston to first lieutenant. President Monroe was in his second term when Sam Houston arrived in Washington for his first session in Congress. For the next two years Houston had his first front-row-seat whole observing a president at work. Monroe had vast experience: combat officer in the Revolution; member of the Continental Congress during the 1780s; U.S. Senator; minister to France; governor of Virginia; minister to Great Britain; Secretary of State; Secretary of War. The nation ran smoothly during Monroe's presidential tenure, and he was enormously popular.

Throughout his administration, Monroe's Secretary of War was John C. Calhoun. The brilliant South Carolinian was a superb administrator, markedly reducing the cost of the War Department during his eight-year tenure. But Calhoun was strong-minded, and in 1817 he upbraided Lieutenant Houston for being out of uniform, dressing instead like the Cherokee leaders he had escorted into the Secretary's office. Houston deeply resented Cal-

---

Presidents of Houston's Acquaintance

Thomas Jefferson (1801-1809)   James K. Polk (1845-1849)
James Madison (1809-1817)   Zachary Taylor (1849-1850)
James Monroe (1817-1825)   Milliard Fillmore (1850-1853)
John Quincy Adams (1825-1829)   Franklin Pierce (1853-1857)
Andrew Jackson (1829-1837)   James Buchanan (1857-1861)
Martin Van Buren (1837-1841)   Abraham Lincoln (1861-1865)
William Henry Harrison (1841)   Jefferson Davis (CSA, 1861-1865)
John Tyler (1841-1845)

---

houn's dressing down, and for years the two men feuded, largely by correspondence. But if Calhoun, one of the nation's most capable leaders, seemed objectionable to Houston, the young man could learn qualities not to emulate, leadership qualities to avoid. Calhoun thus provided Houston a learning experience through negativity.

During his two years in Congress, the young politician and budding orator was exposed to the soaring oratory of Daniel Webster. Webster was a handsome man with penetrating eyes, craggy brows, and a rich voice. A champion of strong national government, Webster was the best known orator of his time. When the great orator addressed the House, Houston doubtless picked up helpful tips, nuances of expression and articulation. In 1827 Webster moved to the U.S. Senate and Houston became governor of Tennessee. When Houston joined the Senate of 1846 as senator for the new state of Texas, Webster still was a senator from New Hampshire. By that time Houston was a polished orator in his own right, and without question he had acquired more than a little of that polish from Daniel Webster.

An even more notable leader than Webster during this period was Henry Clay. A prominent American statesman for four decades, Clay was witty, charming, and eloquent. The son of a Baptist preacher and planter, Clay was born in 1777 in Virginia. Clay was just twenty when he was admitted to the bar, and he practiced law successfully in Lexington, Kentucky, where he built a beautiful home, Ashland. He became active in state politics in his twenties, and on his first day in the U.S. House of Rep-

resentatives in 1841 he was elected
to the first of six terms as Speaker.
Clay also was prominent as a senator and secretary of State, and he
ran for president three times. Long
a force for compromise in Congress,
he became known as the "Great
Pacifier." When Representative
Sam Houston took his first seat in
the House, Henry Clay was elected Speaker. During his first term in
Congress, Representative Houston
watched one of the greatest statesmen in American history maneuver
and facilitate the business of the
House.

Congressman Sam Houston,
already a gifted public speaker,
benefited greatly from hearing
America's greatest orator, Mas-
sachusetts Representative Daniel Webster, address Congress
on numerous occasions for four
years. *Courtesy National Archives.*

Of course, in 1824 Speaker Clay
engineered the presidential victory
of John Quincy Adams over Andrew Jackson, thereby earning the
enmity of Jackson and his supporters, including Sam Houston. But
when Houston returned to Con-
gress as a senator from Texas he developed an appreciation for
Senator Clay's efforts to compromise the nation's growing sectionalism, as well as his support of internal improvements, badly
needed by frontier Texas.

During the four-year presidency of John Quincy Adams (1825-
29), Sam Houston was a congressman (1825-27) and governor
from Tennessee (1827-29). Adams was a brilliant, well-educated
man who had served as Minister to the Netherlands, Prussia,
Russia, and Great Britain, while also serving in the U.S. Senate
and as Secretary of State under President Monroe. But President
Adams came under immediate fire from Jackson supporters after the "corrupt bargain" of the Election of 1824, and certainly
offered an example of resolute endurance under a bombardment
of criticism—a situation which Houston would encounter on oc-

casion in Texas. Former president Adams spent the last seventeen years of his life in the House of Representatives, where he opposed the annexation of Texas and voted against the declaration of war with Mexico. When Senator Houston arrived in Washington in 1846, Representative Adams would serve until his death in 1848, but it is unlikely that Houston had little to say to the former president and longtime political foe.

When Martin Van Buren succeeded Jackson as United States President in 1837, Sam Houston was President of the fledgling Republic of Texas. As a U.S. Senator, Van Buren joined Jackson's political campaign in 1828, which of course was actively supported by Tennessee Governor Sam Houston. Indeed, Van Buren ran for the governorship of New York in 1828 in an effort to improve Jackson's presidential chances in the state. Van Buren won the gubernatorial election of 1828, but resigned after less than three months to become President Jackson's Secretary of State. Houston and Van Buren were acquainted through their Jackson connection. But after Houston shifted his operations to Texas, he found scant cooperation from President Van Buren.

William Henry Harrison defeated Van Buren for the presidency in 1840. Harrison was well-educated and intended to become a doctor, but after his father died he enlisted in the army. Harrison became a professional soldier, rising from ensign to major general, and during the War of 1812 he led a successful campaign against Tecumseh. After the war Ohio sent Harrison to Congress, first to the House of Representatives, then to the Senate. As a senator, former major general Harrison deservedly became chairman of both the Military and the Militia committees and he and Houston had a casual acquaintance.

One of Harrison's sons, Dr. Benjamin Harrison, was educated as a physician. But young Harrison was a hard-drinking adventurer who was attracted to Texas in 1834. In 1836 Dr. Harrison briefly was captured by Gen. Jose de Urrea. Regaining his freedom, Harrison returned to Ohio, where he died at the age of thirty-four in 1840. The following year William Henry Harrison was inaugurated as President, but he died one month later, having no impact on Texas or Houston during his brief presidency.

Vice President John Tyler served out President Harrison's term, and for three of those years Sam Houston was President of Texas. During a long political career Tyler served as Governor of Virginia, Representative to the House, and U.S. Senator. But as President he was unpopular, and as the Election of 1844 approached, Tyler put presidential support behind a treaty to annex Texas, hoping to identify with an increasingly popular issue. The Senate refused to ratify the treaty, but public enthusiasm for the annexation of Texas persuaded Congress to pass a joint resolution to admit the new state. President Tyler signed the measure three days before the end of his term.

Tennessean James K. Polk won the presidency in 1844. Two years younger than Sam Houston, he was ten when his family moved to Tennessee from North Carolina. Polk was intensely ambitious and hard-working, a classic overachiever. An excellent student, he enjoyed debate and public speaking. Polk studied law and was captivated by politics, while his charming spouse, Sarah, enjoyed the social duties of a politician's wife.

Polk was prominent during his single term in the Tennessee House of Representatives, 1823-25. He went from the State Legislature to Congress, joining his friend Sam Houston in the House. In 1827 Houston became Governor of Tennessee, while Polk remained in the House for seven consecutive terms, including the last two as Speaker. Polk strongly supported Andrew Jackson. An ardent expansionist, President Polk sent troops to the north bank of the Rio Grande to

James K. Polk and Sam Houston both were strong supporters and intimates of Andrew Jackson, and in time Polk became known as "Young Hickory." Polk's fourteen years in Congress included the two terms of Congressman Houston. Polk became Speaker of the House and was the ninth governor of Tennessee (Houston was the sixth). Polk was president when Houston returned to Washington as a senator. *Courtesy National Archives.*

press the Texas boundary claim, and he triggered the War with Mexico, which added a vast area to the United States. When Senator Sam Houston arrived in Washington, he promptly paid a call at the White House to visit his old friend from Tennessee.

General Zachary Taylor established a U.S. Army encampment in Texas just north of the Rio Grande early in 1846. From there he launched a victorious campaign into Mexico. His military success in the War with Mexico propelled him into the presidency in 1849, but he died in 1850.

President Taylor opposed the Compromise of 1850, engineered by Senator Henry Clay, but Taylor's successor, Millard Fillmore, placed crucial presidential support behind the measure. Passage of the Compromise relieved growing tensions between the North and South. An important part of the Compromise defined the borders of Texas, with a compensation of $10,000,000 for the Texas surrender of lands far to the west and north. Franklin Pierce of New Hampshire was a veteran of the War with Mexico who earlier had served in Congress as a member of both the House and Senate. Senator Sam Houston helped Pierce to win the Democrat nomination for president in 1852, then campaigned for him as he defeated Whig candidate Winfield Scott.

There was support for Senator Houston as a presidential candidate in 1856. But viable candidates now were selected by national conventions of the Democratic and new Republican parties, and Houston deigned to submit to the convention process. However, he did support his longtime friend, James Buchanan, for the Democratic nomination. Buchanan was almost as tall as Houston and two years his senior. An attorney from Pennsylvania, Buchanan served in he U.S. House of Representatives (1821-1831) and in the Senate (1834-1845). Buchanan was also Polk's Secretary of State, and he served as U.S. Minister to Russia and to Great Britain.

As a young congressman Buchanan supported Andrew Jackson and his policies, beginning with the "corrupt bargain" campaign of 1824. Twenty years later, Senator Buchanan supported the annexation of Texas and the presidential candidacy of James K. Polk. As Polk's Secretary of State, Buchanan made final arrangements for Texas annexation. With a friendship and political alliance that dated back to the 1820s, Houston campaigned strongly for Buchanan's 1856 presidential victory.

Despite Houston's friendship and support for both Pierce and Buchanan, he became disenchanted with the performance of both presidents during the troubled 1850s. "It was thought that Pierce's administration was so poor and low that none could go beneath it," he wrote to his wife in 1858. "Now, Dear, I am sorry to believe that the present Administration will burrow beneath it."[7]

Abraham Lincoln served a single term as a Representative from Illinois from 1847 to 1849, when Sam Houston was in the Senate. Houston was Governor of Texas when Lincoln became President. Short-

Abraham Lincoln served his only term in Congress in 1847-49, when Sam Houston was rapidly becoming a force in the U.S. Senate. A dozen years later there was contact between President Lincoln and Governor Houston on the eve of the Civil War. *Courtesy National Archives.*

ly after Lincoln's election, slave states began to secede from the Union. Because Houston was a staunch unionist, Lincoln began to contact him through emissaries, offering military support if he could keep Texas in the Union. Even after secessionists ousted Houston from the governorship, Lincoln offered him a major general's commission and assistance to resist the loss of Texas to the Union. But Houston could not bring himself to pit Texan against Texan.

In addition to fourteen presidents of the United States, Sam Houston knew the president of the Confederate States of America. Jefferson Davis was a U.S. Senator from Mississippi from 1847 to 1851 and from 1857 to 1861, as well as President Pierce's Secretary of War. Senators Davis and Houston were not close, and sometimes clashed in debate. Jefferson Davis was inaugurated as president of the C.S.A. less than a month before Governor Houston was forced out of office, so there was no meaningful contact in 1861.

Sam Houston also knew the Confederacy's great general, Robert E. Lee. As a young congressman, Houston crossed the Potomac River to the columned mansion, Arlington. There he courted Mary Parke Custis, a descendant by marriage of George Washington. Houston became optimistic that he had found a suitable marriage partner for a rising political figure. But Miss Custis soon told Houston that the suitor who had won her heart was a handsome, impressive West Point cadet, Robert E. Lee.

Houston fumed in the third person that "she might have been Washington's bride and belle of the Washington society."[8] Lee's military career brought him to Texas during the 1850s, as lieutenant colonel and later colonel of the Second Cavalry, a combat regiment organized to battle horseback warriors in Texas and other frontiers. The two men last saw each other in 1860 when Colonel Lee returned to Texas from a long furlough in Virginia, and he stopped in Austin for a visit with Governor Houston before reporting to his regiment.

Beginning in his early twenties, Sam Houston associated with and learned from talented and prominent American leaders. Young Houston had his own leadership gifts and inclinations which matured rapidly. When Houston was in his fifties he returned to Washington, D.C., as a senator with national fame and a myriad of remarkable experiences behind him. Now it was Senator Houston who was listened to and watched by aspiring statesmen.

My God is the man mad?
President Andrew Jackson

Chapter Five

Leader in Disgrace

Handsome and tall, personable and courtly, Sam Houston had been strongly attracted to "the Dear Girls" since his teenage years. While living with the Cherokees the lanky youngster engaged in flirtations with Cherokee maidens. As a twenty-two-year-old officer in uniform in New Orleans, he attracted the attention of young ladies. During a promenade on the public square, for example, he eyed the beautifully-dressed Kent sisters from Virginia. Although he had never been introduced, Houston touched the bill of his shako. "Who was that handsome officer?" whispered one sister to another. The handsome officer bowed elegantly. "Lieutenant Houston, United States Army, at your service."[1]

In New Orleans there were other, less proper, women, and many seductive entertainment venues. When Houston was wounded at Horseshoe Bend, then transported by litter on two long, agonizing trips, the only means of dulling the pain was liquor. The wounds did not heal, and there was more surgery in New Orleans. Houston became accustomed to drinking regularly, including during social occasions. He was a large man and could hold at lot of liquor, but from time to time he became inebriated in public. From colonial times America was a hard-drinking society, and Houston carried on the tradition, from convivial companion to drunken rowdy.

Lieutenant Houston had an affair with "M___," also called "the Princess of E. T." (East Tennessee). But soon he asked a friend to help him break off the romance.[2] As a young congressman he had an affair that seemed to promise a wedding. "For my *single* self I do not yet know yet the sweets of matrimony, but in March or April next I will . . . ," he wrote to a friend in January 1825. But Houston added a revealing condition. "My errand here is to attend to the business of my constituents, and not to spend `honey moons.' *Every thing in due season!*"[3]

And so these romances, too, ended. In April, instead of marrying his latest sweetheart, Congressman Houston left Washington for Tennessee. En route he wrote to his cousin, John H. Houston, who lived in Washington. With a hint of relief, Sam related to his cousin, "I am this far on my way west, in the full enjoyment of the sweets of single blessedness."[4]

Houston sounded the same tone the following January. "I am making myself less frequent in the Lady World than I have been. I must keep my Dignity, or rather I must attend more to politics and less to love."[5]

Houston thoroughly enjoyed "the Lady World," but he did not want the encumbrances of wife and children. Clearly the career that held such promise for prominent leadership was Houston's priority. His world was politics and the military. He needed to attend public events and private meetings. As a bachelor he was free to travel to barbeques, balls, dinners, horse races. He could ride anywhere at any time to make a speech. He could answer any summon to The Hermitage, and stay as long as needed. And if long absences from a sweetheart jeopardized a romance, Houston shrugged and made "myself less frequent in the Lady World."

"I have as usual had 'a small blow up,'" reported Houston to a friend late in 1828. "What the devil is the matter with the gals I cant say but there had been hell to pay and no pitch hot!" But Houston added optimistically that after all "it may be that I will splice myself with a rib."[6]

The "small blow up" that Houston experienced—"as usual"—was with lovely, eighteen-year-old Eliza Allen. But Houston was more persistent than customary, without realizing that the "small blow up" with Eliza was a portent of the future. Enchanted by Eliza's blond good looks and encouraged by her ambitious family, Governor Houston ignored the "hell to pay" quarrel and attempted to repair the romance.

Houston had met Eliza several years earlier, when she was no more than thirteen. Her father, John Allen, was a longtime friend of Andrew Jackson, and his brothers, Robert and Campbell Allen, marched under Jackson during the War of 1812. Robert served in Congress alongside Houston. Between Andrew Jackson and Robert Allen, Sam Houston occasionally visited the Allen family in Gallatin, which was less than thirty miles northeast of Nashville. John Allen's plantation, Allenwood, was three miles south of Gallatin, on the Cumberland River. Andrew Jackson visited Allenwood during the horse racing season, and Houston also enjoyed the gracious society of the plantation on occasion.

As Eliza grew into a young woman, Houston found himself infatuated, and in the summer of 1828 he asked her father for permission to marry. By now Houston was governor of Tennessee, and John and Robert Allen had heard rumors that he might one day succeed Jackson as president. Eliza Allen could soon be First Lady of Tennessee, and quite conceivably she might one day preside over the White House. The Allen family was prominent and ambitious. Eliza had a sweetheart, but no young man was a match for Governor Houston. While Houston was sixteen years older than Eliza, he was handsome and charming—the Governor was the most eligible bachelor in Tennessee. John and Robert Allen were persuasive in convincing Eliza that marriage to Houston was desirable in many ways.

In November 1828, Houston wrote to cousin John Houston about family matters, adding: "I am not married but it may be the case in a few weeks, and should it—you shall hear of it before the newspapers can reach you."[7]

The next month Houston and Eliza had their "small blow up," but the disagreement was patched over, and plans for the wedding continued. Late in the month Rachel Jackson died, and Houston was head pallbearer. He remained at The Hermitage to try to console the grief-stricken president-elect, and Houston must have reflected upon the long, successful marriage of the Jacksons.

On Thursday, January 22, 1829, Sam Houston married Eliza Allen at Allenwood. The ceremony was conducted by Dr. William Hume, a Presbyterian minister who was a member of the Antiquarian Society alongside Governor Houston. The newlyweds spent their first night together at Allenwood. The next morning Sam and Eliza set out for Nashville in bitter weather, and they stayed overnight at Locust Grove, the home of Robert and Martha Martin. The Martins were friends of both Sam and the Allens, and Locust Grove was the scene of an oft-repeated story of the second morning of the Houston marriage. Houston rose early and engaged in a snowball fight with the two Martin daughters. Eliza was the last to rise, and as she came downstairs, Martha Martin pointed out the wintry combat on the front lawn.

"I said to her: it seems as if General Houston is getting the worst of the snowballing; you had better go out and help him. Looking seriously at me, Mrs. Houston said: `I wish they would kill him.' I looked astonished to hear such a remark from a bride of not yet forty-eight hours, when she repeated in the same voice, `yes, I wish from the bottom of my heart that they would kill him.'"[8]

After breakfast the Houstons rode into Nashville, and for a couple of days they were houseguests with Robert McEwen, Houston's cousin, and his family. Governor and Mrs. Houston then move into his two-room quarters on the second floor of the Nashville Inn. These accommodations were a marked comedown from the genteel comforts of Eliza's home at Allenwood. Furthermore, she must have realized that, as a young bride still in her teens, she was in over her head as First Lady of Tennessee. At some point she told Houston that she still loved her early sweetheart. Eliza simply was miserable as the wife of Sam Houston. Houston was a lusty man of the world with a sheltered bride who had just turned nineteen. She was repulsed by the ugly scar on his upper thigh, and by the shoulder wound which continually drained. For Eliza, it was a bad match from the beginning, and her misery grew daily. And with a wife who did not try to hide her unhappiness, Houston's existence was wretched.

Less than a week into the joyless marriage, however, Governor Houston announced his intention to run for re-election. Former governor William Carroll had understood that Houston would serve just one term and step aside, and he campaigned determinedly for a fourth term. In addition to pursuing his own campaign, Houston intended to attend the presidential inauguration of Andrew Jackson on March 4, 1829. Unprecedented numbers of citizens came to Washington to see the president that they had elected, and after the inauguration ceremonies a vast crowd followed him to the White House and nearly took it apart. But Sam Houston, a key member of Jackson's inner circle, was conspicuous by his absence from this sensational day.

Perhaps Houston was too busy with his re-election campaign to go, and most certainly he was preoccupied with his desolate wife. Early in April 1829 Governor and Mrs. Houston visited Judge John Overton and his wife, Mary, at Travelers Rest, their home near Nashville. Among the crowd was Mrs. Mary Lawson Barry, who recalled that Eliza Houston remained silent throughout their stay, refusing the efforts of both Judge and Mrs. Overton, as well as of Houston, to draw her into conversation. Mrs. Barry observed, "She sulked and nursed her wrath to keep it warm all the while."[9]

Shortly after this incident, the two gubernatorial candidates held a debate at Cockrell's Spring, ten miles from Nashville. A large crowd gathered, and Houston performed impressively—he had developed great powers of persuasion over public gatherings. After the debate Houston rode back to the Nashville Inn, but his quarters were empty. Eliza had returned to Allenwood and her family.

Devastated, Houston wrote a disjointed letter to his father-in-law: "Mr. Allen, the most unpleasant & unhappy circumstance has just taken place in the family . . . " Houston penned an impressionistic version of their differences, and offered reassurances of his deep affection for Eliza. "That I have & do love Eliza none can doubt—that she is the only earthly object dear to me God will witness." Houston did not want the separation to become public knowledge. "The only way this matter can now be overcome will be for us all to meet as tho it had never occurred, & this will keep the world, as it should be, ignorant that such thoughts ever were." Houston confided his deepest pain. "She was cold to me,

& I thought did not love me . . . You can judge how unhappy I was to think I was united to a woman who did not love me.' He insisted that "my future happiness can only exist in the assurance that Eliza & myself can be happy & that Mrs. Allen & you can forget the past—forgive all . . . Let me know what is to be done."[10]

Nothing was to be done, not by the Allens, who understandably rallied around their daughter. News of the separation of Governor and Mrs. Houston spread like wildfire. Supporters of William Carroll led a public outcry. Houston was hanged in effigy in Gallatin, and there were subsequent effigy hangings elsewhere. Houston confined himself to his rooms at the Nashville Inn, where he was visited by a few loyal friends, including Judge John Overton, Sheriff Willoughby Williams, and Congressman David Crockett. Seeking the help of God, Houston asked Rev. David Hume—who had married him in January—for baptism. Hume consulted with the pastor of Nashville's First Presbyterian Church, and with a deplorable lack of Christian charity, they declined.

As gossip swirled, Houston refused to defend himself. "This is a painful, but it is a private affair. I do not recognize the right of the public to interfere in it . . . If my character cannot stand the shock, let me lose it. The storm will soon sweep by, and time will be my vindicator."[11] He would never shed light on the reason for

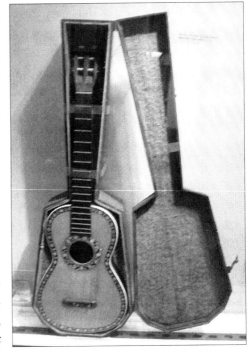

This guitar and case belong to Eliza Allen. On display at the Tennessee State Museum, these items are among the few tangible remnants of her life. Eliza destroyed all correspondence and images, and requested an unmarked grave. *Photo by the author.*

the separation. Years afterward he wrote on the subject in third person: "It is not known . . . to this day, what were the real causes of this unfortunate result, for Houston's lips have never been opened upon the subject to a single human being."[12]

In addition to genuine affection for is lovely wife, Houston understood the grim implications of a separation for his political future. On April 15 he rode to Allenwood and asked to speak to Eliza. She listened to him, in the presence of an aunt, as he took a knee and begged forgiveness. Houston biographer James L. Haley thoughtfully analyzed Eliza, and he concluded that "now she was free of him she had no intention of going back." Haley related that when Houston arrived back in Nashville, after midnight, he sought out longtime friend Frank Chambers. "His face was rigid," described Chambers. "His eyes had a strange stare. he looked like some magnificent ruin . . ."[13]

The next day Governor Houston submitted a letter of resignation. For the next several days he secluded himself at the Nashville Inn, drinking heavily and considering his next course of action. Houston reflected that with his resignation he "gave up all the bright future before him, and exiled himself from all the habitation of man." He decided to commence is exile at "the wigwam of his adopted father, the chief of the Cherokees, in Arkansas . . ."[14]

Houston was deeply wounded. His world had collapsed. Marriage, governorship, public adulation, presidential hopes— all vanished in a dismaying turn of fortune. Now he intended to retreat from the scene of disaster and lick his wounds among the Cherokee in a remote wilderness. Houston borrowed travel funds, and on April 23, one week after his resignation, he emerged from the Nashville Inn. Accompanied by a few friends, Houston walked down a steep street to the river front, where he boarded the little steamboat *Red River*.

The river packet made frequent stops to drop off or take on passengers, mail, and freight. When the *Red River* docked at Clarksville, two armed relatives of Eliza's came aboard to demand from Houston a written statement denying any guilt on her part. Houston flatly refused their demand, because he knew

that Eliza had left him through no wrongdoing of his. But with
the boat's captain present, Houston told Eliza's representatives to
publish in Nashville newspapers a declaration that if "any wretch
ever dares to utter a word against the purity of Mrs. Houston I
will come back and write the libel in his heart's blood."[15]

"I have just this moment heard of poor Houston's disgrace,"
wrote President Jackson to a nephew. "My God is the man mad?"[16]
Jackson was horrified at what had happened to his protégé and
the daughter of his close friend. While Houston evidently never told Jackson any more than he revealed to anyone else, Old
Hickory was so well-connected in Tennessee that he must had
heard versions of both sides of the sad saga. Certainly Jackson
and Houston resumed their close relationship.

"Oh, what a fall for a major general, member of Congress and
a Governor of so respectable a state as Tennessee," wrote Rev.
William Hume with a tone of false sympathy, if not downright
hypocrisy. "And oh what a fall for the cause of Christianity when
a man, heart-weary and broken, had to turn his back on the so-
called representatives of Christ and go to the house of his Indian
foster-parent for solace."[17] Of course, Reverend Hume—who refused Houston's request for baptism at a time of intense emotional and spiritual need—was one of "the so-called representatives
of Christ" who turned his back on a seeker, rather than the other
way around.

But Houston was headed unerringly "to the home of his Indian foster-parent for solace." He cared no more for the disapprov-
al of white society regarding his Indian association than when he
first sought out the Cherokee more than two decades earlier, at
the age of fifteen. Houston was utterly despondent when he departed Nashville, but he perceived an omen that lifted his hopes
for the future. "I was in an agony of despair and strongly tempt-
ed to leap overboard and end my worthless life. At that moment,
however, an eagle swooped down near my head, and then, soaring aloft with wildest screams, was lost in the rays of the setting
sun. I knew that a great destiny awaited me in the West."[18]

Houston rode the *Red River* down the Tennessee River to the
Ohio, and at the Mississippi floated on a flatboat down to the

mouth of the Arkansas. Throughout the journey Houston imbibed uproariously with traveling companions. A small steamboat brought him up the Arkansas to Fort Gibson. Oolooteka learned that Houston was aboard the approaching little boat that would dock just two miles from his home. Houston related their reunion after more than a decade apart.

"It was night when Oolooteka, the rich old chief, full six feet in height, and unbent for his age, bringing with him all his family, hurried to the river bank to meet his adopted son Colonneh . . ." The Raven was greeted with the warmth he yearned for, then was told by his adopted father that the Cherokee needed his services. "The reception was all that the hospitality and simplicity of the Indian character could give such a scene—the old Chief delicately alluding to the dark cloud that had fallen across the path of the white warrior, but assuring him, with the zeal of a prophet, that the Great Spirit had conducted the exile to the Cherokees, who were in great trouble, to give them counsel and to tell their sorrows to their great father, Andrew Jackson."[19]

"My wigwam is yours—my home is yours—my people are yours—rest with us," invited Oolooteka. It was precisely the medicine the Raven needed:

"When I laid myself down to sleep that night, after the gloom and the sorrows of the last few weeks, I felt like a weary wanderer returned at last to my father's house."[20]

It is hard for an old Trooper to forget
the note of the Bugle!

Sam Houston

Chapter Six
Leader Reborn

"We are in trouble, and the Great Spirit has sent you to us to give us council, and take trouble away from us." During his first meeting in eleven years with his adopted son, Oolooteka stated his deepest concerns as principal chief of the Cherokee, along with his fervent hope, to the Raven. "I know you will be our friend, for our hearts are near to you, and you will tell our sorrows to the great father."[1]

Treaties that had been made since the Cherokee removal to the West were constantly violated. Promised cash allotments from the federal government went unpaid. Provisions were under supplied. Liquor was sold. Troubles with other tribes were not mediated. But the sudden appearance of the Raven offered hope.

Since first living with the Cherokee as a youngster, his Native American friends knew that he subsequently had been a warrior, a sub-agent to the tribe, a congressman, and a governor. Most importantly, he was a close friend of "the great father," President Jackson. The Raven may have had troubles in the white man's world, but now he had returned to the Cherokee, and no one could be as powerful an advocate for his Indian friends as Governor Houston. Immediately the Raven began to be visited at Oolooteka's substantial plantation home by other Cherokee leaders and by representatives from neighboring tribes.

Sam Houston had left the office of governor six weeks earlier. He needed an outlet for his leadership gifts to restore himself, and immediately he recognized pressing needs among his Native American brothers. Looking back on this period, Houston proudly recalled, in his favored third person: "Three years' life among these sons of the forest offered him ample opportunity to vindicate the oppressed red men from their wrongs and sufferings, and he proved himself to be what they had always regarded him and still regard him, their friend."[2]

The Raven promptly discarded his Tennessee clothing and donned the colorful Cherokee attire which he always enjoyed. His new outfit featured a white doeskin shirt, handsomely decorated with colored beads. Yellow leather leggings were pulled up to his thighs. The Raven plaited his hair in a queue, adorning his head with feathers or wearing a silk turban. He threw a blanket across his shoulder, changing blankets according to his mood. He spoke the Cherokee tongue, referring to himself in the third person—a Native American trait he employed throughout his life.

The Raven's Cherokee clothing, his hair, his language—all testified to his commitment to use his powers of leadership, his connections in high places, on behalf of the Cherokee and other tribes displaced from their homelands.

Oolooteka hosted a welcome celebration for

Former governor Sam Houston sought refuge among the Cherokee, now re-settled in Indian Territory. Throughout his life Houston would incorporate elements of Cherokee attire into his dress. *Courtesy Sam Houston Schoolhouse Historical Museum.*

his adopted son. Almost immediately afterward an emissary from the Osage tribe persuaded the Raven to ride 100 miles northwest, to the home of Maj. Auguste Pierre Chouteau, a trader and the most trusted white man among the Osage. The tribe was experiencing great problems with their new agent, and the Raven agreed to travel to the agency on their behalf. Creeks soon asked for assistance from the Raven, and Choctaws requested that he write to the Secretary of War regarding their problems.

The Secretary of War was John Eaton, like Houston an intimate of Andrew Jackson. "An old Choctaw Chief called on me today, and complained that the white People were on their lands & were treating them badly," reported Houston to Secretary Eaton. "They take the Choctaw houses, and will not let them go into them. Some [Choctaw] emigrants have lately arrived, and have not houses to go into, and complain that Genl. Jackson, in a treaty with them E[ast] of the Mississippi told them if they would come west that they should be happy, and when they have come that the whites are on their land and they are not happy . . . I have assured him that you will soon grant relief to the Indians . . . "[3]

Houston wrote letter after letter, many seeking aid for the tribes, but some simply to re-establish connections with old friends. Soon numerous letters to him began arriving from the East. The Raven rode across Indian Territory throughout the summer; he represented Oolooteka at meetings; he visited headquarters at Cantonment Gibson; he made his presence known at tribal centers and at Indian agencies. At Cantonment Gibson he became friends with the post commander, Col. Matthew Arbuckle, who appreciated Houston's army background and who enjoyed a convivial companion. Houston and Arbuckle worked together to forestall war factions among the tribes.

The constant activities of the Raven continued from late May through June and July and into August. Although he was busy and aiding the tribes in matters large and small, he drank heavily. Overindulgence in liquor, combined with exertions in the heat of summer, may have contributed to his collapse in mid-August. Houston's biographers generally ascribe his illness to malaria, a common summer malady among white men in Indian Territory.

James Haley agrees with the malaria diagnosis, but he suggests that Houston "was generally losing his battle with alcohol," and that his collapse in August 1829 may have been due to delirium tremens (DTs).[4]

Houston was ill for more than five weeks, and at times he was thought to be on the verge of death. On his good days he read the pile of correspondence that continued to accumulate. As he recovered he began answering his mail, which included a letter from Jackson at the depths of Houston's illness: "My dear Sir," wrote Houston, "I am very feeble, from a long spell of fever, which lasted me some 38 days, and had well nigh closed the scene of all my mortal cares, but I thank my God that I am again cheered by the hope of renewed health. I would not write at this time but that I can not deny to myself the pleasure of tendering to you my heartfelt acknowledgment of your kind favor, which reached me when I was barely able to peruse its contents. It was a cordial to my spirits, and cheered me in my sickness."[5]

Houston's pen continued at length, mentioning to President Jackson "my abando[n]ment of society, my absolute refusal to gratify the inquiring world, my entire silence, because it comported with my notions of honor . . ." Houston wrote on about his efforts among the tribes "to prevent fraud, and peculation, on part of the Government Agents among them . . ." And Houston reflected on the future. "When I left the world I had persuaded myself that I would lose all care, about the passing political events of the world, as well as those of my own country, but it is not so, for as often as I visit Cant. Gibson, where I can obtain News Papers, I find that my interest is rather increased than diminished. It is hard for an old Trooper to forget that *note of the Bugle!*"

Despondent and drinking to excess when he reached the Cherokee Nation in May 1829, Houston had renounced in his own mind any future participation in politics. But his renunciation was shallow. Houston had tasted deeply of political leadership, as prosecuting attorney and adjutant general in Tennessee, as congressman and governor. In every office he had performed with innate confidence, accepting responsibility readily and wielding power skillfully on behalf of his constituents. And so within weeks of resigning his governorship, within days of arriving in the wilderness of the Cherokee Nation, Sam Houston responded without hesitation to the needs and entreaties of the Cherokee, the Osage, the Creek, the Choctaw. Their needs gave him purpose. Houston, the old political Trooper, had not come close to forgetting *the note of the Bugle!*

Finally recovered by summer's end, in the fall the Raven was granted tribal citizenship. On October 21, 1829, "We do . . . Solemnly, firmly, and unrecoverably grant to him for ever all the rights, privileges, and Immunities of a citizen of the Cherokee Nation and do as fully empower him with all rights and liberties as tho he was a native Cherokee . . . "[6]

Cherokee citizenship provided the Raven legal status to represent the Cherokee as an ambassador to the federal government in Washington, D.C. He departed aboard the steamboat *Amazon* late in December 1829. He spent Christmas on the riverboat, and a few days later he wrote Judge John Overton that "I am on my way to Washington, and perhaps New York, before my return to the place of my exile."[7]

The Raven reached Washington on January 12, 1830, and after checking into his former lodging house, Brown's Indian Queen Hotel on Pennsylvania Avenue, he must have felt reborn. His wardrobe, of course, was Cherokee: moccasins, buckskin leggings, hunting shirts, blankets, feathers, beads, traditional turbans. Adorned in Cherokee finery, he answered an invitation to a White House diplomatic reception and was embraced by President Jackson. Most onlookers, unaware that Jackson and Houston had maintained a correspondence, must have been surprised at the genuine warmth between the two men.

In addition to welcoming a protégé and ally, Jackson must have taken special pleasure that Houston would be at his side for a time during his bitter feud with Vice President John C. Calhoun. (Houston's enmity with Calhoun went back to the clash between Lieutenant Houston and Secretary of War Calhoun, who was unnecessarily mean-spirited to the young officer.) Jackson's Secretary of War, John Eaton, married beautiful, vivacious Peggy O'Neale Timberlake. Rumors held that Peggy's first husband, U.S. Navy purser John B. Timberlake, had learned of an affair between his wife and Eaton, and committed suicide while at sea aboard the *U.S.S. Constitution*. When Peggy and John Eaton wed in 1829, the ladies of Washington society, led by Mrs. Calhoun, ostracized Mrs. Eaton.

John Eaton, of course, was a protégé of President Jackson. Jackson found Peggy to be a charming young woman, and he bitterly remembered the slander that had devastated his beloved Rachel. Jackson was infuriated when the "Petticoat Affair" escalated rapidly behind the determined leadership of the wives of his vice president and cabinet members. Vice President Calhoun and other husbands incurred the ire of Jackson during this social feud. But Secretary of State Martin Van Buren was a widower, and he was conspicuously gallant and hospitable to the Eatons.

Van Buren grew in favor with President Jackson, while Vice President Calhoun—surely to the satisfaction of Sam Houston – grew in disfavor. In 1831 John Eaton resigned his secretaryship. But animosity grew between Jackson and Calhoun, cresting over the Nullification Crisis of 1832. Calhoun resigned the vice presidency to accept a U.S. Senate seat from South Carolina, while Van Buren became Jackson's vice president during his second term.

While the Petticoat Affair was playing out, Cherokee Ambassador Houston reported to Secretary of War Eaton regarding allotment payments by certificates (which meant little to Native Americans) rather than gold, inadequate provisions, Indian agents who mistreated their charges, and other problems. Houston succeeded in having five agents removed, but most were reinstated through political contacts.

Backed by a New York financier, Houston submitted a bid to furnish to the Native Americans "full ration, and of good quality . . . "[8] But he did not receive the contract, and political enemies later accused Houston and John Eaton of nefarious collusion (an accusation which Houston refuted with his customary meticulous records).

Houston returned to the Cherokee in May 1830. As he passed through Tennessee, Houston's enemies organized a committee and published resolutions denouncing the former governor's treatment of his bride. The committee declared that "very shortly after the marriage Governor Houston became jealous of his wife, and mentioned . . . that he believed she was incontinent and devoid of affection for her husband." Since then "she has remained in a state of dejection and despondency." The committee also published Houston's letter to his father-in-law, John Allen, written just before Eliza left him to return home.[9]

Houston reacted with bravado in letter to friends. "I am not down," he assured Andrew Jackson. "The affections of the people of Tennessee are with me . . . they have confidence in me, and care nothing about my private matters, which they cannot understand." To another friend Houston stated, "that if I would again return to Tennessee I would beat [Billy Carroll] for Governor . . ." Regarding "Mrs. H.," Houston was as noncommittal as ever: "Tho the world can never know my situation and may condemn me God will justify me!"[10]

Following his return to the Cherokee Nation, Houston established a home among his adopted people. He set up a log trading post a few miles north of Cantonment Gibson. Houston had no more interest in the duties of a merchant-trader than he had as a youngster at the family mercantile in east Tennessee. But the daily activities would be capably handled by the Raven's new wife, Diana (or Tiana) Rogers Gentry. She was a half-sister of John Rogers, boyhood friend of the Raven in Tennessee who now was a likely successor to Oolooteka. Diana had married a white blacksmith named Gentry, but she was widowed when he was killed by Osage warriors. She was a few years younger than Houston. The Raven had known her as a girl in Tennessee, and she may have nursed him during his recent illness.

There had been no divorce between Houston and Eliza, but Cherokee marriage arrangements were informal, especially between a half-blood woman and the white adopted son of a chief. With romantic flair Houston named his Cherokee home "Wigwam Neosho."

From Wigwam Neosho Houston penned a series of articles for the *Arkansas Gazette*. One reflected upon the fate of Native

Americans. "Where stood the Indian of other days? He stood on the shore of the Atlantic, and beheld, each morning, the sun rolling from the bosom of its green waves . . . He was monarch of the wilds," proclaimed the Raven. Then he lamented, "That age has long gone by—the aboriginal character is almost lost in the views of the white man . . . "[11]

Houston went on to list the frauds that had been perpetuated upon the tribes, concluding with "the introduction of ardent spirits among the Indians . . . " Houston insisted that from his trading post, "I never introduced or trafficked in these destructive drinks." He admitted that "I was far from being a practically temperate man myself," and he spoke of "my own occasional indulgences during my visits to Fort Gibson and other white settlements . . ."

By this point Houston's "indulgences" were more than "occasional." Houston understood—as only a problem drinker could—how destructive the effects of liquor were upon his Indian brothers. "I had too much humanity and love for the Red men," vowed Houston at the end of this revealing article, "ever to contribute to . . . their misfortunes by introducing or trafficking in those damnable poisons."

Fort Gibson was a stockaded outpost when Sam Houston sojourned nearby from 1829 through 1831. Houston found convivial drinking companions at the bachelor officers' quarters. *Courtesy Fort Gibson National Park.*

Houston himself all too often indulged "in those damnable poisons." Many Cherokee who knew him as the Raven began to call him "Big Drunk." He stood for a seat in the Cherokee National Council in the spring of 1831, but he was defeated. Soon afterward he boarded a riverboat for a trip to Tennessee, but his reception there was disappointing. Inspired by classical irony—and perhaps a touch of self-pity—he had his portrait painted, clad in a toga, as Marius among the ruins of Carthage. Gaius Marius was a great Roman soldier and statesman, but at a low point in his fortunes he fled to a self-imposed exile in North Africa.

Also while in Nashville, despondency—and probably alcohol—led him to compose and publish a defiant proclamation to the public. "Know all me by these presents, that I, Sam Houston, 'late Governor or the State of Tennessee,' do hereby declare to all *scoundrels whomsoever* that they are authorized to accuse, defame, calumniate, slander, vilify, and libel me to any extent, in *personal or private abuse.*" He went on in this vein for a full page, then planted his tongue in cheek and concluded: "Given under my hand and private seal, *(having no seal of office)* at Nashville, in the State of Tennessee."[12]

Houston returned to Wigwam Neosho, but soon had to travel again. In August he received word that his mother was failing, and he left promptly for the Houston home in East Tennessee. Elizabeth Paxton Houston had reached seventy-four, the stalwart matriarch of a large family. She had been widowed for twenty-four years, but moved her family from Virginia to Tennessee and built a wilderness home. Her oldest son died as a young man, and her second son committed suicide. One daughter died in childhood, and another was mentally unstable. But none of her offspring caused Elizabeth more sadness and disappointment than her free-spirited, gifted, stubborn middle child.

Bristling with promise, Sam had achieved heights which would make any mother proud, but for two years past he had plunged to dismaying depths. Such thoughts must have dogged Sam as he sat by his mother's bedside. She died on September 8, 1831, and Sam helped to carry her pine coffin to the cemetery behind the Baker's Creek Presbyterian Church.

Again Houston's return to Wigwam Neosho was brief. Another Cherokee delegation left for Washington in December, and they were accompanied by the Raven. The party went by riverboat down the Arkansas and Mississippi to New Orleans, then transferred to a ship which sailed around Florida and up the East Coast. En route downriver Houston encountered the inquisitive, observant French traveler, Alexis de Tocqueville. De Tocqueville intended to explore the influence of the American frontier on democracy.

He had heard of Houston.

Sam was present when his mother, Elizabeth Paxton Houston, died at the family house on September 8, 1831. She was buried in the cemetery behind the Baker's Creek Presbyterian Church. *Photo by the author.*

"This man was once Governor of Tennesse [sic]." De Tocqueville related that Houston treated his wife badly and had abandoned her, although some said that she was the cause of their problems. Then he recounted his version of Houston's retreat to the wilderness among Indians. "What's certain is that he left Tennessee, crossed the Mississippi and retired among the Creeks [Cherokees] in the district of Arkansas. There he was adopted by one of the chiefs, and is said to have married his daughter. Since then he has been living in the middle of the wilderness, half European and half savage."[13]

In his conversations with Houston, de Tocqueville engaged him particularly on the subject of Indians. Houston held forth on Christian missionaries and the effects of liquor and the best future paths for Indians. The riverboat reached New Orleans early in January 1832, and Houston led the delegation aboard a seagoing vessel. In Washington, D.C., Houston settled the Cherokee into Brown's Indian Queen Hotel, before going on to New York City.

He visited with capitalists interested in Houston as the front man for a Texas colonization venture. After returning to Washington, Houston sat in the gallery during congressional sessions, he socialized with old friends, and he avidly read current newspapers.

Early in April 1832, Huston read an issue of the *National Intelligencer* that reprinted a March 31 speech by Ohio Representative William Stanbery. An anti-Jackson partisan, Stanbery criticized the administration, including former Secretary of War John Eaton (who had resigned his cabinet position, but accepted an appointment by President Jackson as governor of Florida Territory). "Was not the late Secretary of War removed because of his attempt to give Governor Houston the contract for Indian rations?" Houston was furious when he read this tired old allegation, and he stormed to the foyer of the House chamber to find Stanbery.[14]

Houston was intercepted by his old friend from Tennessee, Congressman James K. Polk. Polk pulled the fuming Houston outside to cool down. But Houston soon sent a formal note to Stanbery which was the first step in initiating a duel. Stanbery refused to respond to the note, but he began carrying two pistols as a precaution.

On Friday, April 13, Houston was walking with two congressional friends when he sighted Stanbery across the street. Houston stalked over to him and asked, "Are you Mr. Stanbery?"

"Yes, sir," replied Stanbery.

"Then you are a damned rascal!" Houston struck Stanbery over the head with his hickory cane.

"Oh don't," cried Stanbery, who turned to run. Houston seized Stanbery and wrestled him to the ground. But Houston's right arm was permanently weakened from battle wounds, and Stanbery, who was nearly as large as Houston, freed an arm and pulled one of his pistols. He pressed the short barrel against Houston's side and pulled the trigger, but the gun misfired. Houston tore the pistol from Stanbery's grasp, stood over him, and beat him repeatedly with the cane. Finishing with a wicked flourish, Houston lifted Stanbery's legs and whipped him across his posterior.[15]

Suffering from a concussion and a fractured hand, along with a colorful assortment of bruises, Stanbery stayed in his quarters the next day. But he sent a note to Speaker of the House Andrew Stevenson, explaining that he was confined to his bed after being "waylaid" and wounded by a "bludgeon" wielded by Samuel Houston. He stressed that he had been assaulted because of words he had spoken in the House, a breach of congressional privilege. After the House voted 245 to 25 to arrest Houston, he engaged the noted attorney (and author of *The Star-Spangled Banner*) Francis Scott Key to mount his defense.

Andrew Jackson provided funds for Houston to acquire a suit and accessories so that Houston would not have to appear in Cherokee garb. Anti-Jackson congressmen used Houston's trial as a political platform, and proceedings in the House dragged on for weeks. President Jackson pointedly invited Houston to the White House during the trial, and he expressed a wish that there were "a dozen Houstons to beat and cudgel members of Congress." Newspapers reported the trial in detail, generating considerable public interest."[16]

Speaker Stevenson called for closing remarks at noon on Monday, May 7. Key's opening summation had been unimpressive, and Houston decided to close his case himself. A group of friends gathered in Houston's quarters Sunday night, May 6, to provide support and planning. Among those allies were Speaker of the House Stevenson and James K. Polk. The event turned into a serious drinking party, and Polk—described by Houston as "a victim of the use of water as a beverage"—departed early.

The next morning Houston suffered from a hangover, but he began drinking coffee and sent for a barber to shave him. Next he dressed in the clothes he had selected with Jackson's funding: "a coat of the finest material, reaching to his knees, trousers in harmony of color and latest style in cut, with a white satin vest to match." Houston announced, "I am all right."[17]

By noon every seat in the gallery was filled. The crowd included ranking officers of the army and navy, members of the diplomatic corps, and notables from Washington society. Resplendent "in my splendid apparel," Houston commanded the room with his impressive appearance and rich voice. "No man has more respect for this body, and its rights and privileges," he declared. "Never can I forget the associations connected with this Hall." He quoted verse, and he dramatically invoked the American flag that draped Lafayette's portrait. "I have violated no law," he insisted, pointing out that it was Stanbery—not Houston—who was armed.[18]

It was a bravura performance. The hall erupted in spontaneous applause. Renowned actor Junius Brutus Booth ran to the defendant, exclaiming, "Houston, take my laurels!" A young lady tossed her floral bouquet from the gallery, and Houston responded with an elegant bow.

Four days later, following partisan wrangling, a vote to reprimand Houston passed. Speaker Stevenson unenthusiastically announced to his friend and drinking partner, "I do reprimand you accordingly." Stanbery promptly had Houston arrested on a charge of assault, and after a long trial he was fined $500 (a fine which President Jackson later remitted).

Vengefully, Stanbery launched an investigation into Houston's efforts, through then-Secretary of War John Eaton, to secure a contract to provide rations to Native American tribes. Houston provided correspondence and records, and after six weeks the committee exonerated both Eaton and Houston.[19]

In July, shortly before departing Washington, Houston published an article discussing the dispute over the proposed rations contract. Regarding William Stanbery, Houston remarked: "His vices are too odious to merit pity and his spirit too mean to deserve contempt."[20]

As Houston left for the West, he was rejuvenated. Following the initial, therapeutic period of his retreat in 1829 to the Cherokee Nation, his existence became increasingly anticlimactic and unsatisfying. He soon realized that the future of Native Americans was limited, which necessarily imposed strict limitations on any future he might have as a leader among the tribes. Still in his thirties, Houston needed a stage suitable for his enormous potential as a public servant, as a national leader. "I was dying out," Houston reflected to a friend more than two decades later, "and had they taken me before a Justice of the Peace and fined me ten dollars for assault and battery, they would have killed me. But they gave me a national tribunal for a theatre, and set me up again."[21]

*Texas is the finest portion of the globe
that has ever blessed my vision.*
Sam Houston

Chapter Seven

Gone To Texas

G.T.T.—"Gone To Texas." During the 1820s and 1830s "G.T.T." was carved or chalked on the doorways or walls of vacated cabins across the South. In the early 1820s Mexico opened Texas to American colonists. A determined mission effort in Texas, launched by the Spanish in the 1690s, had failed to convert Native Americans into productive farmers and taxpayers. Settlers from Mexico also were largely unsuccessful on the Texas frontier. Indeed, by the early 1820s there were only three settlements of any size in Texas. San Antonio, the capital, had no more than 1,500 residents, and Comanche raiding parties boldly rode through the streets while citizens hunkered in their homes. Agriculture and stock-raising were dangerous occupations around San Antonio, and there was little trade. La Bahia and Nacogdoches were villages with only a few hundred inhabitants.

But during the previous two centuries Anglo-American pioneers had settled a succession of frontiers. American frontiersmen regularly transformed wilderness areas into regions of prosperity, and this process would be repeated in Texas. Stephen F. Austin was the first and most effective *empresario*/colonizer. His first colonization contract called for Austin to assign large land grants to 300 families. Austin obtained subsequent contracts for hundreds of more families, while other *empresarios* attempted to populate their own colonies. *Empresarios* received vast land grants for families settled, although Stephen F. Austin was too busy to develop any of his lands. But by 1832, the year of Houston's entry, Texas boasted a population of 20,000, and three quarters were American pioneers "G.T.T."

Sam Houston began thinking about Texas soon after resigning as governor of Tennessee. President Jackson attempted unsuccessfully to purchase Texas from Mexico, and Houston occasionally made observations about Texas in correspondence to his mentor. During private conversations at the White House or The Hermitage, Jackson and Houston certainly must have talked about possibilities in Texas.

During Houston's exile among the Cherokee, he was contacted by former Tennesseans William and John Wharton, who wanted him to visit Texas, where they had become prominent colonists. The Whartons may have influenced another Texan of rising importance, Dr. Branch T. Archer of Virginia, to try to persuade Houston to come to Texas.

Early in 1832 Houston began a two-year correspondence with James Prentiss, a New York financier who was related by marriage to the proprietor of Brown's Indian Queen Hotel in Washington. There were plans for Houston to be the front man of a Texas colonization venture that would secure lands from the Leftwich Grant, a failed effort from the 1820s. The Galveston Bay and Texas Land Company was to be backed by New York financiers, while Houston would receive expense money and stipends.

Houston obtained a passport in September 1832 at Cantonment Gibson. The document described "General Samuel Houston, a Citizen of the United States, Thirty-eight years of age, Six feet, two inches in stature, brown hair and light complexion . . . " Not long afterward Houston met Washington Irving, a noted literary figure and inveterate traveler. In his journal, Irving recorded a writer's impression of Houston: "Gov. Houston, tall, large, well formed, fascinating man—low crowned large brimmed white beaver—boots with brass eagle spurs—given to grandiloquence. A large and military mode of expressing himself."[1]

Houston made final preparations to move to Texas late in the year. He abandoned his relationship with Diana. Cherokee marriage was informal, and so was divorce, but there were firm expectations that provisions would be made for the woman. To Diana, Houston left Wigwam Neosho, adjacent fields, and two slaves. Of course, with Houston's long absence and lack of interest in the trading post and farm, Diana had taken charge of operations and certainly deserved the property. She also deserved greater loyalty from Houston, but throughout his life his activities as a military and political leader, his role in events of the day commanded priority. Although smitten with lovely Eliza Allen, if their marriage had continued Houston almost surely would have expected his wife—and their children—to accommodate the considerable demands of his high-level career. Indeed, the success of his third marriage depended upon the compatibility of Sam and Margaret—and upon her acceptance of the frequent and lengthy absences of Senator Houston.

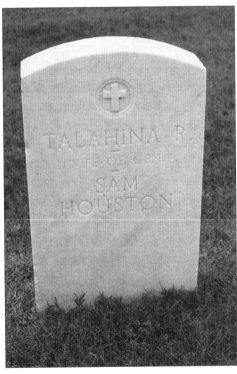

Diana Rogers Houston died in her late 30s on November 17, 1838. She was buried on the Officers' Circle in the Fort Gibson cemetery, which today is Oklahoma's only National Cemetery. Diana also was known as Tiana, which somehow led to the gravestone spelling "Talahina." *Photo by the author.*

Whatever comforts Diana had provided Houston, he cast them aside just as he cast aside the Cherokee community where he had found relief. Now recovered psychologically, Houston sensed exciting possibilities in Texas, and figuratively he chalked "G.T.T." on the door of Wigwam Neosho. Diana stayed behind, married a third time, and died in 1838, two years after Houston's spectacular triumph at San Jacinto.

On the first day of December 1832, Houston rode into Fort Towson, five miles north of the Red River. The next day he wrote to his cousin, John Houston. At the end of a chatty letter, he asked that *Auld Lang Sine* be played for him. "Its notes would even reach me in the

Indian's wigwam, and reclaim me to the civilized world again."[2]

Aware that he cut a striking figure on horseback, Houston wanted to re-enter "the civilized world" astride a handsome mount. Houston rode away from Wigwam Neosho on a bobtail nag named Jack. But en route he encountered Elias Rector, U.S. Marshal of Arkansas Territory, who rode a better-looking animal. Houston and Rector spent a convivial time together, and the former governor persuaded his younger companion to trade horses. Impressed with Houston, Rector insisted upon leaving him a gift, but he had only a razor. Houston accepted the proferred token with an assertion: "mark my words, if I have luck this razor will some day shave the chin of a president of a republic."[3]

After crossing the Red River to Jonesborough, Texas, Houston rode a wilderness trail 150 miles south to Nacogdoches. The *alcalde*, or mayor, of Nacogdoches was an old friend from Tennessee, Adolphus Sterne, and there were other Tennessee acquaintances in town. Houston soon headed farther south, 150 miles to San

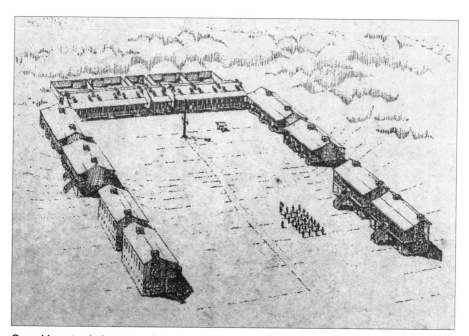

Sam Houston's last stop in Indian Territory was Fort Towson. From this military post just north of the Red River, Houston crossed into his "Land of Promise."
Courtesy Fort Towson State Park.

Felipe de Austin, the log cabin village on the Brazos River that served as headquarters for the colonial enterprises of Stephen F. Austin. When Houston arrived at San Felipe, Stephen F. Austin was out of town. But his efficient secretary, Samuel May Williams, handled Houston's application for a headright of one league, or 4,428 acres.

Houston received his grant on Christmas Eve, and that evening he dined with James Bowie. A land speculator, slave dealer, and gambler, Bowie was better known as a fighting man. His most famous episode was the 1826 Sand Bar fight near Natchez, in which a duel exploded into a general melee. Bowie suffered several wounds but killed an adversary with a large knife. Copies of Bowie's knife, with its brass handguard and double cutting edge, began to be purchased by Texans and other frontiersman. During the previous year, 1831, Bowie and a small party of men fought off a large band of Comanche warriors. Texas was a rough and often dangerous frontier society, and Bowie's violent exploits as a brawler, duelist, and Indian fighter elicited admiration among many Texans.

Jim Bowie and Sam Houston encountered one another in 1833 in San Felipe, and rode together to San Antonio. Both men were frontier adventurers and fond of drinking, and must have become boon companions during their journey. *Author's collection.*

Like Jim Bowie, Sam Houston had battled warriors, and his heroics at Horseshoe Bend were known and admired. In 1826 Houston shot a man in a duel, and in 1832 there was widespread publicity about his caning of Congressman Stanbery. Like Bowie, Sam Houston was known as a brawler, duelist, and warrior. And as a one-time major general of Tennessee Militia, he often was addressed as

"General" or "General Houston." Add the automatic respect customarily extended to a former congressman and governor, and Sam Houston found himself the beneficiary of considerable admiration and respect as he made his way across Texas.

Houston's travels resumed shortly after Christmas when he rode another 150 miles westward, accompanied by Bowie to San Antonio. Bowie's bride was Ursula de Veramendi, whose father was Vice Governor of Texas. (Texas was the junior partner of the Mexican state of Coahuila y Tejas, and Vice Governor Don Juan de Veramendi aided Bowie in various business schemes.)

Houston had told President Jackson he would try to meet with Comanches while in Texas, and in San Antonio he encountered a tribal delegation. But the meeting proved inconclusive, and Houston rode eastward through San Felipe and toward Louisiana.

After more than two months of riding horseback several hundred miles across Texas, Houston emerged from Mexican territory in February, stopping in Natchitoches long enough to write a report to President Jackson. Houston referred to Jackson's hope of bringing Texas into the United States. "That such a measure is desirable by nineteen twentieths of the population of the Province, I can not doubt." He emphasized the willingness and ability of Texas to resist Mexico. "She can defend herself against the whole power of Mexico," insisted Houston, explaining his thoughts on how Texans could accomplish this feat.

Houston was aware of "the late commotions in Texas" between Anglo settlers and Mexican *soldados* at Anahuac. As a result of this clash, in early October of 1832 fifty-six delegates from seventeen colonial districts convened in San Felipe. Stephen F. Austin was elected president of the convention, but little was accomplished. Nevertheless, it was the first effort at unified action by Texans, and another convention was scheduled for April 1, 1833.

"I expect to be present at the convention and will apprise you of the course adopted," wrote Houston to Jackson. "I have traveled near five hundred miles across Texas [the distance was closer to seven hundred miles] . . . and I have no hesitancy in pronouncing it the finest country to its extent upon the globe." Houston added meaningfully, "It is probable that I may make Texas my abiding place!"[4]

Houston reappeared in Nacogdoches in time to be elected one of the community's five delegates to the Convention of April 1, 1833, a selection that took place on March 1. He set up a law practice in Nacogdoches, and he boarded at the story and a half frame house of Adolphus Sterne, located on the eastern outskirts of town. Sterne was an immigrant from Germany who became a successful businessman and landowner. Sterne settled in Nacogdoches in the mid-1820s, and he and his wife Eva became the parents of seven children. Sterne met Sam Houston during a trip to Nashville, and Houston enjoyed the hospitality of the Sterne home while in Nacogdoches. In the Sterne parlor he was baptized into the Catholic church as "Samuel Pablo Houston," while Eva Sterne was listed as his godmother. All new settlers in Mex-

The Adolphus Sterne home was built in Nacogdoches in 1828. Sterne and Houston were friends in Tennessee, and Sam sometimes boarded in the home of his friend, who was *alcalde* (mayor) of Nacogdoches. In the Sterne parlor, Houston was baptized into the Catholic Church, a requirement for land ownership in Mexican Texas. Today the Texas colonial home is a museum. *Photo by the author.*

ican Texas were required to join the Catholic church, although like most Anglo-Texans, "Pablo" Houston was no more than a nominal Catholic.

Another Nacogdoches resident with a Tennessee connection to Houston was Henry Raguet, whose beautiful daughter, Anna, promptly appealed to Sam. She was seventeen and he was forty, but Houston always was attracted to younger women. At the age of thirty-five, Governor Houston wed nineteen-year-old Eliza Allen. When he was forty-seven, Houston married twenty-one-year-old Margaret Lea. So the twenty-three-year age difference between Houston and Anna Raguet posed no problem for him. He was a fine-looking man of great reputation, and Anna entertained his company for several years, before marrying a younger man in 1839.

Delegate Houston was in San Felipe when the Convention of April 1, 1833, was called to order. William H. Wharton was elected president of the convention, and Sam Houston was appointed to chair the committee to write a constitution. The convention met for nearly two weeks. Many of the fifty delegates were activists for a more independent Texas. They voted to request of the Mexican government free immigration into Texas and separate statehood for Texas from Coahuila. To facilitate statehood, a Texas constitution from Sam Houston's committee was approved by the convention. Three delegates were asked to journey to Mexico City to present the petitions and constitution, but travel funds were not available, and only Stephen F. Austin was willing to go.

On the same day, April 1, that Sam Houston was selected to head the constitutional committee, General Antonio Lopez de Santa Anna was elected President of Mexico by the Mexican Congress. The next year President Santa Anna dissolved the Congress of Mexico, explaining that the Mexican people were not yet ready for democracy. *El Presidente* then rapidly became a military dictator.

When Stephen F. Austin arrived at Mexico City, Santa Anna was absent. Little was accomplished on behalf of Texas, and many Mexican officials were irked at the demands from the *norteamericanos*. Austin grew impatient, and after Santa Anna offered various assurances, the *empresario* finally departed for Texas. But in frustration Austin had written a letter advocating that Texans should form a separate government. The letter was intercepted, and when Austin reached Saltillo in January 1834, he was arrested. He was taken to Mexico City and incarcerated, although there were no charges. Austin was not released from prison until December 1834, and he was not allowed to leave Mexico City for several more months.

Attorneys from Texas finally secured his freedom in July 1835, but it took more than a month to journey home. In all Austin was gone from Texas for two years and four months, and during that time Santa Anna's actions toward Texas became increasingly oppressive.

Meanwhile Houston returned to Nacogdoches from San Felipe. The hundreds of miles he had ridden during his first five months in Texas had taken a toll. Houston's shoulder wound was dealing him misery and he also suffered from head sores. So he mounted up again for a trip to the renowned Hot Springs in Arkansas Territory. The thermal springs gave Houston relief. He wrote to cousin John Houston that "my wound was sore and some bones were working out of it when I came here—the inflammation has left it and the bones have escaped. The tetter on my head seems cured entirely!"[5]

Houston returned to Nacogdoches, practicing law and persuading the lovely Anna Raguet to teach him Spanish. Men wanted the legal services of the noted Sam Houston, and he traveled often to court sessions at San Augustine, thirty miles east of Nacogdoches. Although he was promised handsome fees and retainers, there was little cash in circulation in frontier Texas. Houston continued to correspond with James Prentiss, hoping to receive long-promised funds from the Galveston Bay and Texas Land Company. But in the spring of 1834 he traveled to Washington D.C. and New York, only to learn that company owners had decided not to make deals which would require the payment of large fees to individual agents.

It was just as well. Houston's heart was no more in the business and activities of being a land agent than in the activities of a farmer or storekeeper. Before he ever came to Texas he sensed opportunities that stimulated his instincts as a leader. In 1832, after hearing about the clash between Texans and Mexican *soldados* at Anahuac, Houston "indulged in some regrets that I was not there . . ."[6] He was in Texas only a couple of months before he became convinced that "nineteen twentieths of the population" wanted acquisition by the United States. Later, while riding the road from Nacogdoches to San Augustine, Houston courteously bowed and touched the wide brim of his hat when he passed a group which included a few ladies. That evening Houston passed the same group as both parties returned in the opposite directions. Again Houston paid courtesy to the ladies, and one of the women asked a man in the group if he knew the polite gentleman. "That is Governor Houston, and he says there is going to be a war in Texas before long and he means to figure in it."[7]

Of course, it was strongly rumored that Houston was in Texas acting as an agent of the United States, perhaps reporting directly to President Andrew Jackson. True or not, these rumors added an air of mystery and importance to Houston's presence. Hardly had Houston arrived in Texas than he was inserted as a delegate to the Convention of April 1, 1833. Not another man in Texas had the breadth of his experience in high office. A former governor and member of congress, he also had been a confidante of President Jackson, a sub-agent and emissary to Washington of Native American tribes, and adjutant general of Tennessee. Houston also was a military hero and former major general of Tennessee militia, and his reputation as a duelist and brawler only improved his image to most members of the rough and tumble Texas society.

Houston was captivated by Texas and by the looming events of which he might play a part. In a letter to James Prentiss in April 1834, Houston made a bold prediction about Texas: "Within three years I think it will be separated from the Mexican Confederacy, and remain so forever." Four days later he wrote to Prentiss again about Texas. "She cannot, and will not remain as she now is . . . Texas will be bound to look to herself and to do for herself." There were more predictions and speculations before Houston declared his own role: "The course that I may pursue, you may rely upon it, shall be for the true interests of Texas . . . "[8]

On his trips to the eastern United States Houston often visited relatives in Virginia. When he was introduced to a youthful cousin named Narcissa Hamilton, she asked for a remembrance in her autograph book. Houston penned a charming verse:

> *Remember thee?*
> *Yes, lovely girl;*
> > *While faithful memory holds its seat,*
> *Till this warm heart in dust is laid,*
> > *And this wild pulse shall cease to beat,*
> *No matter where my bark is lost,*
> > *On life's tumultuous, stormy sea;*
> *My anchor gone, my rudder lost,*
> > *Still, cousin, I will think of thee.*

Composing rapidly and while he conversed, Houston exhibited the literary skills which colored and elevated his oratory. Meanwhile, Narcissa listened in on the adult conversation, learning that Cousin Sam recently had been in the nation's capital "making plans for the liberation of Texas."[9]

Combined with charm and a commanding personality, Houston at forty also was notably handsome. "Gen. Houston was one of the most magnificent specimens of physical manhood I have ever seen . . . ," recorded a citizen of Little Rock. "I first saw him on the public road a few miles out of town. He was riding a splendid bay horse, and his saddle and bridle were of the most exquisite Mexican workmanship and were elaborately ornamented with solid silver plates and buckles in profusion. He was enveloped in a Mexican 'poncho' which was richly ornamented with Mexican embroidery work."[10]

Late in 1834 Houston spent time in Washington, in Arkansas Territory, about thirty miles northeast of the border of Texas. A jumping-off place for Texas, Washington taverns housed, at one time or another, Stephen F. Austin, James Bowie, David Crockett, and a host of lesser-known G.T.T. pioneers. Englishman G. W. Featherstonhaugh, traveling through the South while gathering material for a book, became aware of peculiar circumstances surrounding the presence of Sam Houston in Washington.

"General Houston was here, leading a mysterious sort of life, shut up in a small town, seeing nobody by day and sitting up all night." Many people thought that there was all-night gambling in Houston's quarters, but Featherstonhaugh was convinced that "a much deeper game . . . was playing. There were many persons at this time in the village from the States lying adjacent to the Mississippi, under the pretense of purchasing government lands, but whose real object was to encourage the settlers in Texas to throw off their allegiance to the Mexican government."[11]

"The mission of Houston was confidential, and nothing, of course, is known of the details," recorded Houston years later in third person. Houston "saw that a great destiny awaited the people who should inhabit that region, that this was a field wherein all the bold elements of his character could find full play . . . "[12]

The bold elements of Sam Houston's character—courage, decisiveness, willingness to shoulder vast responsibility, powers of persuasion—all were about to find full play. His previous military experiences would be mined to the deepest extent. Houston would employ his sense of strategy, as well as his natural inclination to keep his future course of action absolutely to himself. He would call on every measure of physical stamina, and once again he would risk his life in battle. During eight crucial months of 1835 and 1836, Sam Houston would employ all of his leadership qualities, instinctive or acquired, in the service of Texas—and of his own "great destiny."

The work of liberty has begun… The morning of glory is dawning among us.
Sam Houston

Chapter Eight

Revolution

On October 6, 1835, Sam Houston was designated commander in chief of the volunteer soldiers of the Department of Nacogdoches. The appointment was made by the Committee of Vigilance and Safety of the Nacogdoches Department. This committee had been organized for several weeks, as tensions worsened between Texas and Santa Anna's Mexico. There were seven members of the Nacogdoches committee—including Sam Houston, the town's most famous citizen.

There were Committees of Safety or Committees of Correspondence in every colonial town and county during the troubled years preceding the American Revolution. The committees were organized by colonial radicals, who utilized the committee network to keep their revolutionary cause alive and growing. The stirring events of the American Revolution were only half a century or so in the past, and were an inspiration to the revolutionary Texans who wanted independence from Mexico. Throughout the Texas Revolution, there were references in speeches and letters and proclamations to the American Revolution. During the climactic campaign of the Texas Revolution, General Houston fashioned the brim of his hat into a tricorn, a visible reminder of the American Revolution. Perhaps, too, Houston's tricorn was a gesture of homage to his father, who fought in the Revolution.

During 1835 a "War Party" developed among Texans who advocated independence, and there was a "Peace Party" made up of early settlers, who took their lead from the peaceful and influential *empresario*, Stephen F. Austin. War Party men organized committees in various Texas towns and "Departments," and Sam

Houston's participation in the Committee of Vigilance and Safety of the Nacogdoches Department identified him with those who wanted Texas independence. Houston was no wild-eyed revolutionary, but he concluded—and stated—that Texans would seek independence from Mexico. Accordingly, Houston spent considerable time in 1834, as well as early 1835, planning and arranging support for a likely Texas war effort.

Many of the *soldados* sent from Mexico to enforce commercial and immigration regulations were former convicts, who chose service on the Texas frontier over confinement in the notorious Mexican prisons. Texans clashed with the *soldados*, and in 1835 agitator William Barrett Travis triggered an incident which resulted in his arrest and confinement in Anahuac. Texans smuggled goods in defiance of customs laws, and *norteamericanos* flooded into Texas in defiance of immigration requirements.

Sam Houston summed up the situation in Texas by 1835. "The commerce of Texas was now most oppressively restricted, the worst men were appointed to collect the customs, taxation was increased to a ruinous height, justice was refused to the people except at the price of enormous extortions, and the Mexican laws and edicts were made the instruments of wholesale tyranny in the hands of corrupt officials. This was the beginning of the end."[1] The end of Mexican control of Texas—and the beginning of iconic status for Sam Houston.

Following an absence of twenty-eight months from Texas, Stephen F. Austin arrived by schooner at Velasco on September 1, 1835. Promptly he was invited by delegations from Brazoria and San Felipe to address the public at welcome home dinners. The dinner at Brazoria was held at the hotel of Mrs. Jane Long, widow of filibuster Dr. James Long, who had been murdered while in custody at Mexico City in 1820. Austin's cousin, Henry Perry, described the occasion: "There were sixty covers, and despite the short notice, the table was three times filled with men alone. In the evening the long room was filled to a jam. At least sixty or eighty ladies danced until sun up, and the Oyster Creek girls would not have quit then had the room not been wanted for breakfast. You never saw such enthusiasm."[2]

The highlight of the evening, of course, was Austin's address. Texas was moving toward revolution, but Stephen F. Austin always had been the voice of moderation and loyalty toward Mexico. In a Mexican dungeon, however, the influential *empresario* had experienced the despotism of Santa Anna. He was ill from long confinement, and he had become embittered. Aware of the significance of his remarks, Austin prepared his address with care. At the hotel of Jane Long, Austin was greeted warmly by old friends, and he was honored with a succession of toasts.

Austin spoke for only fifteen minutes, and he made one hard-hitting point after another:

- I was arrested, and have suffered a long persecution and imprisonment.
- I fully hoped to have found Texas at peace and tranquility, but regret to find it in commotion; all disorganized, all in anarchy, and threatened with immediate hostilities.
- The object [of Santa Anna] is to change the form of government . . . and establish a central or consolidated government.
- Something must be done, and that without delay.

Austin closed his remarks with a toast: "The Constitutional rights and security and peace of Texas—they ought to be maintained; and jeopardized as they now are, they demand a general consultation of the people."[3]

Four days later Austin made essentially the same speech at San Felipe. A Committee of Correspondence and Vigilance was immediately organized in San Felipe, with Austin as chairman. Committees were created in other municipalities, and delegates were selected for a consultation scheduled to convene on October 15. But on October 2 in Gonzales, a skirmish broke out between Texas volunteer riflemen and a force of Mexican *soldados* sent from San Antonio to retrieve a small cannon. The little gun had been given to the village for defense against marauding Comanches. When Mexican soldiers tried to reclaim the cannon, they were met by a homemade flag proclaiming "Come and Take It." In the ensuing "Battle of Gonzales," one *soldado* was killed, but the clash was an immediate rallying point for Texans.

In September 1835 Stephen F. Austin returned to Texas after more than two years in Mexico, including an undeserved incarceration. Austin's change of heart about Mexican control of Texas was a key step in the Texas independence movement. *Courtesy San Felipe de Austin State Historic Site.*

Volunteers rushed toward Gonzales, including most of the delegates to the consultation scheduled for October 15. When Austin arrived on October 11 he was elected commander in chief, even though he had virtually no military background. On October 13 Austin led several hundred men toward San Antonio, where 1,100 Mexican soldiers were commanded by General Martin Perfecto de Cos, brother-in-law of President Santa Anna. General Austin established camp at Salado Creek, about five miles from San Antonio. On the march and in camp, volunteers arrived and swelled the ranks.

Meanwhile, Sam Houston was selected as Commander in Chief of the Nacogdoches Department and as a delegate to the October 15 Consultation. On October 5 Houston placed a letter in San Augustine calling for military volunteers and promising "liberal bounties of land" for their service. Houston had no authority to promise land bounties, but that did not stop him from pointing out that "We have millions of acres of our best lands unchosen and unappropriated." Aware that there were no military stores in Anglo-Texas, Houston instructed: "Let each man come with a good rifle, and one hundred rounds of ammunition, and come soon."[4]

Houston's eloquent pleas generated public meetings of support and adventurous volunteers from numerous states. The New Orleans Grays, for example, organized and prepared to come to

Texas. A volunteer company was formed in Nacogdoches by Thomas Jefferson Rusk, a well-trained lawyer from Georgia who arrived in Texas only several months earlier, but who quickly became swept up in the independence movement. A decade younger than Houston, Rusk would become a loyal friend and an important figure in the climactic campaign. Rusk promptly led his company from Nacogdoches to Gonzales.

As Houston prepared to leave Nacogdoches, he stored his personal effects: a few items of furniture, clothing, and a library of nearly fifty books. Later he would have three trunks sent to himself containing a frock coat, four dress coats, pantaloons, other clothing, and his books: *The Iliad*, of course, volumes of Milton, Burns, Thucydides, Livy, Taciticus, a classical dictionary, a multi-volume history of England, a book on army regulations, and a Bible.

Before he departed, he met with Anna Raguet, who was swept up in the drama of the movement. "She tied his sword sash, snipped a lock of his hair and sent her soldier to fight for Texas," reported Marquis James.[5]

On October 8 Houston addressed local volunteers assembled before the Old Stone Fort in Nacogdoches. "The morning of glory is dawning upon us. The work of liberty has begun," he declared. "Let your valor proclaim to the world that liberty is your birthright. We cannot be conquered by all the arts of anarchy and despotism combined."[6]

Soon Houston left Nacogdoches, not to join the volunteers gathering before San Antonio, but to begin work with the other delegates at the Consultation of October 15. But on October 15 most of the delegates were on their way to San Antonio or already with Austin's army. Houston knew that it was absolutely necessary to form a government that could equip an army in the field. He rode toward San Antonio to collect enough delegates to do business at San Felipe.

At the rude encampment of the Volunteer Army of Texas, Houston shared his concerns with General Austin. Austin vigorously agreed with the need to organize a civil government and, according to Houston, offered to surrender his command to the more experienced former officer and war veteran. Houston wrote that he "positively declined the magnanimous offer," which might not have been accepted by the volunteers in any event. Austin immediately called a counsel of war, and it was decided to let the volunteers vote on the question of forming a provisional government. The men overwhelmingly voted that all delegates return to San Felipe.[7]

Austin ordered a general parade of troops, who then were addressed by several leaders. Prominent among the speakers was Houston. Vigorously he stressed the need for governmental organization that could procure and provide arms and supplies to the army. And he strongly advised the army to fall back to Gonzales, go into winter quarters, and undergo a training regimen that would prepare them to combat Mexican regulars.

When General Austin spoke, he made it clear that he did not want to retreat over ground already won in order to establish a training camp. But he agreed wholeheartedly with the need to organize a government, and the Consultation delegates dutifully prepared to leave.

The Consultation scheduled for October 15 finally convened on November 3 in a narrow frame building with unplastered walls and no ceiling. Dr. Branch T. Archer was elected to preside, but for the first few days there was constant political bickering. Houston circulated among the delegates, making influential friends and delivering an address designed to focus the efforts of the Consultation. Delegate Gail Borden, Jr., reported to Stephen F. Austin in a letter dated November 5, 1835. "Had a conversation with Gen'l Houston today—I believe he has the interests of our country at heart. He made the best speech yesterday I ever heard; the whole tenour of it went to harmonize the feelings of the people and to produce unanimity of sentiment."[8]

The Consultation set up a Provisional Government, a temporary organization to operate until a formal election could be held across Texas. Henry Smith, a strong supporter of Houston, was elected Provisional Governor. Although passed over for governor, Stephen F. Austin was asked to go to the United States, along with Dr. Archer and William H. Wharton. This three-man commission sought volunteers, money, and munitions.

The Provisional Government would be in charge of affairs until the war ended. Of pressing importance was appointment of a commander-in-chief of the army. Sam Houston had been an officer in the United States Army, a wounded battle hero, and a major general of the Tennessee State Militia. He had a military bearing and a commanding presence, and most people referred to him as "General" or "General Houston." Houston was an obvious choice for commander-in-chief, even though some men—many out of jealousy—disliked him.

When the Continental Congress met after Lexington and Concord, delegate George Washington arrived in his colonel's uniform from the French and Indian War. He had been a ranking officer and a combat veteran, and although he made no campaign speeches, Congress appointed him General of the Continental Army. In the same manner, on November 12, 1835, Houston was nominated as major general and commander-in-chief of the Texas Regular Army. He was elected with forty-nine out of fifty votes. Governor Smith signed his commission, and on the back of the document, Houston signed his name to the same oath of office which the governor and council had taken. Sam Houston once again was a major general.

Major General Houston had long planned a course of action. He composed bills for recruiting and organizing an army, and for raising funds. Immediately General Houston began assembling a staff. On November 13 he wrote to James W. Fannin, offering him the position of Inspector General of the Texas Army. Fannin was a West Point dropout, but before he resigned from the Academy, he was exposed to more than two years of high-level military instruction. Fannin was in his early thirties, a slave trader with a wife and children. He fought at the battle of Gonzales, and campaigned with the Volunteer Army of Texas.

Houston reiterated to Fannin his conviction that the volunteer army should pull back to Gonzales. "The army at present without tents and the necessary comforts for the men, I fear may produce an epidemic and destroy more than would have fallen in storming the place. Recommend the safest course!" Houston underlined a key to his approach as a general, to his style as a leader. *Remember one Maxim: it is better to do well late than never.*[9]

Fannin did not accept Houston's offer, but he remained active as a leader. Later, as commander of nearly 500 men, he would disobey the orders of General Houston, dooming himself and his command. Meanwhile, Austin left for the United States, yielding command of the army to Col. Edward Burleson, an experienced Indian fighter.

There was fighting near San Antonio, but as winter neared volunteers began to drift away to their homes. But early in December Ben Milam, a former filibuster and one-time *empresario*, led 300 men in a bold assault on San Antonio. Although the town was defended by General Cos and more than 1,100 *soldados*, Milam—who was slain during the attack—and his men forced a surrender after five days of house-to-house fighting.

Houston repeatedly had said that San Antonio could not be taken, particularly without artillery support. But following the triumph of these outnumbered "gallant spirits," Houston freely praised the "brave men" who "entered the town at night, made their way from house to house, with crowbars, through the walls," and with relentless effort secured the surrender of San Antonio.[10]

While Austin, Archer, and Wharton attempted to borrow money and recruit volunteers in the United States, General Houston began to secure assistance from "the handful of his fellow citizens, who were embarked in the same cause with himself, and on the generous patriots of the country . . . " He issued a lengthy proclamation to the citizens, explaining the situation in Texas, listing land bounties to be given to recruits, and calling for 5,000 volunteers. "Let the brave rally to our standard."[11]

Houston was directed by the General Council of the Provisional Government to establish headquarters at Washington-on-the-Brazos. Ostensibly he would direct recruiting from Washington, but several members wanted Houston out of the way so that they could exercise influence in military matters. General Houston set out from San Felipe on December 23, 1835, and he stayed in Washington for two weeks. Houston experienced a dull Christmas season, and he wanted it known that he was not drinking. "I am most miserably cool and sober—so you can say to all my friends. Instead of eggnog I eat roasted eggs in my office," he wrote to an ally in San Felipe on the day after New Year's, 1836. General Houston stated his intention to "proceed to the *frontier* and organize the army for the prompt movement in the Spring."[12]

Houston became increasingly aware of the intrigues between members of the General Council and "self-created officers." Officers such as F. W. Johnson, Dr. James Grant, and James Fannin were land speculators. Some of their claims were in northern Mexico, and they hoped to use the Texas Army to secure these regions. Provisions and blankets were beginning to arrive, only to be diverted. More than 400 armed men, many organized in companies, arrived from the United States, and Colonel Fannin took charge as commander of the volunteers. Soon the General Council appointed Fannin "special agent" and gave him authority to attack Matamoros—300 miles below the Rio Grande—or any other point he considered proper. Fannin and Johnson made calls for soldiers to assemble at Refugio, a village south of Goliad. Some members of the General Council attempted unsuccessfully to oust Houston.

"No language can express my anguish of soul. Oh, save our country!" wrote a horrified Houston to Governor Henry Smith. Houston was embarrassed at the self-serving image Texas leaders were presenting. "What will the world think of the authorities of Texas?"[13]

Two days later Houston headed for the southwest, where most of the fighting men in Texas had gathered. Riding hard, he arrived in Goliad on January 14, 1836. The force that had seized San Antonio had disbanded, leaving Col. J. C. Neill with a little more than 100 men in charge of a town with an overwhelming Mexican/Tejano population. San Antonio was almost two days' ride from the nearest Anglo communities, and the principal defense site, the Alamo, was a crumbling old mission. The Alamo had no real fortification features, although there were more than twenty cannons—the largest collection of artillery in Texas.

Word had reached Texas that General Santa Anna was marching at the head of an army to restore Mexican authority. As Houston related, "knowing it was impossible to hold Bexar, he dispatched Cols. Bowie and [James] Bonham, with an escort, to that town, with orders to the commanding officer to blow up the Alamo and fall back to Gonzales, . . . which he intended to make the line of defense."[14] But when Bowie arrived in San Antonio, at the head of about thirty reinforcements, he and Neill decided not to destroy the Alamo. Bowie, whose home was in San Antonio, did not share Houston's strategic vision. Bowie wrote to Governor Smith on February 2:

> *The salvation of Texas depends in great measure on keeping Bexar out of the hands of the enemy. It stands on the frontier picquet guard, and if it was in the possession on Santa Anna, there is no stronghold from which to repel him in his march to the Sabine. Colonel Neill and myself have come to the solemn resolution that we will rather die in those ditches than give them up to the enemy.*[15]

Bowie and Neill deliberately disobeyed the orders of General Houston. Ignoring Houston, Fannin collected most of the fighting men in Texas and, with Johnson and Grant, began planning an expedition to Matamoros, hundreds of miles away. Grant designated himself "acting commander-in-chief." There was no authority, no discipline, no organization, no strategic planning. With a regular army of thousands on the march from Mexico, Major General Houston commanded a military nightmare. "I very soon discovered that I was a General without an army, serving under . . . a pretended government, that had no head, and no loyal subjects to obey its commands."[16]

At Goliad Houston tactfully tried to dissuade soldiers from participating in the Matamoros expedition. "I remonstrated with the officers in a friendly manner, representing the great difficulties they would have to encounter—the futility of the project—and the disasters attendant on failure."[17] Houston addressed the men, vigorously pointing out the impossibility of supplying a column hundreds of miles into Mexico, as well as the dangerous exposure of the invaders. A number of men decided not to go any farther. Shortly afterward, when Acting Commander-in-Chief Grant led a march toward Refugio, Houston rode along, moving among the men and persuading others not to go. He did not stay long in Refugio, but his name was put up as a delegate to a constitutional convention to be held in Washington-on-the-Brazos on March 1, 1836. When the vote was held, soldiers voted for Houston in large numbers, and he won election as a delegate from Refugio.

Having done what he could, Houston decided to ride back to San Felipe, accompanied by Major George Hockley and a few other staff members. Houston was deeply troubled, riding for most of the first day in silence. Painfully he wondered "whether to withdraw once more from the treacheries and persecutions of the world, and bury myself deep in the solitude of nature, and pass a life of communion with the Great Spirit and his beautiful creations—or whether I should boldly mark out a track for myself, and in leading a new people to Independency trample down all opposition." But in recent years he had tried withdrawal into "a life of communion"—and it proved completely unsatisfying. Deep down Houston believed that somehow, in some way he could "trample down all opposition" and lead Texans "to Independency." At the end of the day Houston addressed his companions, outlining the current state of affairs, before dealing "with enthusiasm upon the future prospects of Texas."[18]

No one understood as well as Houston the seemingly insurmountable difficulties posed by political and military officials of Texas. But within a single day's ride his irrepressible confidence asserted itself. The prize of leading Texas to independence was fame and the fulfillment of being the hero, the great leader . . .

The press of events had kept General Houston from an early assignment. A large Cherokee tribe lived north of Nacogdoches, with villages in modern Smith County. The principal chief of Cherokees in Texas was Chief Bowl, a man of eighty years. Twice Chief Bowl had applied without success for title to lands where Cherokees lived, and he assisted Mexican authorities in putting down the Fredonian Rebellion. Concerned that the Cherokee might unite with Mexico against Texans, the Provisional Government authorized General Houston and two other commissioners

General Houston helps Chief Bowl sign an agreement to relieve tensions between Texans and the Cherokee. This statue stands in Nacogdoches. *Photo by the author.*

to make a treaty awarding the Cherokee land titles.

When Houston returned to San Felipe from Refugio, Governor Smith gave the general a furlough until March 1, instructing him to effect the Indian treaty. Houston wrote Chief Bowl, an old acquaintance from Tennessee, and he traveled to Bowl's village with Judge John Forbes, a fellow commissioner from Nacogdoches. Houston presented Chief Bowl a sword and other gifts, and during a three-day conference negotiated a satisfactory treaty. Now General Houston did not have to worry about Texans having to fight Cherokee warriors in the northeast while battling Mexican *soldados* in the southwest.

After signing the treaty on February 26, Houston hurried south to Washington-on-the-Brazos. His name had been presented as one of the delegates from Nacogdoches, but he was not elected. Never mind—he had been elected a delegate from Refugio. For weeks Houston had lobbied for independence from Mexico, and in Washington he would find himself among kindred spirits.

There are but few of us, and if we are beaten,
the fate of Texas is sealed.
Gen. Sam Houston

Chapter Nine

Leading a Strategic Retreat

A number of delegates already had arrived at Washington when Sam Houston rode into the riverside village on Monday, February 29. The large man showed fatigue from the constant travel of recent weeks, as well as from the turmoil he had endured from politicians and ambitious military officers. But there was keen expectancy over the arrival of General Houston, and as he rode up Washington's only street, men swarmed around his horse and shouted their greetings.

"Gen'l Houston's arrival has created more sensation than that of any other man," observed Col. William F. Gray from Virginia, who had been in Washington for three days. "He is much broken in appearance, but still has a fine person and courtly manners; he will be forty-three years old on the [2nd] March—looks older."[1]

Gray was not impressed with Washington. "Disgusting place. About a dozen cabins or shanties constitute the city; not one decent house in it, and only one well defined street, which consists of an opening cut out of the woods. The stumps still standing."[2]

The village stood on a bluff above the west bank of the Brazos River, high enough to be safe from flooding. There was a busy ferry, but even though a few families had lived in the vicinity for more than a decade, a townsite had been surveyed only a year earlier. The population of Washington (it was not called Washington-on-the-Brazos for another thirty years) was about 100. There was a small tavern, but many of the delegates had to camp under a tree. In December 1835 General Houston had established his headquarters in Washington, which became the gathering point for army recruits. Enterprising local entrepreneurs offered an assembly hall free of charge, and it was decided to open the Convention on March 1 in Washington.

The day before Houston arrived, February 28, a courier on a tired horse labored into town. There had been reports that General Santa Anna had marched into Texas at the head of a large army. San Antonio was an obvious target, and the courier brought an alarming, heroic, stirring letter from William Barrett Travis at the Alamo.

> *Commandancy of the Alamo*
> *Bexar, Feby 24th, 1836*
>
> *To the People of Texas and All Americans in the World –*
> *Fellow Citizens and Compatriots:*
> *I am besieged with a thousand or more of the Mexicans under Santa Anna. I have sustained a continual Bombardment and cannonade for 24 hours and have not lost a man. The enemy has demanded surrender at discretion, otherwise, the garrison are to be put to the sword, if the fort is taken. I have answered the demand with a cannon shot, and our flag still waves proudly from the wall. I shall never surrender or retreat. Then, I call on you in the name of Liberty, of patriotism, and everything dear to the American character, to come to our aid with all dispatch. The enemy is receiving reinforcements daily and will no doubt increase to three or four thousand in four or five days. If this call is neglected I am determined to sustain myself as long as possible and die like a soldier who never forgets what is due his honor and that of his country.*
>
> *VICTORY OR DEATH.*

Fighting between Texans and Mexican soldiers had gone on for five months, since October 1835, and now General Santa Anna and an invading army were bombarding the Alamo. It was clear that Texas should declare independence. On Tuesday, March 1, fifty-nine delegates assembled in the hall provided in Washington. The building was unfinished—no ceiling, no interior finish to the walls. A norther struck on March 1, dropping the temperatures nearly to freezing. The delegates were uncomfortably cold in their unheated hall (and so were the defenders of the Alamo, struck by this same norther).

On March 1 a committee was appointed to draft a declaration of independence. Chairman George Childress worked through the night, using the Declaration of Independence of 1776 as a model. The opening words—"When a government has ceased to protect the lives, liberty and property of the people from whom its legitimate powers are derived . . ."—suggest familiarity with the 1776 Declaration. And like the 1776 document, the latter two-thirds comprised a list of grievances against the Mexican government: "It incarcerated in a dungeon, for a long time, one of our citizens [Austin]. . ."

The Texas Declaration of Independence was adopted unanimously and signed on the second day of the Convention. By a delicious historical coincidence, the delegate from Refugio, Sam Houston, affixed his bold signature on March 2, 1836—his forty-third birthday. That afternoon Houston took it upon himself to issue a proclamation. "War is raging on the frontiers," announced the proclamation, which next described the desperate siege at San Antonio. "The citizens of Texas must rally to the aid of our army, or it will perish. Let the citizens of the east march to the combat.

A replica of Independence Hall was built at Washington-on-the Brazos State Park. *Photo by the author.*

Lower half of the signatures on the Texas Declaration of Independence show "Sam Houston" in the right hand column, second from top. Critics felt that he crafted his signature to read. "I am Houston." *Image from Clark, A History of Texas, Land of Promise.*

The enemy must be driven from our soil . . . Independence is declared," Houston announced, "it must be maintained. Immediate action united with valor can alone achieve the great work. The services of all are forthwith required in the field."[3]

With further reports coming in about the Mexican invasion, the delegates worked rapidly to produce a constitution for the newly declared Republic of Texas, as well as an *ad interim* government to replace the widely despised Provisional Government. The new government assumed office at the close of the convention, on March 17, and would serve until general elections could be held.

With the Alamo under siege, it was imperative to provide military relief. On March 4 Houston was nominated as commander-in-chief of all forces, both regular and volunteer, with the rank of major general. He was re-elected commander-in-chief with only one dissenting vote.

Houston "hesitated for hours" before accepting the commission, recalling the myriad of difficulties he had experienced during his first term as commander, just ended. But he could not resist the responsibilities and challenges of being "general-in-chief" of all the Texas rebellion. As Houston recognized his responsibility: "He was to produce a nation; he was to defend a people; he was to command the resources of the country, and he must give character to the army."[4]

Houston's task was daunting and dangerous, but almost since the day he arrived in Texas he had embraced every available leadership responsibility. He seemed confident that he could instill character into an army not yet assembled, that he could find the necessary resources for his men, that he could defend Texas from an invading force, that he could indeed "produce a nation."

Winston Churchill became Prime Minister of England on May 10, 1940. Despite the precarious position of the nation early in World War II, when Churchill went to bed that night he was conscious "of a profound sense of relief. At last I had authority to give directions over the whole scene. I felt as if I were walking with destiny, and that all my past life had been but a preparation for this hour and for this trial."[5] On the night of Sam Houston's election as general-in-chief, he seemed to possess the same sense of destiny that Winston Churchill would feel just over a century later.

On Sunday morning, March 6, the latest—and final—letter from Colonel Travis arrived in Washington. The courier rode up to the assembly hall and hurried inside with the letter. "The spirits of my men are still high, although they have had much to depress them." When Travis penned this note the siege had gone on for ten days, Mexican reinforcements continued to swell the ranks of Santa Anna, and Travis now feared that Fannin was not coming to his aide. "I hope your honorable body will hasten on reinforcements . . . Our supply of ammunition is limited."

Delegate Robert Potter leaped up to make a motion that the convention adjourn and march to the relief of the Alamo. As a young man Potter spent six years in the U.S. Navy as a midshipman, before serving as a North Carolina legislator and congressman. But he was volatile and hot-tempered, engaging in brawls, duels, and adultery. A masterful orator, Potter repeatedly showered ridicule and vitriol on public figures, and his abrasive conduct assured him a steady supply of enemies.

He arrived in Nacogdoches in July 1835, on the eve of revolution, and he immediately asserted himself as an advocate for Texas independence. In Washington on March 4, 1836, Potter was the only delegate to vote against Sam Houston as commander-in-chief of Texan forces.

So when Potter proposed to ad-

Robert Potter, a former congressman and state legislator from North Carolina, played an active role in the Texas independence movement. But Potter was a magnet for trouble and a bitter foe of Sam Houston. *Courtesy Jefferson (Texas) Historical Museum.*

journ the convention and march to the Alamo, Houston promptly responded, denouncing the motion "as treason to the people . . ." Speaking at length, Houston "advised the Convention to remain calmly at their posts and do their duty to the country, by organizing a government," while he would ride immediately to collect an army and advance to the Alamo. Concluding his persuasive remarks, General Houston stalked dramatically out of Convention Hall, and within a few minutes he rode out of Washington.[6]

General Houston was accompanied by Col. George W. Hockley, Aide-de-Camp Alexander "Sandy" Horton from San Augustine, and recruit Richardson Scurry. Houston had appointed the loyal and capable Hockley his chief of staff. Like Hockley, Scurry had been influenced by Houston to leave Tennessee for Texas, and he would fight at San Jacinto as a lieutenant. Judge John Forbes was commissioned a major and sent south to round up volunteers and bring them to Gonzales. General Houston and his small detail arrived in Gonzales on Friday afternoon, March 11.

"I found 374 men," related Houston. "They were without organization and destitute of supplies . . . I at once had them assembled and organized, the men electing their own officers."[7] Camped beside the Guadalupe River, the volunteers were waiting for someone to lead them to the Alamo.

Colonels Edward Burleson and J. C. Neill, who had left the Alamo for home when Lt. Col. William B. Travis arrived in San Antonio, had worked to keep these volunteers together. General Houston rapidly formed a regiment, with Colonel Burleson in command. New recruits were anticipated, and would be placed into established companies. General Houston was authoritative and clearly capable, and he impressed volunteers in other ways.

Sheer physical size is an asset for combat leaders. During the long military eras when hand-to-hand fighting was an integral part of combat, leaders with impressive physiques inspired confidence among their men that they could successfully manhandle enemy soldiers. The greatest military leader of the Early Middle Ages was Charlemagne, fabled to be seven feet tall at a time when the average knight stood perhaps five-feet-four inches. The "seven feet" measurement originated because his height was seven times the length of one of his large feet. Such a calculation obviously is inexact, and examinations of the emperor's skeletal remains indicate that he stood six-feet-two, or perhaps a few inches taller. Even at six-two, Charlemagne was in the ninety-ninth height percentile of men of the period, and he loomed over most soldiers who followed him into battle after battle.

Similarly, General George Washington stood six-feet-two inches and he possessed exceptional muscular strength. Taller and stronger than most men of the 1700s, Washington was a superb horseman and he dressed in an immaculate uniform. General Washington presented an impressive military appearance, which was a significant element in his ability to hold the colonial volunteer army together despite multiple adversities.

As a military leader early in the nineteenth century, Sam Houston likewise benefited from physical size and an imposing appearance. During the War of 1812 the strapping young soldier rose rapidly in rank, and displayed ferocious valor and astounding physical stamina during the Battle of Horseshoe Bend. More than two decades later, Major General Houston's military reputation was highly regarded in Texas.

Now in his early forties, he was six-feet-two-inches and weighed well over 200 pounds. He was a big man and he rode a big horse into battle—a white stallion named Saracen. General Houston was so large and imposing that many Texans said he was six-foot-six—six and a half feet tall. Like seven-foot Charlemagne in an earlier age, Houston *seemed* that tall. Certainly when General Houston, astride his white warhorse and brandishing a sword, rode ahead of the advancing Texas Army toward the Mexican line at San Jacinto, he appeared to be the biggest man on the field of battle.

In addition to an impressive physique, General Houston brought a towering reputation to his Texas command: Governor of Tennessee, combat hero of Horseshoe Bend, Major General of Tennessee Militia, veteran of personal altercations. Now he held a major general's commission from the Texas government. These qualities triggered immediate respect among the citizen-soldiers who served under him.

Houston's imposing physique and his equally imposing background lent him instant credibility among volunteers. Few of the men who marched under Houston during the six-week campaign of March and April 1836 had ever been in an army. They were Texas farmers who volunteered to defend their homes and families, or they were adventurers from the United States. They all were risking their lives, and while most were competent riflemen, they were disorganized and knew nothing of military maneuver.

Sam Houston had spent five years as a junior officer in the United States Army, and he certainly knew how to teach close-order drill and other basic movements. His experience as commander of the Tennessee State Militia had taught him how to organize large numbers of backwoods volunteers. At Gonzales General Houston organized the First Regiment of Texas Volunteer Infantry. Later, as his force grew, he formed the Second Regiment of Texas Volunteer Infantry, as well as smaller units. Houston formed a company of "spies," as scouts were called, and he kept them well-mounted. His most trusted scouts were Erasmus "Deaf" Smith and Henry Karnes, but the entire company of hard-riding backwoodsmen kept a steady stream of observation reports coming to headquarters throughout the campaign.

On Major General Houston's first night in Gonzales, news arrived of the fall of the Alamo (on Sunday, March 6—the day Houston left Washington) and the death of all defenders. Virtually every household in the village had lost a husband or son or brother. Scout R. E. Handy remembered that the night was filled with "the wild shrieks of women, and the heart-rending screams of their fatherless children." Handy added that these spontaneous expressions of grief "sank deep into the heart of the rudest soldier."[8]

General Houston sent scouts Smith, Karnes, and Handy toward San Antonio to gather information. Twenty miles from Gonzales they encountered Susannah Dickinson, whose husband had died in the Alamo. Carrying her baby daughter, the young widow confirmed the Alamo disaster. When she was brought into camp men swarmed around her, and she blurted out the tragic story.

"I was walking alone a few hundred yards from the camp at the moment this stricken and bereaved messenger arrived," recalled General Houston, who often needed to be by himself. "I returned soon after and found her fearful narrative of the butchering and burning [of the Alamo dead], with some of the most stirring details of that dark tragedy, had already struck the soldiers with a chill of horror . . ." Mrs. Dickinson added that 5,000 Mexican soldiers were marching eastward, whereupon "the wildest consternation spread through the camp." Deserters fled Gonzales, other soldiers were stunned, "—others were wild with lamenting—and even officers had set fire to their tents."[9]

Houston commanded the fires to be extinguished and he sent reliable men after the deserters. He gathered his command around him and described their situation. "I announced that we would fall back to a more secure position, as we were at a bend of the river where the enemy, by crossing, could cut off all possible retreat." A letter had been sent to Col. Fannin directing him to pull back from the presidio at Goliad and combine with Houston's column. With the arrival of volunteers and the addition of Fannin's command, Houston expected a force exceeding 1,000 men. Three of the army's four baggage and supply wagons were given to civilians preparing to abandon Gonzales. Houston directed excess equipage to be burned, and, with no way to haul artillery, three cannons were dumped into the Guadalupe River. More than twenty deserters were brought back into camp, although a score continued on toward their families, spreading panic everywhere they went. After Houston established a rear guard, "I ordered the camp to be struck, and the little band took up their line of march."[10]

The army struggled through dense woods for ten miles, and they could see fires as the cabins of Gonzales burned in their wake. Houston called a halt at Peach Creek, where the army was met by one hundred volunteers. Even with the loss of twenty deserters, Houston's force now numbered 450, and within another couple of days the Texas Army had grown to 600. But en route a letter arrived from Fannin stating that he had held a council of war and it had been decided—in direct disobedience of General Houston's orders—to defend the presidio, which had been named Fort Defiance. Houston gloomily realized that there would be no reinforcement from Fannin, and he accurately predicted the doom of the men at La Bahia. Turning to Major Hockley, Houston indicated the men who now constituted the only substantial contingent of the Texas Army.

"Hockley, there is the last hope of Texas," stated Houston. "We shall never see Fannin nor his men—with these soldiers we must achieve our independence or perish in the attempt."[11]

In camp that night, General Houston learned of a blind woman, widow of an Alamo defender, and her six children who lived in the country side and who had been left behind. Houston sent a company of fifty men after them, and delayed the march until these refugees were brought into camp. When the little army reached the Colorado River, Houston halted the column until the women, children, and elderly, along with their livestock, made it to the east bank. Only then did he cross over with the army.

Refugees had been fleeing Santa Anna's army since February. But after word spread of the Alamo disaster and, later, of the mass execution of Fannin and nearly 400 of his men, settler withdrawal rapidly accelerated into the refugee parade that became known as the "Runaway Scrape." A growing number of refugees followed the army, hoping for protection, but other groups fled east and north, carrying their children and provisions and a few possessions on horseback or mule back or wagons. And their path could be followed by the discarded items that littered the trails.

Adding greatly to the problems of retreat were unusually heavy spring rains. Day after day rain fell, often in sheets. Clothing became soaked and stayed wet. Streams were swollen and turbulent. Crossing creeks and rivers was difficult to—at certain places and times—impossible. The rutted trails that passed for roads in early Texas were quagmires. There was little food, for the army or the refugees. Wet and cold and underfed, people sickened, and some – especially the young—died.

Soon Houston learned that Mexican troops were advancing in three divisions. Gen. Antonio Gaona led a column from San

Antonio northeast, toward Nacogdoches, before turning southeastward at Bastrop. Gen. Joaquin Ramirez y Sesma led the central division to Gonzales, then on toward San Felipe, while General Santa Anna followed with a reserve column. The core of the southern division, commanded by Gen. Jose Urrea, defeated and, upon the orders of Santa Anna, executed Colonel Fannin and his men. Urrea led his column to Victoria before angling down to the coast, then moving northward to close in on Houston's army.

Aware of the movement by divisions, Houston realized that even if his army held its own against one column, one of the other columns might flank and destroy the Texas force. And should his army meet a Mexican division of relatively equal numbers, Houston did not believe his untrained volunteers could defeat enemy regulars. "The first principles of drill had not been taught the men," he complained. And yet, "They are eager to meet the enemy."[12]

The spirit of battle was strong in these men of the frontier. They wanted vengeance against the *soldados* who had slain the Alamo defenders to the last man, who had executed the men of Fannin's command, who had burned these hundreds of bodies on funeral pyres. And many of the Texan soldiers had families and homes to defend. Texan officers, mostly elected by the men, were equally aggressive, and some were ambitious to a fault. When General Houston pulled out of Gonzales with only a few hundred men, many volunteers wanted to stay and fight. Houston knew that "it would have been madness to have hazarded a contest."[13]

With the loss of Fannin's command, General Houston decided upon a strategic retreat into the heart of Anglo-Texas, back toward his manpower and supply base. He intended to find opportunity to drill his men, to teach the rudiments of battlefield maneuver. Houston expected his army to grow, and at one point in the campaign he commanded 1,400 men, although desertions continued to take their toll.

W. P. Zuber, not yet sixteen-years-old, joined the army during the campaign. Awaiting the approach of the main column, Zuber and his companions saw the "front guard, a small body of horsemen, emerging from the timber at the west end of the prairie. Then came the wagon train, consisting of six wagons drawn by oxen, then the unmounted infantry, and, lastly, the mounted infantry. The cavalry, being divided into two parts, formed the flank guards on the right and left of the central column." The column stretched out for more than half a mile, and Zuber was "stricken with admiration . . . , since I had previously never seen more than three hundred persons at one time."[14]

Zuber was immediately impressed by Houston who, although conspicuous by his size, was dressed plainly in "coarse jeans, a white wool hat, and mud boots." But Zuber recognized a born leader: "I thought that he was the noblest-looking man that I had ever seen." Zuber testified that many "of our men reposed unlimited confidence in General Houston and were willing to follow him blindly and to do whatsoever he commanded."[15]

Zuber praised Houston's "inflexibility, confidence of success, and courtesy to his soldiers. Also he kept no bodyguard." No guard was posted at his tent. "When we were encamped, the door of his tent generally stood open, and any soldier who wished could enter at liberty." General Houston did not engage in light conversation, but when a soldier addressed him on business, "he courteously answered necessary inquiries and gave needed advice and encouragement. He was skilled in inspiring men with hope, and his sympathy with his men was remarkable."[16]

Many men griped and complained about retreating in the face of the enemy, about marching through the rain and mud on empty stomachs. Some of the officers talked openly about finding a new commander, one who would turn and fight Santa Anna's legions. Some officers spoke mutinous defiance, apparently within earshot of General Houston. But Houston ignored them. He appeared not to hear taunts. He remained aloof from petty critics. He did not consult his officers. Indeed, he wrote to his friend and ally, Secretary of War Thomas J. Rusk: "I consulted none—I held no councils-of-war. If I err, the blame is mine."[17]

Although some of his men continued to desert—mostly to be with their families—General Houston's army remained intact.

Despite their complaints, despite the criticisms of some of their officers, the soldiers continued to follow the directions of Houston. He had impressed them from the start, and his tight-lipped assurance in himself somehow added a touch of authority.

Despite weeks of retreating through mud and rain, of miserable refugees, of scant provisions, the core of the army did not lose confidence in their imposing general. Like Washington at Valley Forge, Houston kept his army together. George Washington may have been the only man in early America with the background, reputation, character, and commanding presence who could have kept the Continental Army in the field throughout the long years of the Revolution. Perhaps, too, Sam Houston was the only man in frontier Texas with the necessary background, reputation, character, and commanding presence to keep the Texas Army together and on the march during the difficult, discouraging, dangerous campaign of 1836.

On March 17 General Houston and his army reached Burnam's Crossing (near present-day LaGrange) on the Colorado River. It was raining and the Colorado was swollen, so it was necessary to take the army across the river at Burnam's, utilizing a ferry that was burned after everyone had reached the east bank. Houston then continued downstream, slogging alongside the Colorado almost thirty miles to Beason's Ford near Columbus. Measles had broken out among the men, which often happened when large numbers of soldiers gathered from isolated country homes and were exposed to communicable diseases. Houston encamped for eight days at Beason's, placing scouts for miles along the river to watch for Mexican soldiers. Houston's large number of sick men had time to heal, while reinforcements and supplies and ammunition had a better chance of reaching the army when not on the move. And General Houston had time to drill his army, beginning to make battlefield soldiers of them.

A veteran of the War of 1812, sixty-year-old Wyly Martin, joined the army in the camp at Beason's Ford. He was an officer at Horseshoe Bend, settled in Austin's colony in 1825, and was appointed a major in the Texas Army. Martin had been an officer in the United States Army of higher rank, captain, and longer duration than Lt. Sam Houston, and he was Houston's senior in age. Major Martin immediately joined the critics of General Houston.

Houston had greater problems with Capt. Moseley Baker. More than a decade Houston's junior, Baker was a journalist and politician who became Alabama's Speaker of the House. But after forging a $5,000 check, he fled Alabama, settling in Austin's colony in 1833. At the Consultation of 1835, Baker made a motion to dissolve the convention, prompting Sam Houston to stand in opposition.

Houston emphatically believed that there was key work to be done by the Consultation, and he ended his remarks by belittling Baker: "I had rather be a slave, and grovel in the dust all my life than a convicted felon."[18] Houston kept the Consultation together, but the combative Moseley Baker became his lifelong enemy, as he proved during the campaign of 1836.

Also problematic was David G. Burnet, selected as president *ad interim* by the wartime government on the last day—March 17 – of the Convention at Washington. Burnet had a failed record as an *empresario* and attorney, and he was not elected as a delegate to the Convention. But he attended as a visitor, and the delegates, who did not think it proper to elect one of their own as president, selected Burnet, who lobbied behind the scenes. President Burnet immediately moved the seat of government from Washington to Harrisburg, close to the small but effective Texas Navy headquartered at Galveston.

David G. Burnet, as interim president of Texas, was critical and jealous of General Houston, while offering scant assistance to the army. *Author's collection.*

The removal of the government was unsettling to Texans and accelerated the Runaway Scrape. On March

23 General Houston wrote his friend Thomas J. Rusk, congratulating him on his recent appointment as Secretary of War. In the course of a lengthy report he asserted, "The retreat of the government will have a bad effect on the troops, and I am half-provoked at it myself." Later in the letter he blurted, "Oh, why did the cabinet leave Washington?" And he confessed to Rusk, "You know that I am not easily depressed, but, before my God, since we parted, I have found the darkest hours of my past life! . . . for forty-eight hours, I have not eaten an ounce, nor have I slept."[19]

Whether or not he slept, General Houston beat tattoo every night, as well as reveille an hour before dawn each morning. He had learned these drum beats as a teenager hanging out with an eastern Tennessee militia company called the "Mounted Gunmen." It was one more military proficiency that reinforced his leadership role. Each evening he inspected sentinel posts, met with his staff, wrote reports and letters and dispatches, and tried to read himself to sleep. The predawn reveille and early readiness was especially important after General Sesma's central division reached the western bank of the Colorado River and began probing for a crossing.

On March 26 General Houston ordered the army to pack up and break camp, resuming the march eastward. Houston assembled his men and reminded them that, with the surrender of Fannin's command, they comprised the only army in Texas.

"There are but few of us," he stressed, "and if we are beaten, the fate of Texas is sealed. The salvation of the country depends upon the first battle had with the enemy. For this reason, I intend to retreat, if I am obliged to go even to the banks of the Sabine."[20]

General Houston realized that his ill-trained, poorly disciplined army of volunteers had one chance at victory. He had to continue his strategic retreat, buying time to better prepare his men and to await an opportunity to strike a Mexican column with a reasonable shot at victory. Regarding his mention of the Sabine River, there were widespread suspicions that Houston had arranged, perhaps with the cooperation of Andrew Jackson, to have troops of the United States Army waiting on the east side of the Sabine. Houston welcomed any rumor that might encourage his army to continue with his strategy.

Predictably, Moseley Baker led the opposition to another re-treat, especially with a Mexican force within striking distance. Captain Baker talked loudly of changing commanders the next day. But the men dutifully took up the march at sundown, leav-ing campfires burning to fool Mexican scouts that the camp re-mained occupied. Houston led his disgruntled army for six miles through the darkness, although as many as 200 men deserted into the night.

The soldiers bivouacked without campfires for a few hours, before resuming the march at dawn. Houston set a steady, re-lentless pace, with the help of aides who constantly rode up and down the column. That night, Sunday, March 27, the weary men camped about a mile west of San Felipe, which stood on the west bank of the Brazos River. Since the previous evening, Houston's army had marched thirty miles through mud, moving from the Colorado River to the Brazos within a single day.

Losing no time, the next day Houston commenced a march northward up the west bank of the Brazos. General Houston had decided to encamp his army across the Brazos from Bernardo, a large plantation house built by Jared Groce in 1822. One of Aus-tin's Old Three Hundred, Groce came to Texas with nearly 100 slaves and a large wagon train bearing, among many other items, a small cotton gin. Groce received vast acreage from the Mexican government, and he became the wealthiest of Austin's colonists. In 1833, Groce built a new plantation home, Groce's Retreat, sev-eral miles to the north. His son, Leonard Waller Groce, made Ber-nardo his family home.

When General Houston launched a northward march, Mose-ley Baker and Wyly Martin refused to advance with their compa-nies, and soldiers from other units who wanted to wait no longer to fight fell in with them. Houston realized that there was "much discontent in the lines" even among the men who obeyed his or-der to march.[21] He faced the greatest challenge yet to his authori-ty as commander-in-chief.

General Houston responded with a masterful solution. He detached Moseley Baker to guard the San Felipe ford across the

Brazos River. Captain Baker commanded the largest company in the army, Company D of the First Regiment. With his recent "reinforcements," Baker had about 150 men to establish a strong point. Wyly Martin, with about forty-six soldiers, was asked to hold four crossings and ferries below San Felipe. These two mutinous captains actually anchored Houston's right flank.

A week later General Houston wrote to Captain Baker, pointedly admonishing him that "the utmost harmony of action, subordination, and discipline, must be observed. The safety of the country requires it, and the commanding general orders a rigid adherence to it."[22]

With torrential rain cascading onto his men and drenching the line of march, it took the Texas Army three days to reach Houston's destination, arriving opposite Bernardo on March 30. The steamboat *Yellow Stone* loaded with cotton bales, stood at the landing. General Houston promptly commandeered the riverboat, placing a substantial guard aboard to secure the vessel, while promising that the captain and his men would be compensated with generous land grants from the Republic of Texas.

Jared and Leonard Groce had strongly supported the independence movement. Indeed, after President Burnet led the *ad interim* government out of Washington, they spent the next three nights at Groce's Retreat before moving on toward Harrisburg. General Houston established "Camp West of Brazos" beside a lake that shielded the army from frontal attack. A nearby stand of timber provided wood for campfires. A hospital was set up on the east side of the river to deal with cases of measles and dysentery, pink eye and mumps. Buildings of the plantation complex east of the river were used for shelter, and supplies of corn and beef and other foodstuffs were made available for the army. These soldiers were tough frontiersman, and many were in their teens and twenties, with resilience and rapid recuperative powers.

General Houston and his staff made sure the men washed their mud-caked clothing and cleaned their weapons. Weapons were repaired and rifle balls were molded at the plantation blacksmith shop. "Camp West of Brazos" was arranged by units, and "an entire organization of camp duty and discipline" was established, with day and night inspections by Houston and Hockley. A program of drill was instituted—Houston wanted his men to be able to advance in lines and fire by volley and execute other battlefield maneuvers. Of considerable help were more than forty men who had been discharged from the U.S. Army or who were recent deserters who came to Texas to claim land grants promised to recruits. These experienced soldiers could lead or demonstrate drills. Maj. George W. Hockley praised "the exertions of the officers and obedience of the men."[23]

Eight "Redlanders" from East Texas arrived in camp, and other reinforcements were expected, along with supplies and ammunition. Word soon reached Houston that two six-pounders—which would be nicknamed the "Twin Sisters" by the soldiers—had been sent by boat by citizens of Cincinnati, and now were en route overland to the army.

A reinforcement of special importance to General Houston was Secretary of War Thomas Jefferson Rusk, who arrived in camp on April 4. Earlier in the day Houston had dispatched another report to Rusk, asking him yet again to visit the camp: "It will inspirit the troops."[24]

President Burnet, greatly alarmed by the advance of Mexican troops with no resistance from the Texas Army, sent an oft-quoted letter to Houston through Rusk: "The enemy are laughing you to scorn. You must fight them. You must retreat no further. The country expects you to fight. The salvation of the country depends on you doing so."[25]

President Burnet disliked Houston and had given Rusk instructions to take command if it seemed advisable. But Rusk was Houston's friend and admirer, and the two men conferred on war conditions and strategy. Secretary Rusk held the rank of colonel, and he decided to stay with the army as Houston's second-in-command.

Meanwhile, General Santa Anna learned that President Burnet had moved the government to Harrisburg. Deciding upon a bold stroke, Santa Anna decided to lead a column to Harrisburg and capture Burnet and other government officials, which presumably would end the war. His column was smaller than Hous-

General Houston fashioned his hat into a tricorn, reminiscent of the American Revolution and depicted by the equestrian statue in Hermann Park. *Photo by Dr. Berri O'Neal.*

ton's army, but the Texans had been in constant retreat, and after his devastating triumphs at the Alamo and Goliad, Santa Anna was contemptuous of the Texas Army and its leader.

The Mexican column reached San Felipe in April 7. San Felipe had been burned, apparently by Moseley Baker. General Houston had sent reinforcements to Baker, who dug in on the east bank. When Santa Anna arrived, deadly rifle fire denied the Mexicans use of the ford. After two days Santa Anna led his men downriver, seizing a ferry at Fort Bend and rapidly crossing to the east bank. Wyly Martin and his little command hastened north, connecting with Baker at San Felipe. Captains Baker and Martin, facing a superior Mexican column, executed a movement they had harshly criticized General Houston for—they retreated.

Texans fled their homes by the thousands. At Lynchburg, at the mouth of the San Jacinto River, 5,000 desperate refugees camped. With Santa Anna on the march in Anglo Texas, Houston had to intercept the invading army.

"I have, under the most disadvantageous circumstances, kept an army together," observed Houston.[26] He knew that the ultimate purpose of an army is to fight. On the night of April 11 Houston and Rusk talked strategy. The next morning the order went out to break camp and move the army across the swollen Brazos. After nearly two weeks at Camp West of Brazos, the Texas Army readied itself to march in the direction of the Mexican Army.

We go to conquer.
Gen. Sam Houston
April 19, 1836

Chapter Ten

San Jacinto

At ten o'clock on Tuesday morning, April 12, General Sam Houston and his staff began directing the Texas Army in crossing the turbulent Brazos River at Groce's Landing. There was no ferry, but the 130-foot steamboat, *Yellow Stone*, and a yawl—a small sailboat—made trip after trip on Tuesday and Wednesday. Aside from the soldiers and baggage, some of which could be handled by the yawl, the *Yellow Stone* had to bring "eight or ten wagons, ox-teams, and about two hundred horses . . . "[1] By Wednesday afternoon the entire army was on the east bank.

From his new headquarters on the east bank of the Brazos, General Houston wrote orders to detachments to unite with the main force, as well as a proclamation "To the Citizens of Texas." He informed the public of the situation, and at this crucial point he appealed for more recruits: "Protect your wives, your children, and your homes . . . Come and free your country at once; and be men!"[2]

Awaiting the army on the east side of the river were the two six-pounders from Cincinnati, which the soldiers dubbed the "Twin Sisters." Lt. Col. J. C. Neill knew artillery, and so did Maj. George W. Hockley. Each man would be in charge of a cannon and its crew, and Lieutenant Colonel Neill was appointed commander of the "Artillery Corps." In the blacksmith shop lead and old horseshoes were converted to grape shot.

A few days earlier General Houston and his staff had reorganized the army, creating a second regiment, as well as a battalion of "Regular Infantry." The hard-working General Staff was headed by Major General Houston and Colonel Rusk. The Medical

Staff was composed of nine physicians, including Dr. Anson B. Jones. The Artillery Corps boasted the Twin Sisters and more than thirty men. The First Regiment of Texas Volunteers, organized in Gonzales at the start of the campaign, still was commanded by Col. Edward Burleson. There were eight companies in the First Regiment: A, B, C, D, F, H, I, and K. But B and I were transferred to the new infantry battalion, which also had Regular Company A and Volunteer Company B. This four-company battalion of Regular Infantry was commanded by Lt. Col. Henry Millard.

The Second Regiment of Texas Volunteers included the Spy Company, commanded by Capt. Henry W. Karnes. This company had more than forty spies, or scouts. The best-known scout was Deaf Smith, but all of these men were hard-riding frontiersmen who were constantly on the roads or in the countryside. The scouts kept Houston supplied with information about the movement and size of Mexican columns, the condition of rivers and streams, and countless other items. At San Jacinto several of these scouts would be away on duty, but others would ride into battle as cavalry. There also was Cavalry Company J, comprised of about thirty mounted rifleman.

The heart of the Second Regiment was ten companies of infantry, although some of those "companies" had only twenty-odd men apiece, barely the size of a modest platoon. The largest company in any unit was Company C of the First Regiment. Commanded by Capt. Moseley Baker, this troop normally had more than sixty men.

Commanding the new Second Regiment was Col. Sidney Sherman, who had gone to considerable effort and expense to lead men into battle on behalf of Texas independence. He was a successful entrepreneur from Newport, Kentucky, where he was captain of a state militia troop. In Newport Sherman had founded the first company to produce machine-made cotton bagging, and he also fashioned sheet lead. But when the Texas Revolution erupted in the fall of 1835, Sherman sold his cotton bag company to finance a band of volunteers.

The thirty-year-old militia captain equipped fifty-two men, while donning a uniform that would be the sharpest military at-

Lady Liberty was the silk flag made by the ladies of Newport, Kentucky, for the Texas-bound company raised by Capt. Sidney Sherman. By the time Houston led his column to San Jacinto, Colonel Sherman commanded the Second Infantry Regiment, and Lady Liberty served as the battle flag of the Texas Army. *Author's collection.*

tire in the Texas Army. The ladies of Newport made a silk flag of Lady Liberty for the company. Sherman and his men departed for Texas on the last day of 1835. Captain Sherman and his Kentuckians had reached Gonzales by the time General Houston arrived, and when the First Regiment was organized, Sherman became second-in-command as lieutenant colonel. When the Second Regiment was formed, Sherman was the obvious choice to take command as colonel. Like the men, Colonel Sherman had joined the army to fight, and he would prove aggressive in combat.

The same could be said for a volunteer who enlisted as a private when the Texas Army was at Camp West of Brazos. Mirabeau Buonaparte Lamar was a native of Georgia who was five years Houston's junior. In Georgia Lamar received a good education, served in the legislature, started a family, wrote poetry, painted in oils. Restless after the death of his wife, Lamar came to Texas in 1835. He declared himself for Texas independence and returned to Georgia to arrange a move. When he learned of combat in the Texas Revolution, he hurried back and found the army encamped on the Brazos River. Private Lamar immediately tried to recruit men to take the *Yellow Stone*, fortified with cotton bales, downriver to attack Mexican positions. Soon learning of the scheme, General Houston posted notices around camp that anyone who tried to organize an unauthorized expedition would be regarded as a mutineer and shot. Private Lamar lowered his profile and, within days, distinguished himself in battle.

On Friday, April 15, the Texas Army, after two fruitful weeks in camp, advanced southward in a new and better organized line of march. Houston ordered a bivouac after six miles. When the column was joined by the retreating companies of Moseley Baker and Wyly Martin, more than 300 men were incorporated into the army.

But Martin immediately resumed open criticism of General Houston, who reassigned him to supervise the refugees following the army. Martin—and his vicious calumnies against Houston—thus was removed from the presence of the army. Captain Baker also continued to carp, but he remained to lead his company into battle. Well over 200 men had seen action under Baker at San Felipe, and Houston avoided the controversy that would have erupted if he had removed a captain who, although disruptive, had proved himself in action.

On Saturday, Sunday, and Monday, April 16-17-18, Houston pushed his men hard. During the march the army approached a fork in the road marked by a gnarled old oak. To the left of the "Which-way Tree" a road went northeast toward Nacogdoches—another retreat. The right fork angled southeast, toward Harrisburg and the reported presence of Santa Anna. Houston's critics always claimed that the men in the lead determined the route by marching down the right fork without orders, and the rest of the men followed purposefully. But General Houston knew his men well enough to know that an attempt to send the army on a retreat to Nacogdoches would spark disobedience and mutiny.

General Houston led more than one thousand men in a march that approached a gnarled oak—similar and near to this tree in New Kentucky Park west of Tomball. At the "Which-way Tree" the column marched steadfastly along the right fork, toward the reported presence of Santa Anna. *Photo by the author.*

He pulled his horse up at the right fork, indicated the Harrisburg road, and watched his army march past. Houston was pushing his men in a forced march straight toward the Mexican force. Now was the time to close with Santa Anna.

Houston had more than 1,000 men, but many could not keep up with the main column. Despite foul weather and miserable road conditions, Houston drove the Texas Army fifty-five miles in two and a half days. On Monday, April 18, the Texan soldiers reached the north side of Buffalo Bayou opposite Harrisburg, which was in ashes.

Santa Anna and his advance division already had passed through Harrisburg, hoping to capture the interim government. But the town was abandoned, and Santa Anna ordered it burned. Burnet had led his cabinet to the hamlet of New Washington, about twenty miles south on Galveston Bay. Santa Anna sent a detail of lancers to New Washington, post haste, but Burnet and the others escaped just ahead of them in a rowboat, which was picked up by a little warship of the Texas Navy.

Mexican couriers were captured by Houston's scouts. Their dispatches revealed that Santa Anna's advance column numbered only about 750 men, but that General Cos had been directed to join him with 500 men. Houston now moved to corner the self-styled Napoleon of the West. A rear guard was established near Harrisburg, with 250 Texan soldiers, many of them ill, guarding refugees, supply wagons, and camp equipage. Houston's combat force would travel light. An old ferry was repaired to take across men and horses and, of course, the Twin Sisters.

General Houston was part of the first crossing, at mid-morning on April 19. Houston took up a position astride his white stallion, Saracen, which had been acquired from a farmer during the march. Colonel Rusk stayed on the opposite side to supervise the loading of the ferry. Buffalo Bayou was about fifty yards wide and over twenty feet deep at this point. "The passage over the Bayou was difficult and perilous," reported Houston, "and yet I was determined to make it that morning."[3]

Before resuming the march, Secretary of War Rusk and General Houston penned a proclamation to the People of Texas. "Enthusiasm prevails in the army," stated Rusk, who also reported: "Your general is at the head of a brave and chivalrous band, and throws himself, sword in hand, into the breach to save his country and vindicate her rights."

Houston asserted: "We view ourselves on the eve of battle. We are nerved for the contest, and must conquer or perish." The General signed off: "Liberty and our country."[4]

Houston also dashed off a letter to Henry Raguet in Nacogdoches, doubtless hoping that his lovely daughter, Anna, also would read it. "Sir: This morning we are in preparation to meet Santa Anna. It is the only chance of saving Texas." Houston described the situation and the army. "The troops are in fine spirits, and now is the time for action." And he stated flatly: "We go to conquer."[5]

Both Rusk and Houston recognized the readiness, the eagerness of the army to fight. Young W. P. Zuber, at this same time, said that "the prospect for the main army to engage Santa Anna

was certain, and none doubted victory." When Zuber was assigned to the rear guard, in part because his rifle was broken, he
wept bitterly. In vain he scrambled to acquire a good rifle from
someone, and he offered his only ten dollars to hire one of his
comrades to trade assignments. "My mortification at being pre-
vented from being under fire in the approaching battle was truly
great."[6]

Aware that his men were spoiling for a fight, General Houston
assembled the army and delivered a resounding speech. "Victory
is certain," he boomed out in closing. "Trust in God and fear not.
And remember the Alamo! Remember the Alamo!" The battle cry
was shouted back at him, while Maj. Alexander Somervell ex-
claimed prophetically, "After such a speech, but damned few will
be taken prisoner—that I know."[7]

"My policy was to concentrate, retreat, and conquer,"[8] Houston later related, in analyzing his strategy during the six-week
campaign. His orders to Fannin to withdraw from Goliad had
been ignored, to the detriment of the Texas Army and to the doom
of Fannin's men. But Houston had managed to concentrate about
1,400 men, and he held most of them together during a long retreat. And now, as he declared to Henry Raguet two days before
the decisive battle: "We go to conquer."

Houston led a march through the night, calling a halt for a
brief rest. But there were no campfires, no tents, few blankets, no
rations, and the men "rested" on soggy ground. At dawn Houston again took up the march, soon stopping for breakfast. Three
cattle, grazing on the prairie, were butchered, and beef was roasted. But scouts rode in with the news that Mexican scouts had
been encountered and that Santa Anna's column was marching
from the south toward Lynch's Ferry. The beef was packed up
and the column arrived at Lynch's Ferry ahead of the Mexicans.
A flatboat was intercepted, carrying provisions from New Washington—which Santa Anna had just burned—for use by the Mexican Army at Lynchburg, above the ferry.

Houston positioned his army in timber that lined the east
bank of Buffalo Bayou. The Twin Sisters were unlimbered and
placed at the edge of the oak grove. The Mexican column would

have to march, right to left, on the prairie in front of Texan rifles and artillery protected by timber. A flour barrel was rolled off the flatboat and flour cakes were made to go with the beef. The Texas soldiers enjoyed a late breakfast while awaiting the appearance of Santa Anna's *soldados*.

Early in the afternoon the Mexican column appeared, impressive with uniformed infantry, mounted lancers, and marching music from drums and bugle. Twice Santa Anna ordered that the chilling *Dequello* be played (the verb *degollar* means "to slit the throat," and the cutthroat song had been played at the Alamo).

Mexican scouts reported that the Texas Army blocked the approach to the ferry. Houston had his men lie flat so that their positions and numbers could not be determined. Santa Anna set up his lone artillery piece, a brass twelve-pounder, and began to pepper the oak grove with grapeshot. General Houston ordered Lt. Col. J. C. Neill to answer with the two six-pounders. The Twin Sisters wounded a captain, knocked an ammunition crate apart, and killed two mules and a horse. But Lieutenant Colonel Neill caught a grapeshot in the hip, and George Hockley took command of the battery.

As the artillery duel continued, Colonel Sherman persuaded a reluctant General Houston to grant him permission to try to capture the Mexican cannon with Texas cavalry. Houston gave explicit orders to Sherman to conduct merely a reconnaissance, and not engage in general combat. Sixty-one men, including Colonel Rusk, rode with Sherman, who promptly led a charge straight for the cannon. But the gun carriage had been damaged and the twelve-pounder already was being dragged out of range.

Sherman's "cavalrymen" were nothing more than mounted riflemen. After firing one shot at Mexicans, most of these men rode back a distance, dismounted, and began to reload their long-barreled rifles. Immediately Santa Anna's lancers charged Sherman's scattered command, and a large number of infantrymen rushed out to cut off a Texan retreat. Houston disgustedly ignored pleas for help, refusing to commit infantry to a spontaneous, unplanned battle. But Capt. Jesse Billingsley defiantly led his company out of the timber line, and other men followed, ignoring Houston's shouts to counter-march. Before they advanced very far, however, Sherman's men raced back to the safety of the main army.

Scrambling back into their saddles, the makeshift cavalry force spurred away from their pursuers. Colonel Rusk and a dismounted, wounded rifleman seemed about to be killed or captured, until Pvt. Mirabeau B. Lamar galloped to the rescue, knocking one lancer from his saddle with a collision and extricating his two comrades. Houston commended Lamar's courage, promoted him to colonel in front of the army, and gave him command of the cavalry. General Houston furiously roared a scathing condemnation at the disobedient Sherman, who was publicly humiliated and who hated Houston until the day he died—a decade after his sharp-tongued General.

Santa Anna established camp several hundred yards east of the Texan position. There was timber behind his camp and Peggy's Lake, surrounded by marsh, and to the north there was timber and marsh and the San Jacinto River. The camp site was on a higher elevation, and knee-high prairie grass sloped down toward the Texas camp. Rows of tents stretched east to west, and Santa Anna's spacious marquee stood in front of the tents. Santa Anna did not know the size of the Texan Army, but he knew that his own column was small.

He feared that the Texans might launch a dawn attack, and he ordered his men to build a barricade in front of the camp. After erecting their tents, the *soldados* spent most of the night arranging supply crates, saddles, and brush into a ramshackle fortification about five feet high. The twelve-pounder was placed in the center of the barricade.

Houston's men found sleeping spots, spread out a blanket—if they had one—and stacked arms. General Houston ordered pickets to be set out. Houston had never been to this area, and he studied the terrain and talked to his scouts. He stayed up late, as usual, planning a battle and considering possible moves. The General arranged for the camp to be awakened at four a.m., in case Santa Anna launched a dawn attack.

General Houston had been in the saddle all day, exposed for

hours to enemy fire. He had worked deep into the night. Most nights Houston caught only a few hours of sleep, and several times during the past six weeks he had led night marches. Now a climactic battle loomed. But the General had planned extensively, his men were at a fighting pitch, and he felt able to relax.

Someone had made off with the Indian blanket he had worn during the rains, and he contributed his saddle blanket to be cut up for wadding in the artillery charges. Houston, in his own words, "laid himself under an oak to rest, with his saddle for a pillow, and without covering, slept undisturbed through the whole night, and when he awoke in the morning it was remarked that every shade of anxiety had disappeared from his brow."[9]

A shade of anxiety may have returned to his brow at mid-morning, when General Cos marched a large column across the prairie to reinforce Santa Anna. Houston sent out Deaf Smith and Henry Karnes, who soon returned with a count of approximately 540 new *soldados*.

Hoping not to alarm the men, Houston loudly announced that the troop movement was "a mere ruse on the part of Santa Anna."[10] But word soon spread throughout the camp that the morning column indeed were reinforcements, and the Texas Army now was outnumbered. Colonel Rusk and Adjutant General John Wharton requested a council of war with senior officers. There had been nothing resembling a council of war during the campaign, but Houston agreed, calling the meeting for noon.

At twelve o'clock General Houston, "seated on the grass beneath a post oak tree, submitted the proposition whether they should attack the enemy in his position, or whether they should wait for him to attack them in theirs." Houston's proposition was debated at length. Two of the seven officers wanted to assault the Mexican camp. Secretary of War Rusk counseled against such an attack, and the other officers also recognized "that charging a disciplined army in position by a raw soldiery, advancing in an open prairie . . . was an unheard-of-thing."[11] The majority of these seven senior officers wanted to fight on the defensive from the cover of the trees. General Houston, inscrutable as ever, dismissed the council without announcing his decision.

Houston knew from personal experience about attacking a defensive position. As a young lieutenant he had been severely wounded while charging over a barricade at Horseshoe Bend. Later that day, Lieutenant Houston was shot twice more when he rushed a redoubt. And yet the barricade, although taller and far more stoutly built than Santa Anna's makeshift obstruction, had been carried by a determined charge, and the redoubt had been destroyed. Furthermore, John Wharton had been going from company to company exhorting the men to vote to attack, while Capt. Moseley Baker loudly urged his men to do the same.

General Houston, quietly riding around the camp, observed company after company vote to attack. Now. After an arduous six-week campaign, he knew these men. He had known such men all his life. These frontier volunteers did not like to take orders; they felt at liberty to leave the army whenever they pleased; they were undisciplined. But they had come together to fight, and the enemy—led by the hated Santa Anna—were camped within sight. The General decided to ignore the council. Writing in third person, Houston revealed that he "at once determined on his own responsibility, to give battle."[12]

Houston summoned Deaf Smith and another scout, armed them with axes, and ordered them to cut down Vince's Bridge, eight miles to the south. Both armies had marched over Vince's Bridge on the way to the battle ground, and with the bridge gone there would be no retreat for the Mexicans—or, if they lost, for the Texans. Houston urged the scouts to hurry back, because the armies would be engaged in combat.

During the hard march from Groce's, volunteers had joined the column. Even with these late additions, after Houston assigned a substantial camp guard, he reported a combat force of just 783 men. Colonel Sherman's Second Regiment would anchor the left flank, moving adjacent to the timber along the north side of the battle ground. Secretary of War Rusk would command the left wing, and would be a check to the impulsive Sherman. Colonel Burleson's First Regiment would occupy the center, with General Houston in front. Major Hockley would command the Twin Sisters, which would be manhandled by the men of the Artillery Corps. To the right of the Twin Sisters would march Colonel Millard's battalion. On the right flank, newly-promoted Col. M. B. Lamar commanded sixty cavalrymen. This mounted force was assigned to cut off retreat to the south, which was the sole escape route.

In the Mexican camp, the expected dawn attack by the Texans did not materialize, and at mid-morning General Cos arrived with substantial reinforcements. There was little activity in the Texan camp, and by afternoon it seemed that Houston intended no action on April 21. Probably there would be combat early on April 22. Meanwhile, Santa Anna's men had worked most of the night putting up a barricade, while the men of General Cos had marched through the night. Santa Anna retired to his striped marquee, and his command engaged in badly needed *siestas*. So contemptuous was Santa Anna of Houston's timid performance that he did not post pickets or even sentinels.

At three-thirty General Houston formed his men to attack. "Our troops paraded with alacrity and spirit," observed Houston, "and were anxious for the contest."[13] A black soldier, who had beaten taps and reveille while Houston slept, was joined by three fifers to play marching music. But this unlikely combo did not know martial tunes, only a few popular songs. They agreed upon a tavern ballad: "Will You Come to the Bower? (I have shaded for you? Will you, will you, will you, will you come to my bower?)." The drummer tapped out a steady beat on the song that soon would become known in Texas as the "San Jacinto Quickstep."

The Texas Army stepped out of the oak grove in unit columns—left to right: Second Regiment, First Regiment, Twin Sisters, Regular Battalion, and, on the right flank, Cavalry. General Houston rode his white stallion about twenty yards in advance. He had not been in combat for twenty-two years, when he was wounded three times while twice leading his men to the attack. Now he was forty-three, but in battle he was none the wiser—and no less brave. Like young Lieutenant Houston at Horseshoe Bend, Major General Houston at San Jacinto would lead from the front.

The columns marched through the knee-high grass about half the distance to the Mexican camp. Except for the light strains of the little band, the march was quiet, as men contemplated the coming assault. At the halfway point the columns fanned out, forming a line 900 yards wide and only two ranks deep. The advance continued, with the Texas soldiers carrying their rifles at Port Arms. General Houston must have been gratified that the fortnight of drilling at Groce's was bearing fruit on the field of battle. The battle flag of the Texas Army was the Liberty Flag presented to Sidney Sherman by the ladies of Newport, Kentucky.

A slight grassy ridge west of the Mexican camp blocked the Texas line from view during its approach. At 200 yards Houston ordered Hockley to discharge the Twin Sisters at the breastworks. The first round of grapeshot sent pieces of the barricade flying. The infantrymen continued to advance, and the artillerymen manhandled the two six-pounders forward.

Ben McCulloch commanded one of the gun crews: "We advanced after each discharge, keeping in advance of the infantry, until we were within less than 100 yards of their breastworks." With General Houston riding in front, McCulloch had to take care not to trigger his cannon while Houston was in the line of fire.[14]

On the left Colonel Sherman bellowed, "Remember the Alamo!" His regiment took up the war cry, "Remember the Alamo! Remember Goliad!" The 9th Company of Sherman's Second Regiment was comprised of slightly more than twenty Tejanos, displaced from their San Antonio homes by Santa Anna. Their war cry was in Spanish: "¡ *Recuerden el Alamo!* ¡ *Recuerden La Bahía!*" These words *en español* had a chilling effect on Santa Anna's *soldados*.

Mexican officers were trying to form up their *soldados* when General Houston ordered a rifle volley. On the left Sherman's men already had broken into a run while shouting the Texan war cry, and they fired sporadically, on the move. But Burleson's First Regiment and Willard's Regulars responded with a volley at close range.

American riflemen had learned to "shoot for the braid" during the American Revolution, knocking out officers in fancy uniforms. At San Jacinto Brigadier General Manuel Fernández Castrillon was killed. Also killed or wounded were nine Mexican colonels, five lieutenant colonels, two majors, twelve captains, and thirteen lieutenants. Not all of these officers were shot in that devastating first volley, but many were, and most of the rest were hit during the next few minutes. Just when the officers were trying to mount a belated defense, many of them were gunned down. Leaderless *soldados* became a disorganized rabble.

General Houston wanted a second volley, but now the entire Texan line charged. The Second Regiment already had turned the Mexican right when the First Regiment and the Regulars piled into the barricade, clambering over and through the flimsy fortification, already riddled with grapeshot. General Castrillon stood defiantly beside the brass twelve-pounder, which had fired a round of grapeshot that sailed above the heads of the Texans. Castrillon was overwhelmed and slain, and so were *soldados* who tried to make a stand. With no time to reload, the Texans clubbed their rifles and wielded bowie knives.

"The conflict in the breastwork lasted but a few moments," noted Houston, " . . . our riflemen used their pieces as war-clubs, breaking many of them off at the breech."[15] Mounted on a white stallion in the forefront of his army, Houston was an obvious target. Several balls thudded into Saracen. The great horse went down, but an aide offered Houston his horse. Within moments, however, a copper ball ripped through his boot and shattered his left ankle. Houston ignored the wound and kept his attention on the fast-paced battle.

Lamar and his cavalry swept out of the woods and struck the enemy's left flank. Within moments the battle became a rout. Santa Anna emerged from his marquee, took in the collapse of his army, mounted his horse, and galloped off to the south. His men fled into the marshlands behind the camp and bogged down in Peggy's Lake. Texans furiously shot these trapped *soldados*, while wounded Mexicans met the same fate. The battle was over in less than twenty minutes, but the slaughter went on for an hour. Houston and several of his officers tried to halt the killing, but the men were filled with pent-up blood lust, and orders to "Parade" were ignored.

The only hope of escape was to the south, backtracking over yesterday's entry route. Texan cavalry cut off many of the fleeing *soldados*, and Henry Karnes led a mounted pursuit party all the way to the destroyed bridge, eight miles away. Colonel Juan Almonte gathered hundreds of *soldados* southwest of the camp and surrendered this large group to Thomas Rusk. Houston, concerned that his men were scattered all over the battleground and beyond, was conferring with several officers when he saw a Mexican column in the distance. For a terrible moment Houston thought that a fresh Mexican division was arriving, until he was told that they were prisoners of Rusk.

"The conflict lasted about eighteen minutes from the time of close action until we were in possession of the enemy's encampment, taking one piece of cannon (loaded), four stands of colors, all their camp equipage, stores, and baggage," announced a report prepared by General Houston for *ad interim* President David G. Burnet four days after the battle. "The rout commenced at half-past-four, and the pursuit by the main army continued until twilight. A guard was then left in charge of the enemy's encampment, and our army returned with their killed and wounded."

Eight Texans died and about two dozen more were wounded. Houston reported 630 Mexican dead and 730 captives, including 208 wounded. About 600 Mexican muskets were collected, along with 200 pistols, 300 sabres, hundreds of horses and mules, and nearly $12,000 in silver. Aware that the only payment the Texas government could make to his soldiers would be land grants, Houston ordered the money distributed among the men.

Toward the end of the Battle of San Jacinto, Houston rode back into the Texan camp, his left boot filling with blood. Thomas Rusk brought Colonel Juan Almonte to present this high-ranking prisoner to General Houston. At this point Houston could no longer stay in the saddle. He was bedded down where he slept the night before, and physicians were summoned.

Early the next morning Texan soldiers began scouring the countryside for escaped *soldados*, with General Santa Anna a special target. At mid-afternoon on April 22 Sgt. James Sylvester spotted a ragged escapee on foot near Vince's Bridge. Sylvester brought him back to camp, whereupon numerous *soldados* began calling out, "*¡El Presidente! ¡El Presidente!*" As word spread of this notable capture, Texan soldiers began to lust for a lynching. The prisoner was taken to Houston, who raised himself on an elbow on the pallet beneath an oak tree.

In Spanish, the captive "announced himself to be the President of Mexico and Houston's prisoner of war." Houston sent for Colonel Almonte, Secretary of War Rusk, and Tejano Lt. Lorenzo de Zavalla, Jr. as interpreters.

Santa Anna grandly pointed out, "The conqueror of the Napoleon of the West is born to no common destiny, and he can afford to be generous to the vanquished."

Houston the conqueror coldly retorted, "You should have remembered that, sir, at the Alamo!" Santa Anna tried to elude responsibility for the slaughters at the Alamo and La Bahia by blaming "orders from my Government."

"You are the Government yourself, sir," insisted Houston, adding, "A dictator, sir, has no superior."[16]

Santa Anna shakily requested opium. Houston directed that the prisoner's marquee and baggage be restored to him. Santa Anna returned better dressed and somewhat calmer, but Texans still wanted to hang him. Houston, however, had sized up his man. Santa Anna feared the vengeance of the Texans, and *El Presidente* was invaluable as a live prisoner.

Santa Anna quickly agreed to order the withdrawal of all Mexican troops

Gen. Antonio Lopez de Santa Anna, the self-styled "Napoleon of the West." *Courtesy Alamo Museum – DRT Library, San Antonio.*

from Texas, to recognize Texas independence, to agree to an enormous expansion of Texas borders, and to make other generous concessions.

Houston wrote that he "had great difficulty in preventing his assassination," but he "saved his soldiers from themselves"— and in the process saved the Revolution. With Houston "suffering excruciating pain from his wound, he was moved into Santa Anna's marquee. Santa Anna was moved eight feet to the tent of General Cos, where an eight-man "Santa Anna guard" was on duty twenty-four hours per day.[17]

Santa Anna's orders promptly were delivered to General Vicente Filisola, now the ranking Mexican officer in the field, and encamped just twenty-five miles away. Filisola dutifully gathered 2,900 *soldados* and headed south, collecting other contingents along the way. He marched back into Mexico with 4,600 men, enough to have overwhelmed the Texas Army, had there been some way to supply the *soldados*. Meanwhile, volunteers for the Texas Army now arrived in large numbers. But Houston was too ill and too agonized to command an army, and he asked that Thomas Rusk be appointed to succeed him. M. B. Lamar replaced Rusk as Secretary of War.

When Houston left the army he was too weak and feverish to address the men, so on May 5 he dictated farewell remarks that were read to the soldiers. "In taking leave of my brave comrades in arms," began the last paragraph, "I can not suppress the expression of that pride which I so justly feel in having had the honor to command them in person . . . At parting my heart embraces you with gratitude and affection."[18]

Dr. Alexander W. Ewing, Surgeon General of the Army, insisted that Houston travel to New Orleans for more sophisticated medical care than was available in Texas. President Burnet and his cabinet had made their way to San Jacinto, where their jealousy and hatred of Houston was ill-concealed. Secretary of Navy Robert Potter proposed removing Houston from command because he had distributed the $12,000 in silver to the soldiers instead of turning it over to the government. By the time this spiteful idea was rejected, Burnet and the others were preparing to take Santa

Anna to Galveston on the *Yellow Stone*.

Dr. Ewing insisted that his patient start his journey to New Orleans, but Burnet vindictively refused General Houston permission to leave the army! Captain John Ross of the *Yellow Stone* refused to depart without Houston, but when Dr. Ewing accompanied his patient, Secretary of War Lamar dismissed him from the army (he was reinstated a few months later by President Houston).

After reaching Galveston, General Houston was refused passage on the Texas warship *Liberty*, which was headed to New Orleans for repairs. At last Houston made his way to New Orleans aboard the trading schooner *Flora*. Having received no pay as Commanding General, Houston was forced to persuade the schooner's captain to extend him credit for his ticket.

Delayed by storm, the *Flora* did not dock at New Orleans until noon on May 22, a month after the spectacular victory. A crowd estimated at 5,000 had gathered to welcome the wounded hero, who stood on crutches to acknowledge their cheers and the lively airs of a band. He spoke a few words of appreciation before fainting into the arms of his companions. Part of the throng was a group of schoolgirls from Marion, Alabama, in New Orleans for a holiday. Seventeen-year-old Margaret Lea shed tears.

William Christy, an old friend of Houston from their days in the U.S. Army, met the *Flora* at the dock. He had Houston carried to his coach. Christy had prospered and generously supported the Texas Revolution. Christy took Houston to his spacious house, where three physicians removed more than twenty bone fragments from the General's inflamed ankle. Desperately ill when he arrived, Houston recovered steadily amid the comforts of his friend's home.

General Houston was showered with accolades and became aware that he was a national hero. Indeed, his victory had national implications, as stated in the final paragraph of the lengthy inscription on the San Jacinto Monument:

> *Measured by its results San Jacinto was one of the decisive battles of the world. The freedom of Texas from Mexico won here led to annexation and to the Mexican war, resulting in the ac-*

quisition by the United States of Texas, New Mexico, Arizona, Nevada, California, Utah, and parts of Colorado, Wyoming, Kansas and Oklahoma, almost one-third of the present area of the American nation, nearly a million square miles of territory, changed sovereignty.

In the nation's capitol building, Houston's first mentor, Senator Thomas Hart Benton, compared the Texas general to Mark Antony. On the morning after the battle the wounded Houston wrote a letter and immediately dispatched it by courier to his most important mentor, President Andrew Jackson. Twenty-one years earlier, General Jackson triumphed at the Battle of New Orleans. Badly outnumbered but fighting from a strong defensive position, in just thirty minutes the Americans inflicted almost 2,100 British casualties, while suffering merely seventy-one killed, wounded, and missing. Now Houston had led his own triumph, attacking a superior force but generating 630 dead and 730 prisoners, while absorbing only eight dead and fewer than thirty wounded. Of course, Houston was one of the wounded, and like his injuries at Horseshoe Bend, he would feel his San Jacinto wound the rest of his life.

This etching of General Houston was made in 1837. *From Wharton, The Republic of Texas.*

In Texas Houston became an iconic hero, "Old Sam Jacinto." Aside from a few disaffected officers and men who continued to regard him a coward for retreating—or who permanently resented his scorching rebukes—General Houston suddenly was the idol of the army. The day after the battle, Houston on his pallet produced an ear of corn from a pocket to gnaw. Nearby Texas soldiers asked to divide the corn, kernel by kernel. "We'll plant it and call it Houston corn."

The public speaker in Houston sensed a valuable anecdote. He handed over the ear of corn, asking each man to "take it home to your own fields." Houston added pointedly, "You may not call it Houston corn but call it San Jacinto corn."[19]

I would rather vote for you than any man.
Thomas J. Rusk
August 9, 1836

Chapter Eleven

President of Texas

The Hero of San Jacinto returned to Texas early in July 1836. Sam Houston had recuperated from surgery on his shattered ankle at the New Orleans mansion of an old friend, William Christy. While recovering at Christy's, Houston received a stream of letters, gifts, and visitors. When he set out overland for Texas, letters and gifts followed. Houston crossed the Sabine River and halted for a time in San Augustine, hosted by another old friend, Judge Philip Sublett. Houston had many friends in San Augustine, and he enjoyed an active social life, even though he still was on crutches. Indeed, Houston had friends and admirers throughout the entire country, and a great many of them tried to contact the new national hero.

During Houston's convalescence, the new Republic of Texas was beset by problems and uncertainty. The public debt already exceeded $1,000,000. Although most of the veterans of San Jacinto had returned to their homes, the Texas Army had swelled to more than 2,000 men, mostly new arrivals. There was no pay for them, few rations, rumors of Mexican Army invasions, and talk of Texas soldiers marching on Matamoros for booty.

The Texas economy was colonial in nature: most settlers were subsistence farmers who engaged in barter, while planters exported cotton against imported goods. There was little cash in circulation, but the interim government had no power of taxation anyway. Santa Anna remained in custody, and there was a continuing clamor to execute him, which would have caused an international furor. *Ad interim* President David G. Burnet proved incapable of dealing with these and other problems, and there was an effort from the army to force him to resign.

Although the interim government was supposed to operate until December 1836, on July 23 a harried Burnet and his cabinet called for an election to be held on Monday, September 5. The election would determine ratification of the constitution that had been written at Washington-on-the-Brazos, as well as whether the Republic of Texas should seek annexation to the United States. And assuming that the constitution became law, officials would be elected: president, vice president, fourteen senators, and twenty-nine representatives.

Henry Smith, selected as governor when the revolution started, announced his candidacy for president, hoping to have another chance at leadership. At the urging of friends and supporters, Stephen F. Austin agreed to run, primarily to attain annexation. But Austin had not recovered his health after his long incarceration in Mexico, not to speak of years of relentless overwork as *empresario*. And during the crucial months of the revolution Austin was absent from Texas—sent to the United States by the government—causing his popularity to wane.

Riding a crest of popularity, of course, was Old Sam Jacinto. Houston was widely implored to run. There were spontaneous meetings on his behalf. A petition bearing 600 names in support of a Houston candidacy was delivered to Columbia, serving as a ramshackle capital village. At a public gathering in San Augustine on August 15, Phil Sublett nominated Houston for president.

As he had done during the Runaway Scrape, as had become his leadership custom in matters large and small, Sam Houston delayed his decision to see how conditions developed. But he "was pressed on all sides to consent to take the office . . . " Tom Rusk expressed the feeling of most Texans when he wrote, "I would rather vote for you than any man."[1]

"I wish to retire from public life . . . ," Houston mused at one point. "I am, therefore, disinclined to mingle in the turmoil of public life." Despite this unconvincing protestation, Houston was irresistibly drawn to the "turmoil of public life." It became clear that he would win the presidential election overwhelmingly, and at last he made a dramatic entrance to the race.

Eleven days before the election he announced his candidacy. "The crisis requires it." Houston had assumed command of the Texas Army in March 1836, confident that somehow his leadership abilities could overcome all odds, and that same self-assurance applied to the presidency of the nascent Texas Republic. When told by supporters "that the time had come for him to save the new Republic, a second time," he confidently accepted the opportunity.[2]

On Monday, September 5, 1836, almost four out of every five Texans who voted supported Houston for president. Old Sam Jacinto received 5,119 votes, while Smith took just 743 votes and a suddenly forgotten Austin collected a paltry 587 votes. The constitution, of course, was approved, while only ninety-three voters opposed annexation. Houston regarded his elevation to the presidency as "almost by acclamation,"[3] and he considered the even more lopsided vote in favor of annexation as a mandate for his administration.

Ad interim President Burnet called the newly-elected First Congress to assemble in Columbia on Monday, October 3. According to the Constitution the President-elect would not assume office until the second Monday in December, but Houston felt that he should be present in Columbia during the congressional session. Burnet continued to flail in office, and with the people's choice in town, the *ad interim* president suddenly resigned on Saturday, October 22. At mid-day Houston was told that he would be inaugurated that afternoon at four o'clock in the two-story frame building known as Representative Hall.

There was no time to prepare the customary two- or three-hour inaugural address. After taking the oath of office from the Speaker of the House, President Houston spoke extemporaneously as a stenographer took down his remarks. "We are only in the outset of the campaign of liberty. Futurity has locked up the destiny which awaits our people." Destiny. Houston long had held an unshakable belief in his personal destiny, which plainly was now tied to the destiny of the Texas people. Houston spoke of the Battle of San Jacinto, which had happened only six months earlier and which always was a welcome topic for a Texas audience. Not so welcome were his pleas to maintain peace with Indians on the frontier. Most Texans considered Indians trespassing vermin, but Houston would never waver from his policy of treaties and trade instead of military action against the tribes.[4]

Houston closed his impromptu performance with a dramatic gesture, a gesture from which his actor's gifts extracted deep response. He unsheathed the sword he had brandished at San Jacinto. "It now, Sir, becomes my duty to make a presentation of this sword—this emblem of my past office!"[5]

The stenographer noted that Houston "was unable to proceed further . . . " During this emotional pause the President clutched his sword "with both hands, as if with a farewell grasp, a tide of varied associations of ideas rushed upon him in the moment; his countenance bespoke the workings of the strongest emotions, his soul seemed . . . to dwell momentarily on the glistening blade . . ." The stenographer continued to describe Houston's "eloquently impressive" pause, before recording the end of the speech in which the President laid "his sword upon the civil altar."[6]

The civil altar demanded a great deal from the new president, but Houston responded with decisiveness. Within days President Houston formed a new cabinet. To the most prestigious cabinet position, Secretary of State, he appointed Stephen F. Austin. Although dejected after finishing a distant third in the presidential race, Austin now could work directly toward his principal presidential goal, annexation by the United States. Houston's other presidential opponent, Henry Smith, was appointed Secretary of Treasury. By appointing recent political opponents, Houston was magnanimous in trying to heal old wounds. President Houston reappointed his trusted ally, Thomas J. Rusk, as Secretary of War. The able lawyer John Pinckney Henderson agreed to serve as Attorney General, while Houston's friend William Wharton was sent to the United States to represent Texas.

Houston dealt quickly with the two problem posed by the continuing presence of General Santa Anna. After the Battle of San Jacinto, General Houston had promised Santa Anna safety from the soldiers who wanted to execute him, while extracting promises regarding a treaty from the worried captive. General

Houston informed President Burnet of these two-way promises before departing for New Orleans on May 11. Three days later Santa Anna signed treaty agreements greatly favorable to Texas, but a large and vengeful army faction still wanted him to die. It was countered that if Santa Anna continued to be held prisoner, Mexico would not again invade Texas. With his life constantly threatened, Santa Anna was spirited to Orizombo, the plantation home of Dr. James Phelps. Orizombo was twelve miles from Columbia, and a twenty-man guard was posted.

When President Houston assumed the presidency, Santa Anna had been held captive in Texas for six months. Houston visited Orizombo prior to his inauguration, and Santa Anna urged that he be permitted to return to Mexico by way of Washington, D.C., where he would attempt to transfer Texas to the United States. The Texas Congress already had asserted the right to dispose of the prisoner, so President Houston requested permission to send Santa Anna to Washington and then to Santa Cruz. But Congress, incited by Houston's enemies, passed a resolution ordering the prisoner to be kept in Texas. President Houston vetoed the resolution.

Colonel Almonte was released to accompany Santa Anna, along with a three-man escort led by George Hockley. On November 25 this delegation sailed for New Orleans, where a large crowd gathered to see Santa Anna. Curious crowds turned out all along the way to Washington. President Jackson was courteous but noncommittal, and six days later Santa Anna was sent to the *U.S.S. Pioneer.* On February 23, 1837, the *Pioneer* delivered Santa Anna to Mexico and a government that had repudiated him and his treaty.

Meanwhile, Stephen F. Austin died in Columbia on December 27, 1836. Contracting pneumonia while working in his unheated quarters, Austin had little physical resistance left. He was only a few months younger than Houston. The President immediately announced the sad news. "The Father of Texas is no more. The first pioneer of the wilderness has departed. General Stephen F. Austin, Secretary of State, has expired this day."[7] Many admirers of Old Sam Jacinto already were calling Houston the "Father of

Texas," but his magnanimity permanently assigned the title to Stephen F. Austin.

Austin's final letter as Secretary of State was to President Andrew Jackson, urging recognition of the Republic of Texas by the United States. Northern states of the Union strongly opposed the annexation of such a potentially huge new slave state as Texas, and there were constitutional doubts that an independent nation could be annexed.

Texas delegate William Wharton seemed to make no progress with annexation or even recognition, even after Memucan Hunt arrived from Texas in February 1837 to assist. Houston's entreaties to Jackson—"My great desire is that our country Texas shall be annexed to the United States"[8]—had little effect. On March 4, 1837, Jackson's hand-picked successor, Vice President Martin Van Buren, would be inaugurated as president. On March 2 Southern congressmen engineered passage of a bill giving Texas recognition and appropriating funds to pay the expenses of a minister to the new republic. The next day, President Jackson's last in office, he signed the bill, appointing as minister an official from Louisiana. Shortly before midnight Jackson summoned Wharton and Hunt, told them the news, and shared a toast to the Republic of Texas and to its first president, his friend Sam Houston. Houston always was proud that "the last time Gen. Jackson ever put his pen officially to paper, was to sign the resolution of Congress"[9] recognizing Texas. But Houston continued to press for annexation.

The unruly Texas Army, commanded by Gen. Felix Huston, remained in camp, while talk of marching on Matamoros continued. President Houston sent Albert Sidney Johnston, a West Point graduate, to replace Huston. But Huston angrily challenged Johnston to a duel. After several exchanges of shots, Huston finally drilled his opponent in the hip—and stayed in command of the army.

President Houston next dispatched Secretary of War Rusk to furlough the army, making it clear to them that they might be recalled. All but 600 of the soldiers were sent by companies to Galveston and other ports. The troops had received no pay, and most of them returned to their homes in the United States or the Republic of Texas. "In thirty days they had all disappeared."[10]

By this time the capital no longer was in tiny Columbia. In the fall of 1836 Augustus C. Allen and John Kirby Allen began advertising the new town of Houston. The Allen brothers were from New York, and in Texas they were enterprising businessmen and land promoters. Acquiring half a league of land on Buffalo Bayou, they decided to develop a town and name it Houston. The Allens had the townsite surveyed by Gail Borden, and they offered free town lots to churches, schools, and important individuals. Sam Houston, of course, received lots in his namesake city. The Allens lobbied the government to move to Houston, promising to erect a two-story capitol building.

The government began the move to Houston early in 1837. President Houston, who had only a single drafty room in Columbia, was provided a two-room cabin with a dogtrot. One room was his office, the other his bed chamber. When a dignitary or friend visited, President Houston gave his bed to the guest and slept on a pallet.

The President was in Houston for the first anniversary of the Battle of San Jacinto, April 21, 1837. A blue silk flag with a gold

The ramshackle "Executive Mansion" inhabited by President Houston in 1837.
Courtesy Ed Eakin, Austin.

The Capitol of Houston in 1837. When the seat of government was moved to Austin, the big frame structure became the Capitol Hotel. *From Wharton, The Republic of Texas.*

star in the center was hoisted on a new flagpole. President Houston gathered a large number of Indians to perform a ceremonial dance around the flagpole. Many veterans of the battle had come for the occasion, camping just outside Houston, which as yet offered few accommodations. The highlight of the grand celebration was a ball, to be held in the nearly completed capitol building. Although the population of the new town included no more than eighty women, riders were sent to nearby towns, plantations, and farms to invite young ladies to the festivities.

President Houston's "striking and somewhat unique" attire was described by a newcomer to Texas, twenty-two-year-old Francis R. Lubbock. "His ruffled shirt, scarlet cassimere waistcoat and suit of black silk velvet, corded with gold, was admirably suited to set off his fine, tall figure . . ."[11]

During the day he led a parade of veterans and various dignitaries to the flagpole. That evening he gallantly escorted Eliza Baker—the lovely wife of Moseley Baker, who deeply disliked Houston, but who was out of town. Houston happily danced with Eliza and others, and he mingled freely with the crowd. Dancing was interrupted by a midnight supper served buffet-style at a nearby hotel, after which the music and dancing continued until dawn.

Anna Raguet did not come to Houston for the ball. She had not made the much shorter journey from Nacogdoches to San Augustine when Houston was recovering from ankle surgery. From the San Jacinto battlefield he had fashioned "laurels of victory" from magnolia leaves and dispatched them by courier to Nacogdoches. Houston corresponded faithfully to Anna, mentioning on one occasion that in Nacogdoches "I may look out for a 'spare rib' appropriate to myself."[12]

But Anna only responded perfunctorily to Houston's long courtship. Although she was just fourteen when she met the forty-year-old Houston in 1833, he applied for a divorce from Eliza Allen through a petition from Jonas Harrison, an experienced attorney and Texas patriot. The Mexican government, connected with the Catholic Church, ignored the divorce petition. But in 1837 President Houston authorized Judge Shelby Corzine to consider his petition of divorce in the district court of San Augustine County.

The divorce from Eliza Allen—who seems to have made overtures to her husband through third parties after his triumph at San Jacinto—was granted on April 8, 1837. But the realization of Houston's first marriage, coupled with the great difference in their ages, made young Anna turn her back on any notion of marriage to her famous but middle-aged suitor. Soon she began to be courted by Dr. Robert Irion, Houston's Secretary of State. Irion had delivered many letters to Anna from Houston and happily began his own courtship. He was much closer to Anna's age, and they married in 1840. Dr. Irion practiced medicine in Nacogdoches, and he and Anna had five children.

President Houston casually began to see other women. He had stopped drinking during the military campaign of 1836, but now President Houston was imbibing heavily again. Drinking was a major pastime with many men in early Texas, and Houston often joined his fellow Texans in public and in private. He long had enjoyed roistering with companions, and at dinners he happily drank to the multiple toasts that were customary. In November 1838 Thomas F. McKinney, a highly successful Texas merchant, observed that President Houston was "nearly all the time drunk."[13]

Houston must have had a fine time earlier that year, on the second anniversary of the Battle of San Jacinto. At this and other events the orchestra saluted President Houston with *Hail to the Chief*. Again the highlight of the celebration was a ball, with two to three hundred men and about fifty women in attendance. The night-long revelry produced a great many drunken participants.

Houston moved his new friend, Dr. Ashbel Smith, into the Executive Mansion, conversing and reading Smith's books deep into the night. This statue stands in Baytown. *Photo by the author.*

During this period Houston met Dr. Ashbel Smith. A native of Connecticut, Smith was a graduate of Yale Medical School with a deep interest in literature, mathematics, and geology. In his early thirties, Dr. Smith left his medical practice to come to Texas. Arriving in Houston in May 1837, Smith presented letters of introduction to President Houston. The President wasted little time in nominating this highly qualified physician as Surgeon General of the Army. Immediately drawn to this well-educated, congenial man, Houston invited Smith to share the modest Executive Mansion. Smith moved his trunks into the bedroom.

Often President Houston would return to the Executive Mansion after an earthy evening with companions and select a book from one of Ashbel Smith's trunks. Smith sometimes recited poetry to Houston, or they engaged in the kind of discussions favored by two well-read men. Smith provided Houston needed medical care and invaluable companionship, and they were friends until Houston's death.

In June 1837 President Houston wrote the Texas Congress about a crucial financial matter. "Since the commencement of the constitutional government, no pubic officer has received any salary. Their personal expenses are great, from the fact of their having to pay an exorbitant price for board. Their individual means are quite exhausted."[14] President Houston had pledged his personal credit, put up land and lots he owned, to cover various governmental expenses.

By 1838 Texas was collecting substantial customs duties, and in February more than $5,900 in wartime expenses submitted by Houston—salary ($200 per month), clothing, rations, forage for horses, etc.—was approved. Apparently payment was sporadic, because within three months he wrote Ashbel Smith: "My cash is exhausted!!!"[15]

The Texas Constitution mandated that the first president would serve a team of two years and could not succeed himself. Thereafter presidential terms would last for three years, although presidents could not serve consecutive terms. There were no political parties in the Republic of Texas—no Democrats or Whigs—but there were "Houston" and "Anti-Houston" factions. Sam Houston, his fame, his leadership abilities, and most of his policies (his humane, live-and-let-live approach to Indian affairs had little support among frontier Texans) generated widespread backing for the Houston faction. The anti-Houston faction was driven by malicious enemies of the President.

Near the top of that list was Vice President Mirabeau B. Lamar, who was strongly backed for president by the anti-Houston faction. Stephen F. Austin would have been the obvious choice of Houston and his supporters. With Austin dead, James

Collinsworth and Peter Grayson were encouraged to run. Both men had been sent by President Houston to influence the United States favorably toward Texas, but both received harsh criticism from Lamar and his supporters during the campaign. Both men died within two days early in July—Grayson was a suicide, and Collinsworth drowned in Galveston Bay. With no opposition Lamar was swept into the presidency, while another leading Houston-hater, David G. Burnet, was elected vice president.

During his two-year inaugural term, President Houston

led the creation of the first twenty-three Texas counties, along with the establishment of a system of courts and a postal system. He ordered the surveying of public lands into traditional American sections of 640 acres each. He cleverly reduced the size of an unpaid and undisciplined army. President Houston attempted to borrow $5 million for operating capital, although the only substantial loan, $457,380, was arranged with the Bank of the United States in Philadelphia. Active collection of customs duties soon would produce as much as $300,000 in annual revenue.

This imposing statue of Sam Houston wearing his Masonic apron stands beside the west entrance to the Texas State Archives Building. The statue depicts President Houston as Chairman of the Convention of Freemasons that established the Grand Lodge of the Republic of Texas in the Senate Chamber in the Capitol at Houston on December 20, 1837. *Photo by the author.*

Despite obvious accomplishments in creating a new republic, President Houston became despondent when comparing fledgling Texas with what Andrew Jackson had accomplished as President of the United States. Houston wrote his mentor compliment-ing the unprecedented "monuments to Glory" that Jackson had left to his country. "But you had an organized government, and men who were accustomed to civil rule while I had to command a Government from chaos, with men who had never been accus-tomed as a community to any rule, but their passions, nor to any government but their will." Of course, these were the same kind of men who had made up his army in 1836, and these were the qualities that made Houston's task far more difficult—as general and as president.

Houston closed this letter on a note that proclaimed his deep-est conviction as a statesman. "The principles of holy patrio-tism which you inculcated upon me, in my early life have never ceased to abide, nor can they ever cease to remain with me while life lasts."[16]

Mirabeau B. Lamar assumed the presidency on December 10, 1838. An educated man who liked to write poetry, Lamar com-posed an eloquent inaugural address. But the outgoing presi-dent characteristically decided to play a memorable role in La-mar's big day. Houston arrived at the two-story capitol building dressed for a Gilbert Stuart portrait. He wore a powdered wig and a colonial suit, including knee breeches and stockings. A large crowd had gathered in front of the capitol for the inaugura-tion, and when Houston in his costume stepped onto the porch, "wild shouts of enthusiasm rent the air." Houston had prepared a sweeping farewell address, and he spoke for three hours with his usual command of the audience. When Houston finished, "he extended his broad arms, and poured down upon them from his great heart the benediction of the patriot and the soldier, as the tears streamed down his cheeks."[17]

Lamar's frustration had grown by the hour, and Houston's dramatic ending literally rendered him speechless. Realizing that his inaugural address now would be anticlimactic, he handed the speech to an aide to be read to the crowd.

The speech outlined Lamar's policies, and the new president followed through on a course "diametrically opposite to that of President Houston's . . ."[18] Lamar recommended replacing Indian trading posts with a line of forts, and he succeeded in creating a regiment of 840 soldiers to protect the frontier. President Lamar ordered Chief Bowl to lead his Cherokees out of Texas, and the army was sent to enforce this edict.

The two sides clashed in July 1839, and Chief Bowl was slain at the Battle of the Neches. The elderly chief carried the sword Houston had presented him. The Cherokee retreated from Texas, and by the next year aggressive policies erupted into hostilities against a more dangerous foe, the horseback warriors of the Comanche and Kiowa tribes. President Lamar's Indian policies cost Texas more than $2,500,000, while during the five years of his two presidential terms, Sam Houston spent less than $200,000 in his dealings with Indians.

President Lamar changed the flag and seal of Texas, and he was instrumented in moving the capital westward, from Houston to the new frontier community that was named Austin. President Lamar dreamed of extending the Republic of Texas all the way to the Pacific coast. Toward that end, he determined to send an expedition to Santa Fe, which stood east of the Rio Grande, the boundary claimed by Texas. A profitable trade had grown up along the Santa Fe Trail, and Lamar intended to blaze a route from Austin across the Llano Estacado to attract a share of this commerce. When the Texas Congress refused to fund the expedition, Lamar acquired private funding. In June 1841 321 merchants, teamsters, journalists, soldiers, and Texas officials set out, with twenty-one ox-drawn wagons hauling $200,000 worth of goods. Attempting to cross the Staked Plains in the blazing heat of summer proved to be a disaster. Many died and survivors were imprisoned in Mexico.

Nevertheless, Europeans liked Lamar's imperious style. During his presidency Great Britain, the world's greatest power, recognized Texas as a nation, and so did France, Belgium, and the Netherlands. But in his three-year term, Lamar's policies cost the Texas government almost $5 million, while Texas collected just $1,083,661 in revenue. The Texas national debt grew precipitously.

Congressman Sam Houston opposed the Santa Fe Expedition

and most of Lamar's other policies. Houston was elected to a two-year congressional term (1839-1841), which allowed him to oppose Lamar's program from a position of influence. "Things had even been worse if Houston had not been in Congress," reflected Houston years later, still irked over Lamar's "three years of misrule and maladministration . . ."[19]

President Lamar's first year in office was free of direct opposition from Houston, a compulsive traveler who departed Texas for an extended trip to the United States soon after his presidency ended. Houston was involved in a partnership to develop a new town, "Sabine City," at the mouth of the Sabine River. He intended to meet with potential investors in Mobile, before traveling northeastward to see family and to The Hermitage to visit with Andrew Jackson.

In Mobile he met brothers-in-law William Bledsoe and Martin Lea, who invited the noted Houston to his home outside Mobile. There Houston met Lea's mother, Nancy, and his pretty sisters, Antoinette Lea Bledsoe and Margaret Lea.

Margaret was twenty, with a good education and a profound sense of religion—her deceased father had been a Baptist minister. Margaret brought out the best in the courtly Houston, and she told him about having seen him brought ashore in New Orleans three years earlier. They took a walk, and that night—May 31, 1839—Margaret composed poetry in her room. The romantic poem was about a flower Houston had picked for her, and was eight stanzas of four verses each.

"Why have I sought thee out—loved flower?" she began. Later she explained that this floral gift exercised "some tranquilizing power" and that "Thy form doth recollections bring/ Of bright hours passed away." The final stanza reflected deep affection:

> *Thou sweet memento! Gentle flower!*
> *Say will he cherish me.*
> *And love me too in that dark hour*
> *As I now cherish thee?*[20]

Houston also was smitten. He, too, had a romantic streak, and he was easily attracted to much younger women, such as Eliza Allen and Anna Raguet. For years he had spoken of his desire to find "a spare rib" and "a fair, sweet 'wee Wifie,' as Burns says. . ." During his first term as president, Houston reflected upon his presidential levees: "How sad the scenes must be at my Levees, no Mrs. H --- there . . ."[21]

For all his apparent longing for a wife, both of his marriages had been brief. Houston had lived most of his life as a single man, free to travel and carouse, to work or drink until all hours. Responsible for the support of no one but himself, he could devote his efforts to political or military activities that offered scant remuneration, often relying upon personal loans for even small sums of cash. But in middle age, Houston again focused his affections on a bright, lovely young woman, perhaps sensing a final opportunity for a successful marriage and family. He called Margaret "Esperanza," pointing out to her that the word was Spanish for "the one hoped for." Houston and Margaret corresponded when he resumed his travels, and at least once she signed: "For-

The Greek Revival home of Henry Lea in Marion, Alabama. After the death of his father, Henry's mother and teenage sister, Nancy and Margaret Lea, moved into his spacious house, where Margaret's wedding later was held. *Photo by the author.*

ever thine own, Esperanza."²²

On his trip Houston enjoyed seeing his relations, especially those who had been born during the past several years, since his last visit. He renewed himself, as always, in the company of Jackson. In August he returned to Alabama, purchasing seven blooded horses before traveling to Marion, where Margaret lived at the handsome antebellum home of her brother, Henry Lea. Houston stayed across the street at the Eagle Hotel, a two-story boarding house. Townspeople were interested in the famous Houston, who made a public speech from the porch of the Eagle. Despite his age, despite his record of divorce and hard drinking, Margaret accepted Houston's proposal of marriage.

Houston returned to Texas, having been elected to the Fourth Congress *in absentia* by citizens of San Augustine. But it was 250 miles to Austin, and Houston despised the new capital. "This is the most unfortunate site upon earth for the Seat of Government . . . ," fumed Congressman Houston. "Our eating is very plain, and no society to enjoy this place.²³ Austin had only

When Sam Houston visited Marion to court Margaret, he stayed across the street at this building, then a boarding house. On occasion crowds arrived to demand an impromptu public address. *Photo by the author.*

800 residents, and most lived in log cabins. The capitol building was a single-story frame structure surrounded by a stockade, because Comanche war parties were a constant menace.

Houston wanted Margaret to come to Texas for the wedding, but Nancy Lea and her sons would not hear of it. "My daughter goes forth to marry no man," Nancy Lea sternly informed her prospective son-in-law. "He who receives her hand will receive it in my home and not elsewhere."[24]

Margaret was gentle but firm—a trait that was part of her nature—in agreeing with her family. Sam and Margaret were married in Henry Lea's home on May 9, 1840. Mr. and Mrs. Houston arrived in Galveston with Margaret's trousseau, her rosewood piano, miscellaneous possessions, and Aunt Eliza, a household slave devoted to Margaret, who was a decade younger than Eliza.

Nancy Lea had moved to Galveston to investigate investment possibilities, and Margaret and Sam stayed at her rented home. Sam showed his bride around Houston, where they stayed with Francis Lubbock and his wife. Back in Galveston Nancy stayed with her mother when Sam had to spend time in Houston on business. He wrote constantly: "I love you *veerie much*," and in the next line " . . . be assured of my devoted love and imperishable affection."[25]

Before they married, Margaret pointed out to her fiancée that she had little interest in politics—"I prefer my books, music and needle-work."[26] Margaret was a

A beautiful and well-educated Southern belle, Margaret Lea was twenty-one when she married forty-seven-year-old Sam Houston. *Courtesy Huntsville Chamber of Commerce.*

gifted homemaker and a warm hostess, but she wanted no part of life in a political center. Late in their first summer together, Mr. and Mrs. Houston commenced a trip to Nacogdoches and San Augustine, where Houston expected to do a great deal of legal business. En route, however, Margaret came down with malaria. William and Antoinette Bledsoe had moved to Texas, and Houston delivered his ailing wife to their home in nearby Liberty before resuming his journey to East Texas and a busy court docket.

In November Congressman Houston was back in his seat at the capitol building in Austin. The Lamar administration was in shambles, and for a time the President turned the government over to Vice President David Burnet. By 1841 congressmen were so frustrated, matters seemed so hopeless, that most members were ready to adjourn *sine die* —for an indefinite period, in effect dissolution of the government. Houston stood up "in the midst of the tempest, as the members were leaving their seats, and addressed the speaker." The impressive presence of Houston commanded attention and a possibility of hope. "The crowd began to return—members gradually resumed their seats and dropped their hats—they pressed up around me—the House became still. I spoke to them awhile and then said, 'I move that the House adjourn till tomorrow at the usual hours.' Not a member voted against it."[27]

The crisis was averted, thanks to Houston's timely and authoritative action. As the government limped along, Houston wrote constantly to Margaret, sometimes from his desk while a representative was addressing the House. He always expressed a deep longing for his wife, but he knew his presence was needed in Austin, and as always Houston responded to the call of duty.

By 1841 there was a widespread call for Houston to succeed Lamar as president. David G. Burnet began a strong campaign for the presidency by writing anti-Houston articles in friendly newspapers, using the *nom de plume* "Publius." Houston replied with articles signed as "Truth." These men were enemies, and articles and speeches of both candidates ranged from harsh to vicious. Each accused the other of cowardice during the Revolution and of drunken behavior, and Houston repeatedly said that

David G. Burnet's middle initial stood for "Grog" (it actually was an abbreviation for Governeur).

The election was no contest. Despite furious assaults by Houston's perpetually angry and jealous foes, most Texans had far more regard for Sam Houston's leadership abilities than any other public figure. In September 1841, Houston was swept back into the presidency. Three out of every four voters cast their ballots for Old Sam Jacinto, 7,915, to 3,616 for Burnet. Col. Edward R. Burleson, a tower of strength under Houston during the Revolution, was elected vice president.

Sam and Margaret had spent much of the summer at Cedar Point, a property Houston had acquired that fronted Galveston Bay (a few miles from present-day Baytown). Houston had a one-room log cabin built at Cedar Point, and the cabin was expanded as the family grew. Houston's close friends, Dr. Ashbel Smith and George Hockley, had farms in the vicinity. Cedar Point became Houston's favorite retreat.

In November the president-elect and his wife were welcomed in Houston by cheering crowds and booming cannons and a ball. When Houston set out for Austin, Margaret stayed behind. She apparently had a miscarriage earlier at Cedar Point, and she did not feel up to an arduous journey followed by duties of a First Lady in a frontier town. The pattern of their married life was set. Houston would be in the capital—in Texas or in Washington—at least half of each year. He and Margaret were devoted correspondents, and because of his long absences he seemed to enjoy his family all the more when he was at home. During Houston's second presidential term, on May 25, 1843, his first child was born, Sam Houston, Jr. Between 1843 and 1860 Margaret gave birth to eight children, four boys and four girls. Much of the time that Houston was absent from home, Margaret was pregnant or giving birth or nursing a baby.

Inauguration Day was Monday, December 13, 1841. An audience of 1,000 gathered outside the capitol building late in the morning, watching as the Travis Guards militia company escorted Houston and Lamar and other dignitaries to the site. Judge R. E. B. Baylor, Speaker of the House, administered the oath of office. President Houston kissed the Bible as one of the Twin Sisters boomed out a salute. Houston addressed the crowd for more than an hour, then hosted members of Congress at dinner. That evening there was an inaugural ball in the capitol building. President Houston attended, but at three o'clock in the morning he wrote Margaret a lengthy report of inaugural events. "O did not dance," he assured her, "tho' importuned by all to do so."[28]

During his second term, President Houston had three years to attack the desperate problems he had inherited. While spending millions of dollars the Texas government did not have, Lamar had resorted to the printing press. As a result, Texas currency plunged in value, reaching a low of three cents on the dollar. President Houston launched a series of measures to reduce spending, while instituting a pay-as-you-go policy. Houston reduced government salaries, including his own—a selfless case of leadership by example. (The presidential salary was cut from $10,000 to $5,000, and other salaries were reduced by half or more, but soon there was no money for Houston or anyone else.) He eliminated many government offices, and took a great deal of paper money out of circulation. Houston reversed Indian policies, halting aggressive military actions while sending agents to re-establish trade with the tribes. Houston therefore was able to reduce the Texas Army to a small band of Rangers, to patrol the frontier.

Houston attempted to sell the little Texas Navy at a public auction, which would cut a major expense while raising considerable money from the sale of four warships. But the Texas Navy was based at Galveston, where angry citizens blocked the auction, and in 1846 the little warships were turned over to the U.S. Navy. Nevertheless, Houston's policies greatly reduced spending during his three-year term. His administration spent barely one-tenth—about $500,000—of Lamar's expenditures. But even these impressive savings could not pay back the overwhelming national debt.

Houston faced several crises during his second term. In March 1842, Mexico vengefully sent an invasion force into Texas. A column of 500 men under Gen. Rafael Vasquez captured San Antonio, but stayed only two days. Smaller Mexican forces took the villages of Goliad and Refugio. But within days all Mexican soldiers withdrew below the Rio Grande. In July there was another hit and run raid along the Nueces River. On September 11 Gen. Adrian Woll arrived at San Antonio with 1,400 men and took fifty-three captives before withdrawing.

Texan volunteers rushed to San Antonio, and on September 18 attacked Woll's force at Salado Creek. Texan riflemen inflicted heavy casualties and Woll retreated under cover of darkness. That same day Mexican cavalrymen caught more than fifty would-be Texan reinforcements on an open prairie. All but three of the Texans were killed or captured. But within nine days all Mexican troops had left Texas.

These repeated strikes alarmed Texans, and many people from Austin fled eastward. Congress voted President Houston "dictatorial powers" and "ten millions of acres of the public domain"—since there was no money available—to conduct a campaign. Houston regarded himself as "the last man in the world to offer such authority to." With no intention of revisiting the grim days of 1836, he vetoed the bill, thus defying "a storm of opposition . . ."[29]

The Mexicans had no logistical support, and their advances proved to be nothing more than probes. To allay public cries for retaliation, President Houston sent Gen. Alexander Somervell and 750 men toward the Rio Grande in November 1842. But after seizing Laredo, Somervell delayed, as instructed by President Houston. Impatiently, 300 of these volunteers elected a colonel and marched into Mexico, taking Mier before being overwhelmed by a Mexican Army force. The most notorious incident of the Mier Expedition was the drawing of the black beans, with seventeen luckless prisoners executed.

Houston must be credited with deftly and courageously avoiding war, in the face of fierce opposition. But he took advantage of the Mexican raids to try to move the capital from frontier Austin to Houston, his namesake city. During the brief invasion of March 1842, the president called a special session of Congress to meet in Houston. He declared a public emergency and ordered the state archives moved to Houston. But angry Austinites, facing a certain drop in real estate values, set up patrols on the roads, and President Houston dropped the idea. But with General Woll's invasion in September, the President sent Capt. Thomas Smith and twenty men to bring the archives to Houston. Three wagons were loaded with records, and during a stormy night Captain Smith led the way out of town. But a score of Austin citizens rode in pursuit, and the Archive War ended with the archives still in Austin.

Meanwhile, civic leaders in Washington-on-the-Brazos, aware of the high rent charged for Austin's capitol facilities, offered accommodations if the government would move back to the site of Texas Independence. Sessions of Congress were held for the next two years in Washington-on-the-Brazos. Margaret came with Houston to Washington, where the presidential office was in a one-room lawyer's office. Typically, he left the front door open to all comers. The House met in Independence Hall and the Senate in a saloon, while a carpenter's shop and other structures housed various departments.

When Houston again assumed the presidency, he quietly reopened talks with the United States regarding annexation. Artfully he played off the reluctant United States against acquisitive Great Britain and France. "Supposing a charming lady had two suitors," Houston explained, pointing out that young women, as practitioners "of Cupid's court," often used one suitor to light a fire beneath a slow-moving but more desirable sweetheart. "If ladies are justified in making use of coquetry in securing their annexation to good and agreeable husbands, you must excuse me for making use of the same means to annex Texas to Uncle Sam."[30]

Toward the end of his second term, President Houston dealt decisively with a vicious blood feud in East Texas. Houston's leadership throughout his presidency was artful, wily, commanding, confident, and authoritative. He began to be called the "Talleyrand of the Brazos," after the brilliant, crafty foreign minister of France. While recounting Houston's presidency, biographer James Haley stated, "The Talleyrand of the Brazos was at the height of his powers."[31]

Sirs — You will immediately take the proper steps to have your command in readiness for marching orders, armed and equipped for any emergency.

President Houston to militia officers

Chapter Twelve

Lessons in Leadership for the Regulators and Moderators

During his second term as president, Sam Houston employed consummate leadership skills in halting the murderous Regulator-Moderator War in East Texas. The first of many blood feuds in Texas, the Regulator-Moderator War erupted late in 1840. During the next four years, in addition to the vendettas which followed, thirty-one men were slain. The conflict took place in the wilderness of rural Shelby County and in newly-organized Harrison County. There were ambushes and lynchings and skirmishes. By 1844 Regulators in Shelby County, reinforced by mounted allies from Harrison County, numbered 200 men, while there were 100 Moderator riders.[1]

The Regulator leader was "Colonel" Watt Moorman, who wore a cutaway-style jacket and carried a brace of pistols, a Bowie knife, a Bois d'arc stick used as a cudgel, and a hunting horn employed to summon men from the forests. Still in his twenties, Moorman had a powerful physique, but he drank heavily and he was a vicious killer. He knew that the Republic of Texas had no standing army, and with 200 men under his command, Moorman began to have delusions of taking over all of Texas. Colonel Moorman, already commander of the "United Regulating Forces of Harrison, Panola and Shelby Counties," now envisioned county after county sending companies to swell his army.

Moorman's "Regulating forces" would be larger than any

other army in the Republic of Texas. Like Haden Edwards and Dr. James Long and other filibusters who had dreamed of seizing control of Mexican Texas, Watt Moorman "now fondly imagined that the auspicious moment had arrived which was to place him in the proud position then occupied by Sam Houston."

Colonel Moorman began to see himself as General Moorman or President Moorman. He confided his dreams to his most trusted followers, and selected twelve men who would gov-

Watt Moorman, the ruthless, hard-drinking leader of the Shelby County Regulators. *Courtesy Shelby County Historical Museum.*

ern Texas as a Provisional Committee until "a new constitution should be ordained and established." Colonel Leonard Straw was elected as the president of the committee; Moorman served as commander-in-chief of the military—and presumably as president after the new constitution was in place."[2]

President Sam Houston, raised in Virginia and the backwoods of Tennessee, was a Southerner and a frontiersman, touchy about his honor and courageous in combat. He understood the Southern frontiersmen who engaged in the Regulator-Moderator conflict of East Texas and he seemed inclined to let them fight it out as long as the disturbance was confined to a limited area. When the first two Regulators were killed in Harrison County in 1840, Houston, having completed his first term as president of the Republic of Texas, practiced law in Nacogdoches and San Augustine and served as a congressman from Nacogdoches. In 1841, while the conflict heated up and spread to Shelby County, Houston won his second term as president and was inaugurated in December.

In 1842, the first full year of President Houston's second administration, Senator Robert Potter was killed by Regulators in Harrison County. The death of Potter, a chronic troublemaker and a bitter political enemy, could not have surprised or bothered Houston greatly. Otherwise, only a handful of East Texas ruffians died in a few incidents in 1842.

During this year Houston had to deal with two brief but troubling invasions by Mexican forces. He also reopened annexation negotiations with the United States and pursued stringent measures to reduce government expenses. One key reduction involved limiting the Texas military to a few Ranger companies and unpaid

Col. Alexander "Sandy" Horton of San Augustine years after his involvement In the Regulator-Moderator War. Horton was General Houston's aide-de-camp and fought at San Jacinto, and came to President Houston's side at the climax of the East Texas conflict. *Courtesy John and Betty Oglesbee of San Augustine.*

militia units in various counties. President Houston had scant military power to employ in East Texas and more pressing matters elsewhere demanded his attention. Furthermore, there were only three Regulator-Moderator fatalities the next year, in 1843. During the first two years of his three-year term—December 1841 to December 1844—Houston largely ignored the Regulator-Moderator conflict to concentrate on larger events.

Then, early in 1844, Judge John Hansford was murdered in Harrison County by a posse of Regulators. Violence rapidly escalated in Shelby County, and by summer the two factions were clashing with large bodies of armed men. With surprising speed, news of each fight was "carried to all the surrounding country in eastern Texas, which caused many persons in the adjacent counties to have strong feelings in favor of one or the other side; so that there was really danger in the spirit of hostile antagonism spreading beyond the limits of Shelby County." This observation was made by San Augustine District Attorney Oran M. Roberts, who was aware that this "spirit of hostile antagonism" also had wracked Harrison County. "This feeling was becoming very strong in San Augustine County, which caused Judge William A. Ochiltree and many prominent citizens residing there to interest themselves to have this war stopped."

President Houston found a courageous ally in Judge William B. Ochiltree of San Augustine. *Courtesy Shelby County Historical Museum.*

Judge Ochiltree, Roberts, and others wrote to President Houston in Washington-on-the-Brazos, requesting him "to come to San Augustine to take steps to have the combatants lay down their arms." Houston had ignored a petition from San Augustine in 1841, and in the summer of 1844 he again "seemed very tardy about coming . . ."[3]

The great man did come, finally, in mid-August. Likely Houston had heard rumors of Watt Moorman's plans to lead a revolution. Dr. Levi Ashcroft of Shelbyville, the log cabin village that was the seat of Shelby County, stated that the substance of the meeting of Moorman's Provisional Committee "was soon made known in the most remote portions of the country . . ."

President Houston at last responded to the entreaties of old friends in San Augustine, traveling from Washington-on-the-Brazos to Nacogdoches, where he enlisted a former comrade-in-arms, General Thomas J. Rusk. As secretary of war, Rusk had fought alongside Houston at San Jacinto. Elected to represent Nacogdoches in the Second Congress of the Republic, Rusk was selected to chair the House Military Committee.

Houston's staunch friend, Thomas J. Rusk, helped plan and organize the decisive militia campaign against the Regulators and Moderators. *Courtesy East Texas Research Center, Stephen F. Austin State University, Nacogdoches.*

In that capacity he sponsored the Militia Bill, and Rusk currently served as major general of militia. Riding together from Nacogdoches to San Augustine, Rusk and Houston discussed a plan of action along the way.[4]

Arriving in San Augustine on Friday, August 16, Houston established presidential headquarters at the Mansion House, a two-story frame hotel with a large gallery across the front. There Houston greeted Judge William Ochiltree, District Attorney Oran M. Roberts, Colonel Travis Broocks, and several other trusted men from the area. Houston led the way to a woodpile out back where the group whittled and discussed the situation. Plans were formulated, messages dispatched, and correspondence drafted. Late that evening Roberts rode back by the hotel and "saw two very large men—Houston and Rusk—arm in arm, promenading in that long piazza, with beaming faces and cheerful talk, in mellow mood, indicating that they had undergone a spirited communion after the council of war."[5]

Couriers rode into Shelby County with a predated presidential proclamation:

Executive department, San Augustine,
August 15th, 1844.

It having been represented to me that there exists in the county of Shelby a state of anarchy and misrule — that parties are arrayed against each other in hostile attitude, contrary to law and order. —

Now therefore, Be it known, that I, Sam Houston, President of the Republic of Texas, to the end that hostilities may cease and good order prevail, command that all citizens engaged therein to lay down their arms and retire to their respective homes.

Given under my hand and seal this day and year above written,

Sam Houston[6]

Jeff Cravens, Shelbyville attorney and deputy sheriff, had been elected "Commandant" of the Shelby County Moderators, and thereafter he was called "Colonel" Cravens. Colonel Cravens was planning a dawn attack on the Regulator camp near Shelbyville when one of Houston's couriers reached him. Cravens immediately abandoned his attack plans, "hoping that good order and quiet might yet be restored" by President Houston without further bloodshed.

"In truth, all parties were glad of the turn events had taken," stated Dr. Ashcroft. "They had nothing to gain by continuance of the struggle and many of them had much to lose." Colonel Alexander Horton, who marched in with the first company sent by Houston, noted the same relieved attitude: "All parties in Shelbyville hailed the militia with joy as a sure way out of their troubles."[7]

When Colonel Watt Moorman learned of the presence of President Houston and that militia units had been dispatched, dreams of revolution vanished. "Watt gave a few blasts on his horn" to summon his men, related Regulator Eph Daggett. "We will have to disband for a while," announced Moorman, who described the approach of "several companies" of militia. "Every man take the open course and take the best care of himself."[8]

"Such a stampede I never saw before," reported an amused Daggett. "The pine knots flew ten feet high, knocked by the horses' feet as the rowels entered their sides. The woods were the nearest way home. Some did not go home for a long time, and some left the country, I for one." John Middleton and several others fled across the international border into Louisiana. Colonel William Boulware led his company back toward Harrison County. Watt Moorman, accompanied by as many as thirty loyal riders, went north to a redoubt recently constructed at Hilliard's Spring.[9]

President Houston followed his initial, brief proclamation with a longer "Letter to My Countrymen." Houston emphasized that it was his duty "to suppress all insurrectionary movements," and he announced his intention to use militia to restore order. He pointed out that he had not yet had time to evaluate the total situation, and that he could take "a mild and advisory course" in dealing with conditions in Shelby County:

San Augustine, August 16, 1844

My Countrymen: It has been communicated to me from various sources, that much excitement has existed among the citizens of Shelby, and that they are generally arrayed under different leaders, in opposition to each other, and to the great terror and alarm of peaceful inhabitants. Such acts and doings are contrary to the constitution and laws of the country. I have been invested with power and authority, as Chief Magistrate, to suppress all insurrectionary movements, and to that end the militia of the country have been placed subject to my orders. All those concerned, must be aware of the deleterious influence that such associations will have upon our national character abroad, as well as the destructive influence which such acts must have upon our social and political institutions, where disorders of such character exist. All classes and conditions of life must feel insecure in their personal safety and property. If persons in society have rendered themselves above the laws, it remains with the laws to punish them – but not for individuals to place themselves above the law, and assume authority to themselves powers which belong to the constitutional authorities of the country alone.

It has not been in my power to possess myself with all the causes which led to this condition of things. Therefore, I abstain from making decisions as to the merits or demerits of the parties. At the same time I feel it to be my duty, for the discharge of which I am responsible to my country, to admonish those who are now arrayed against each other, in violation of the peace of the community, to disperse and return to their respective homes, and to abstain from all acts of violence toward those who are under the protection of the laws. This is a mild and advisory course; and I trust will be regarded in such manner as will render it unnecessary to have recourse to such measures as would be unpleasant to myself as they would be indispensible to arrest the unhappy condition of things, which I am informed now exists in Shelby County.

Sam Houston[10]

During his first week in San Augustine, August 16-23, President Houston sent a stream of correspondence to the colonels of militia in San Augustine, Nacogdoches, and Sabine counties, and to Brigadier General James Smith, whose plantation was in the center of what became Rusk County. Houston directed the three colonels and their various companies to serve as a "brigade" under General Smith.

At fifty-two, James Smith was six months older than Sam Houston, and like Houston he had served under General Andrew Jackson during the War of 1812. Smith came to Texas from Tennessee in 1834, and when the Texas revolution broke out, he returned to Tennessee to organize a company of volunteers. During the Cherokee War of 1839 Smith again raised a company. This able warrior was a personal friend to both Sam Houston and Thomas J. Rusk, as well as future governor J. Pinckney Henderson. When Rusk County was organized, Smith donated land for a county seat, stipulating that the town be named "Henderson."[11]

President Houston wrote at least three letters to Colonel Travis G. Broocks, a prominent citizen of San Augustine who commanded the county militia. Colonel Brooks could have received oral instructions, but the president wanted him to hold official authorization on paper, Broocks received two brief communications on Monday, August 19, including one that went to all three colonels:

San Augustine, August 19, 1844

To Colonels T.G. Broocks, San Augustine; W.M. Means, Sabine; John Todd, Nacogdoches:

Sirs,— You will immediately take the proper steps to have your command in readiness for marching orders, armed and equipped for any emergency. You will consider this order sufficient, after any notification from authority, and act as it may command.

Sam Houston

The other note received on Monday by Colonel Broocks ordered him to take immediate action. "You will forthwith proceed to the scene of contest in Shelby County, and enforce the laws of the country, with the force that you command. Order must and shall be restored in the county . . . " During the few days since Houston's arrival, a sizable company had gathered in San Augustine. Large numbers of men were soon expected from other counties, but the president decided that Broocks and the San Augustine men could make an initial show of force. Broocks would be accompanied by Colonel Alexander Horton, acting in the capacity of marshal of Texas.

Colonel Broocks and about eighty mounted men rode twenty miles north to Shelbyville and pitched their tents just south of town and within view of the Moderator camp. Presumably Colonel Broocks and Marshal Horton held discussions with Colonel Cravens during the evening. The next morning, seemingly by prearrangement, Broocks demanded a surrender in the name of President Houston.

"Cravens immediately ordered his men to lay down their arms, and submit themselves to the order," related Moderator surgeon Levi Ashcroft. "The men cheerfully obeyed the command and the marshal produced the writ and proceeded to arrest ten of the leading men," including Colonel Cravens and Sheriff Amon Lewellyn.

Marshal Horton and an escort rode with these ten Moderator leaders toward San Augustine. The other Moderators were instructed to remain in camp "until further orders from the proper authorities," while Colonel Broocks marched to the Regulator camp, which had been abandoned.[12]

Other militiamen continued to reach San Augustine by the hundreds. The call to arms had been issued by Sam Houston, victor of San Jacinto. Houston, a larger-than-life man of legendary accomplishments, was enormously admired. He had been a combat hero at twenty-one, a U.S. Congressman, major general of Tennessee militia, governor of Tennessee, protégé of Andrew Jackson, general of the Texan army, the first elected president of the Republic of Texas, and the only man to twice win election as president. Although reviled by numerous political enemies, Houston commanded deep respect and popularity among the great majority of Texans.

When this man of almost mythical reputation and towering achievements called for volunteers, his fellow Texans surged to his summons. Some—perhaps many—had served under him in 1836; others, too young eight years earlier, now had their opportunity. Some volunteers probably had never drilled with a military unit. The county militia companies were informal and unfunded; members provided their own guns, ammunition, supplies, horses, and horse feed.

Colonel Broocks repeatedly asked if the Republic could furnish provisions for his men and horses, or if ordnance might be procured from the U.S. Army at nearby Fort Jesup in Louisiana. President Houston's reply was almost apologetic over the lack of available resources, and he insisted that the militia should not worsen conditions in Shelby County:

San Augustine, 23rd August, 1844

To Colonel T.G.Broock[s]:

Sir, —I have the honor to acknowledge your dispatches of the 20th and 23rd instant. After noting their contents, I have to remark, that it would not be possible to obtain either ordnance or any other supplies from Fort Jesup. The regulations of the United

States army inhibit any officer to loan or dispose of any public arms, or stores, on pain of being dismissed from the service.

As related to the subject of supplies for the army now in camp, I can only assure you Congress made no appropriation for such service, and I dare make no expenditure not sanctioned by law. Considering the scarcity of corn for the inhabitants of Shelby County, the horses should be grazed on grass, but not fed with corn – or it may greatly distress the community.

I have written to Gen. Smith, to whom you are referred, as I am greatly pressed for time.

Sam Houston

More than 500 men eventually assembled in San Augustine. They were organized into a brigade by General Smith and by their colonels, and this formidable column marched into Shelby County. General Smith linked up with Colonel Broocks at the deserted Regulator camp, producing a combined force of 600 fighting men. This army, expertly led by combat veterans, dwarfed any force the Regulators or Moderators could hope to put in the field. President Houston intended to stage a martial demonstration that would intimidate the warring factions and halt the violence and any revolutionary plans.

With Colonel Cravens and other Moderator leaders in custody, a search was launched for Watt Moorman and prominent Regulators. Soon a drunken Moorman blundered into the hands of a militia party. By that time Moorman was the tenth Regulator taken into custody, while ten Moderators already had been delivered to San Augustine.[13]

General Smith and President Houston kept a team of couriers racing back and forth between the army and San Augustine. General Smith intended to keep the president informed of his movements, of the arrests, and of "negotiations" with the captives. On Friday, August 23, President Houston expressed his gratitude, along with the conviction that "the appearance of the military was necessary to suppress the insurrectionary movements which had for some time existed in Shelby County." Emphasizing the importance of "maintaining the majesty of the constitution and the laws," he suggested that a company be left in Shelbyville "subject the orders of the Honorable W. B. Ochiltree," who also sent instructions. Conscious of expenses, President Houston urged "that the greatest care and economy should be used in sustaining the troops," and that the army soon would be discharged. "You will be careful to secure all who surrender, their persons and property inviolate from any indignity."[14]

Sam Houston resourcefully and decisively halted the murderous Regulator-Moderator War. *From Wharton, The Republic of Texas.*

Couriers must have met each other on the road, because that same afternoon General Smith sent a note which reached Houston that night at nine o'clock. The president wrote an immediate reply. Three days later, with order restored, Houston instructed General Smith to leave in Shelbyville "a company of mounted men, to consist of at least fifty-six rank and file," who would be led by a captain and two lieutenants. The company would be stationed in Shelbyville for three months. The rest of the army was discharged, following a final night in camp outside Shelbyville. But in case of further "insurrectionary purposes," General Smith was to raise another force and, if necessary, "proclaim martial law . . . as the emergency may demand."[15]

Captain Leonard Mabbitt of San Augustine agreed to remain camped at Shelbyville with a militia company. Although the men under his command totaled only about half the number suggested by Houston, the presence of thirty armed cavalrymen was a daily reminder of the power that could be exercised by the Republic of Texas. It was understood that Mabbitt's company was in Shelbyville "to keep the peace and assist the civil officers if it became necessary."

The militia company remained quartered at Shelbyville until late December 1844, a deployment of four months instead of three. The San Augustine militia members found month after month of guard duty to be boring and personally unprofitable, and Captain Mabbitt had to issue an appeal for volunteers to keep his ranks filled.[16]

After the Regulator and Moderator leaders arrived in San Augustine, they were confined in the courthouse. "The courthouse was quite full of the Shelby prisoners," described Sandy Horton, "in from their camp life without changing their clothes." The disheveled prisoners were addressed by President Houston, who intended to extend leniency after impressing upon them the force of his personality and authority.

"Houston, in the zenith of his glory, appeared before them," related Horton; "he talked to them as a loving father would talk to a lot of bad boys who had been quarreling among themselves." Judge Ochiltree assigned bail "in heavy sums," which they provided. Then, pointedly, "they were told to go in peace.[17]

When the militia company withdrew before the end of 1844, most Shelby County men still habitually carried guns, but no one envisioned another general outbreak of violence. "The 'Regulators' and 'Moderators,' as organized bodies, ceased to exist," proclaimed Oran M. Roberts, "and the 'Shelby War'. . . was ended."[18] Shelby County had been overwhelmed by a 600-man army and by a caliber of leadership—Houston, Rusk, Smith, Horton, Broocks, Ochiltree, Roberts—that could not be matched in a rural county.

For a nation divided against itself cannot stand.
Sam Houston to the U.S. Senate, 1850

Chapter Thirteen

Senator Houston

Dr. Anson B. Jones was a surgeon in Sam Houston's army at San Jacinto. During the Republic of Texas he served as a congressman, as President Houston's minister to the United States, as a senator, and, in Houston's second term, as secretary of state. He had handled President Houston's maneuvers in playing off Great Britain, France, and even Mexico against the United States—a calculated effort to make Texas seem more desirable for annexation. By September 1844, when a presidential election would produce Houston's successor, annexation was the dominant issue in Texas. The diplomatic background of Anson Jones under President Houston made him seem an ideal candidate, even though he did not speak or write about the subject during the campaign season. Dr. Jones won the election, and was inaugurated in December.

Dr. Anson B. Jones, last president of the Republic of Texas and veteran of San Jacinto. *Courtesy Washington-on-the-Brazos State Park.*

Houston had toiled diligently throughout his presidency and, as at the end of his first term, he yearned to travel. In May 1845 Houston, accompanied by Margaret and two-year-old Sam, Jr., journeyed to New Orleans, where he was cheered and feted and asked to deliver speeches. He intended to make another pilgrimage to The Hermitage and introduce his wife and little boy to Andrew Jackson. When word reached Houston that Jackson was on his death-bed, the little family headed north with all haste. At six o'clock Sunday evening, June 6, Jackson died. Three hours later the Houston carriage clattered up to The Hermitage. Houston wept over his mentor's still form, and urged two-year-old Sam: "My son, try to remember that you have looked upon the face of Andrew Jackson."[1]

On their way back to Texas, Margaret and little Sam stopped in Alabama for a month with her family. In Texas Houston bought a plantation in rolling country fourteen miles east of Huntsville. Harking back to his Cherokee connection, he named the new Houston home "Raven Hill." Houston traveled to Austin for the ceremony celebrating Texas annexation, held on Monday, February 16, 1846.

James K. Polk, Houston's old friend from Tennessee and an ardent expansionist, won the U.S. presidency in 1844 with the promise to annex Texas. Polk's opponent, Henry Clay, opposed annexation—and lost. Observing the mandate for the annexation of Texas, lame duck President John Tyler secured a joint resolution to annex Texas, which was acted upon favorably by the congress of each nation. Texas President Anson B. Jones called a special session of the Texas Congress, which unanimously endorsed annexation and wrote a state constitution. This constitution was ratified in October 1845 by popular vote, and in December J. Pinckney Henderson was elected as governor and a legislature was selected. The U.S. Congress approved the new state constitution on December 29, 1845, and President Polk promptly signed the Texas Admissions Act.

The First Legislature of Texas convened in Austin in mid-February. On February 19 the legislators and Governor Henderson swore the oath of office. President Jones closed his farewell address with an emotional observation. "The final act in this great drama is now performed. The Republic of Texas is no more."

President Jones lowered the Lone Star flag himself, and it was replaced by the Stars and Stripes. Sam Houston—who else?—

reached out to gather the Texas flag lest it touch the ground.

As statehood for Texas approached, it was widely assumed that General Houston—hero of San Jacinto and two-time president of the Republic—was an inevitable choice for the Senate. United States senators were not yet subject to popular election, but were selected by state legislatures. On February 21, 1846, the First Texas Legislature chose Sam Houston and Thomas J. Rusk as U.S. Senators.

If Margaret would not go 200 miles to Austin with President Houston, she had no intention of traveling to Washington, D.C., with Senator Houston. She was pregnant again—Nancy Elizabeth would be born in September—and she decided to stay at Raven Hill with little Sam. Margaret's faithful companion, Eliza, was by her side, and another slave from Alabama, Joshua, ran the farming operations.

Senators Houston and Rusk soon traveled to Washington, D.C. In the Senate they drew lots to determine length of terms: Rusk would serve a full six-year term, while Houston would need reappointment to a full term after just two years. In the Senate Houston again would serve, as when he was a young congressman, with Henry Clay and Daniel Webster. Thomas Hart Benton, the first man of influence to help him, also was a senator, and so was Houston's oldest political enemy, John C. Calhoun. Although a freshman senator, General Houston was appointed chairman of the Military Affairs Committee. The former governor of Tennessee and U.S. (and Texas) congressman and two-term president of Texas ignored the Senate tradition that a rookie senator could not address the Senate for a year. Senator Houston spoke often and with authority.

One young man who was impressed was Oliver Dyer, a Senate staff member from New York. He was in his teens in 1836 and tried to join a company being organized to fight for Texas Independence. Dyer's outfit did not make it to Texas, but he admired Old Sam Jacinto from afar, and in the Senate Houston lived up to his image.

"It was easy to believe in his heroism," reflected Dyer, who was impressed that Houston was "a magnificent barbarian, somewhat tampered by civilization. He was of large frame, of stately carriage and dignified demeanor and had a lion-like countenance capable of expressing fiercest passions."

Like many other observers, Dyer was struck by Houston's attire. "His dress was peculiar, but it was becoming to his style. The conspicuous features of it were a military cap, and a short military cloak of fine blue broadcloth, with a blood-red lining. Afterward, I occasionally met him when he wore a vast and picturesque sombrero and a Mexican blanket."[2]

Houston sometimes wore a colorful blanket over his suit, probably in part to irritate John C. Calhoun, who once furiously upbraided Lieutenant Houston for dressing in Indian costume while serving as an Indian agent. On his first day in the Senate, Houston dressed in a nice suit, but his vest was made from the hide of a Mexican jaguar—an exotic garment that would become one of his most famous items of clothing.

Shortly after arriving in Washington, Senator Houston paid a call on his old friend and Jacksonian ally, President Polk. Political parties had not yet been established in Texas, but Houston assured Polk—a die-hard Jacksonian Democrat—that he would vote with Democrats rather than Whigs. Indeed, Houston soon spoke in support of, and voted for, Polk's treaty with Great Britain to end joint occupancy of Oregon, with more than half of Oregon now to become territory of the United States.

Polk's next expansion involved the vast region of Mexico that had been ceded by Santa Anna—as *presidente* and prisoner of war—to Texas. But the Mexican Congress vigorously disputed this claim, and President Polk sent a significant U.S. Army force under General Zachary Taylor to the north bank of the Rio Grande. Mexican soldiers were on the opposite bank, and when they crossed the Rio Grande on patrols there were skirmishes. President Polk thereupon asked for a declaration of war, which was approved by Congress in May 1846.

The President offered Houston a major general's commission, and Rusk also was proffered a commission, but both senators from Texas declined. In Houston's case, he would not be the commanding general, as he had been at San Jacinto. When

Congress adjourned in August, Senator Houston returned to Texas—to Margaret and Sam, Jr., and his first daughter, baby Nancy Elizabeth.

Houston was back in Washington when Congress opened its December session. There was considerable opposition to the War with Mexico, especially in northern states, which regarded the conflict as an attempt by the South to expand slavery. Senator Houston spoke strongly on behalf of the war, in the Senate and in New York and in other cities of the Northeast. In New York City in 1848 he defined the expansionism that had been labeled "Manifest Destiny" a few years earlier. Houston emphasized that "there is an instinct in the American people which impels them onward, which will lead them to pervade this continent, to develop its resources, to civilize its people and receive the rich bounties of the creating power of divine power." For emphasis he added: "The Americans regard this continent as their birth-right."[3]

The War with Mexico was a superb feat of arms by United States military forces. Outnumbered in every battle, the U.S. Army was victorious in every clash. West Pointers distinguished themselves and their academy. Texans volunteered in large numbers, fighting with such ferocity that Mexicans called the Texans, *Los diablos Tejanos.*

In February 1848 Senator Houston voted for the Treaty of Guadalupe Hidalgo, by which Mexico accepted $15,000,000 from the United States, in exchange for the northern region of their country, basically the southwestern quarter of today's continental U. S., amounting to 500,000 square miles.

The war's first popular hero, Gen. Zachary Taylor, had won a series of battles along the Rio Grande and in northern Mexico. The only president the Whig Party had ever elected was an aging hero from the War of 1812, Gen. William Henry Harrison. General Harrison was elected in 1840, although he died early the next year at the age of sixty-eight. Whigs sensed another winner in General Taylor, even though he was a Louisiana slave holder and a political novice. Taylor was nominated by the Whig Party and won the presidency just months after the U.S. triumph that had brought him national fame.

The election of 1848 was held while Senator Houston was still in Texas. Another baby was about to be born, a daughter named Margaret. She was born at the family's new home in Huntsville, where the Houstons settled in February 1848. At Raven Hill Margaret was unhappy living so far from Huntsville and the Baptist church there. In December 1847 Houston traded Raven Hill to Capt. Frank Hatch for a 233-acre farm and one-room cabin just south of Huntsville. "It is a bang up place!" wrote Houston proudly.[4]

Soon he added a second room to the cabin, with a dogtrot separating the rooms. One room was the parlor, while Sam and Margaret used the other chamber as their bedroom. A dogtrot stairway led to two sleeping rooms under the roof. As the family grew, the boys slept in one loft and the girls in the other. Two small ground-level rooms connected by a gallery were added to the rear. One was for guests and the other for Margaret's mother.

Woodland Home, also called the Wigwam, was begun in 1847 as a one-room log cabin. The Houstons added a second room separated by a dog-trot, then created two sleeping rooms under the roof for the children. *Courtesy Sam Houston Memorial Museum.*

A rosewood piano dominated the parlor at Woodland Home. Margaret Houston was an accomplished pianist who taught her children to play. *Courtesy Sam Houston Memorial Museum.*

Surrounded by trees, the house was dubbed "Woodland Home," and Houston sometimes called it his "Wigwam."

In the yard a one-room log building served Houston as a law office. There also was a kitchen, smokehouse, barn, stable, carriage house, chicken coup, privy, and slave quarters. Woodland Home remained the principal Houston residence for a decade. Four children were born here, and Margaret and her growing brood stayed at Woodland Home during Senator Houston's long trips to Washington.

Houston's residence was Woodland Home when he made a statement regarding his hospitality and his democratic inclinations: "[Houston] lives in a log cabin, the latch string of whose door is not only pulled in, but whose door itself is always wide open to invite the wayfarer in."[5] Of course, his door at other homes was "always wide open" as well—even his tent flap during the 1836 campaign.

Houston derived deep pleasure from his home life, at Raven Hill or Woodland Home or Cedar Point. A third daughter, Mary, was born in 1850. In May 1851 Houston was at Woodland Home,

Two small rooms were added to the rear of Woodland Home. At right was the sleeping room for Margaret's mother, Nancy Lea. The room to the left was for overnight guests. *Photo by the author.*

planting vegetables with four children underfoot. "When I am at home in my woodland residence with my wife and brats," he opened a letter to a friend in New York, "I feel no disposition to return to scenes of official conflict and disputation." Next he discussed a proposed congressional session that would keep him in Washington for several extra months. "This is too long an absence for a man who loves his home and family!"[6]

But he did return to Washington, over and over for thirteen years. Houston could never resist "scenes of official conflict and disputation." No longer was he president of a struggling frontier republic, nor commanding general of a ragtag army which won a spectacular and momentous battle. But if Houston was not the man at the top, as a United States Senator he could debate subjects of importance to a larger and more stable nation than the Texas Republic had been, and he was in wide demand as a speaker on issues of the day. Indeed, Houston often was touted as a candidate for president.

And so he left Texas for Washington at least twice a year. It

Houston's log law office remains in the yard at Woodland Home. *Photo by the author.*

took two or three weeks of hard travel to reach Washington, and two or three weeks to return. Sometimes he rushed back to Texas, and sometimes he lingered at home and had to hurry to make the opening session of Congress. In December 1848 he arrived in Washington just before the Senate convened. "For seven days I never had my clothes off me and only lay down just one time, and that for the space of four hours," he wrote Margaret. Later in the letter he speculated, "I do not think we will have a quorum tomorrow."[7]

Senators and congressmen were paid for each day they were present while Congress was in session. The wage was six dollars a day, which added up to about $900 annually. Traveling expenses also were paid, which amounted to a considerable sum annually for a senator from faraway Texas. Unlike expenses turned in to the Republic of Texas, the United States government paid dependably. A U.S. senator's income was not spectacular, but it was reliable. Although Sam Houston possessed and exercised towering gifts, money-making was not one of them. During Houston's hand-to-mouth years as political leader of the Republic of Texas,

Nancy Lea sometimes had to come to the financial rescue of her daughter's family. But during the thirteen years Houston was a senator, his family was financially stable.

Senator Houston was an absentee husband and father for about half of each year. When he was away he wrote Margaret almost daily, and he devoured her letters to him. "From day to day, I read and peruse your letters. They are to me a solace, and when I peruse them, I feel, at moments, as tho' I were in sweet communion with you . . ."[8]

Like many another young wife, Margaret considered her hard-living husband an object of reform. She could not force Houston to do anything, but she let him know how badly heavy drinking bothered her, and repeatedly he assured Margaret from afar that he had refrained from indulging in "sprees." She was even more concerned about his soul, and from early in their marriage Houston decorated his letters with pieties. "Oh my love! For the sake of our dear Savior, I pray you to be sustained until we meet!" During their first Christmas as a married couple, Houston was in Austin for a session of Congress. "This was Christmas night," he wrote dutifully. "To day I was in church."[9]

Margaret's campaign to improve her husband was largely a success. Houston cut back greatly on his drinking. He wrote to a friend in 1851 that "for years past I have been a whole souled tee-totaler, and so intend to be as long as I live. It suits me!" Houston joined the Sons of Temperance, and in 1853 he made a statement on abstinence to a delegation of ministers. "I believe that total abstinence is the only way by which some intemperate drinkers can be saved. I know it from my own personal experience."[10]

Even dearer to Margaret's heart was her husband's status as a Christian. Houston long had read the Bible and committed passages to memory. After years of written religious utterances and attending church services, he consented to be baptized. A large crowd gathered at Rocky Creek near Independence on Sunday, November 19, 1854, to watch the baptism of Sam Houston. The officiating minister was a Texas Baptist stalwart, Rufus Burleson, pastor of the Independence Baptist Church and president of Baylor University. When Burleson remarked that Houston's sins had

been washed away, Sam fa-
mously quipped that God
should help the fishes.

In middle age Sam Hous-
ton had a loving wife who
provided him with a warm
and accommodating home
environment. She also provided him with a houseful
of sons and daughters, while
ridding him of his most
self-destructive habit and
instilling religion into his behavior. But she was content
to let him spend half of his
time apart from the family in
the high-level political activities that was meat and drink
to his soul.

Senator Houston, there-
fore, was free to participate
in the momentous national
affairs of the 1850s. It was

This painting of Sam Houston's baptism
by Rev. Rufus Burleson is prominently
displayed in the Texas Baptist Museum
in Independence. *Photo by the author.*

a contentious decade, with the nation descending into sectional strife exacerbated by slavery and economic differences, and a
growing threat of civil war. Houston stated that, "I went into the
Senate a national man, and every act of mine, from then on, was
as an American statesman with the broadest impress of nation-
ality."[11] Senator Houston wrote to his friend Henderson Yoakum
from Washington about hardline sectional positions. "It is 'the
Union,' or 'disunion.' You know that I am as unionfied as General Jackson was . . ."[12]

Unlike most politicians from slave states, Houston refused to
place states' rights—even those of his beloved Texas—above the
Union. As he claimed, he was thoroughly "unionfied." Houston
courageously emphasized the needs of the Union above those of
slave states, but his statesmanlike behavior eventually cost him

his senate seat.

In 1849 Senator Houston introduced a resolution to build a railroad to the Pacific. As a man who had spent much of his life on the frontier, he understood how badly western territories needed infrastructure, or "internal improvements" in the parlance of the day. But would a transcontinental railroad extend west from southern states or from the more extensive northern railroad network? Throughout the 1850s congressmen quarreled over whether there would be a northern or southern route, so Houston's vision of a transcontinental railroad would not become reality until years after he left the Senate.

The acquisition of vast southwestern territories from Mexico created the divisive issue of slavery for these new territories. By 1850 it seemed to many that the nation might break apart, despite the conciliatory efforts of Houston and a few other statesmen. But on January 29, 1850, Henry Clay—playing his last great role on the national stage—rose in the Senate to propose a series of compromise measures.

Senator John C. Calhoun, soon to die, opposed this "Compromise of 1850." Senator Daniel Webster eloquently supported the measure, and so did Senator Houston, on February 8. Houston had his lengthy, thoughtful speech printed for advance distribution. He pled for "satisfactory reconciliation" and for "calming the agitated waves that are lashing at the base of our Capitol . . ." Passionately Houston cautioned against "the hazards of civil broils—of a war of dissolution—the worst of all wars; a war, not a language, or of tongue, or of religion, but a war of brother – the most sanguinary of mortal strife." Eight years before Abraham Lincoln's famous "House Divided" speech, Houston thundered, "For a nation divided against itself cannot stand."[13]

Houston, like Lincoln, was familiar with passages from the King James Bible. Mark 3:25 reads: "And if a house be divided against itself, that house cannot stand." There is a similar statement in Matthew 12:25. Lincoln made reference to these verses in a speech of less note in 1843, while he delivered his "House Divided" speech on June 16, 1858, in the Illinois State Capitol in Springfield. But Sam Houston concluded his powerful advocacy of the Compromise of 1850 with this notable biblical reference in the U.S. Senate, only days after Henry Clay introduced his conciliatory measure.

There were as many hotheads in Texas as any other state, and Houston was strongly criticized for his stand. J. P. Henderson, first governor of Texas and a radical supporter of states' rights, wrote that Houston's action was "the damnedest outrage yet committed upon Texas."[14] But after the Compromise of 1850 passed, Texas proved to be a major beneficiary. One of the five compromise measures reduced the area of Texas from 379,000 to 264,000 square miles—regions far to the west and north where no Texans yet lived.

Senator Houston delivered a "House Divided" speech in the 1850—eight years before Abraham Lincoln's better-known delivery on the same theme. *Courtesy Matthew Brady Collection, National Archives.*

In return Texas received $10 million to pay the public debt contracted by the Republic of Texas. Payment came to Texas in annual installments. Texas built its first substantial capitol building, as well as a handsome Greek Revival Governor's Mansion just across the spacious capitol grounds. For six years, beginning in 1852, ninety percent of taxes were returned to counties, providing local funds for two-story brick courthouses to replace primitive log structures. Houston's support of the Compromise of 1850 paid off in substantial physical improvements for the frontier state.

As a man of the frontier and a former soldier, Sam Houston was aware of the evolution of Samuel Colt's revolving pistols

This two-story antebellum house was across the street from the home of Nancy Moffette Lea in Independence. After the death of Sam Houston in Huntsville, Margaret moved with her children into this house. Photo by the author.

in Texas. Texans were the first Anglo settlers to battle horseback warriors, Comanche and Kiowa. During the 1840s Texas Ranger Captain Jack Hays recognized in Colt's little five-shooters a repeating weapon that could be used from horseback—like the bows and arrows of the warriors. Arming his men with two pistols each, Hays carried the fight to the warriors. Texas Rangers soon ordered crucial improvements, guns of larger caliber that could fire six rounds, with structural developments such as plowgrip handles and loaders beneath the barrels. "There is no arm of comparable utility to Colts Revolvers," stated Houston in the Senate on August 6, 1850. "They are certain, simple of construction and the great number of discharges render them terrible to an enemy." Houston recommended "the use of Colts Pistols on the frontier" by the Army.[15]

In 1852 the publication of *Uncle Tom's Cabin* roiled the sectional waters. The author, Mrs. Harriett Beecher Stowe, had never visited the South, but she penned a moving novel in which a cruel overseer, Simon Legree, viciously mistreated the plantation slaves, including noble Uncle Tom. Southerners were incensed at the image presented to the nation, while Northerners were revolted by the novel's portrayal of slavery. Houston had no patience with anyone who exacerbated the precarious relationship between North and South. On the evening of April 17, 1856, Houston attended a party at the residence of the Speaker of the House, and the next day he wrote Margaret from his Senate desk. He reported that he "saw 'Uncle Tom's Cabin,' alias Madam Beecher Stowe. She is certainly a hard subject to look on." He added a reassurance regarding his behavior. "I was at the Party an hour; ate an ice cream and left."[16]

In 1856 Senator Houston met Harriet Beecher Stowe, author of the powerful but divisive novel, *Uncle Tom's Cabin*. *Courtesy National Archives.*

In 1852 Senator Houston assisted Franklin Pierce in gaining the nomination for president at the Democrat convention. A member of both the House and Senate, Pierce had supported the Compromise of 1850, and Houston campaigned on his behalf. Houston therefore felt free to offer president-elect Pierce advice on how to select his cabinet members. Houston's unsolicited advice was ignored, and Pierce appointed a strongly pro-Southern cabinet. Also ignored were the requests by the two Texas senators for patronage appointments. Back in Texas in June, Houston fumed in a letter to a Washington friend that "we have no President . . ." Houston complained that "I discovered that Rusk and myself were to get nothing nor to be consulted about anything . . . Not an auditor or permanent clerk at Washington could we get appointed out of many hundreds in office! I did too much for Pierce and he is jealous of me." Having brought his own blood to a boil, Houston underlined the next sentence. "If God wills, I will make him more so!"[17]

Pierce proved to be a weak president, unable to head off the increasingly bitter sectional conflict. Although Southern political leaders wielded great power in the Democrat Party, there was growing concern that more free states were being added to the Union than slave states. When expansionist Senator Stephen A. Douglas of Illinois proposed a bill to create the territories of Kansas and Nebraska, these territories—and future states—would prohibit slavery, as a geographical requirement of the Missouri Compromise of 1820.

But Southern senators informed Douglas that his bill would be blocked unless slavery was made optional in the new territories. The ambitious Douglas wanted to maintain Southern support for himself, and he met with President Pierce and Secretary of War Jefferson Davis of Mississippi. Accordingly, the Kansas-Nebraska bill was adjusted to repeal the slavery restriction of the Missouri Compromise, so that settlers in these new territories could make their own decisions about slavery.

A storm of protest exploded throughout the North about the proposed cancellation of a sacred compromise that had been in effect for thirty-four years. The South was virtually unanimous in defense of the repeal of the limitation on slavery in the Missouri Compromise. Although Sam Houston owned slaves, he was a kind master, and he understood the vital importance of slavery to the Southern economy and way of life. But he recognized the devastating effects the Kansas-Nebraska bill would have on the North-South conflict.

Senator Houston opposed the bill. He warned that "if this bill passes, there will be tremendous shock; it will convulse the country from Maine to the Rio Grande." In a long speech on the Senate floor, he expressed opposition on the ground that the region in question had been promised to Indian tribes, a position that persuaded almost no one. But his purpose was to avoid the path to armed conflict. "Can any doubt that agitation will be consequent upon the adoption of the measure?"[18]

Other opposition came from Northern politicians, as well as

the public. But Senator Douglas defended his bill aggressively and skillfully, and he guided it through the Senate, thirty-seven to fourteen. Later it passed the House, 113 to 100. The Kansas-Nebraska Act triggered violence in "Bleeding Kansas," along with contentious reactions throughout the nation. With the Democrat Party controlled by Southerners and the Whig Party in severe decline, Northerners organized the Republican Party. The northern-based, anti-slavery party was born from the controversy of the Kansas-Nebraska Act, and posed a mortal threat to Southern control of the government.

Sam Houston was the only senator from the South to vote against the Kansas-Nebraska Act. He was vilified by Southerners, while Texans—embattled against Comanche war parties—objected almost as vehemently to Houston's position on Indians. Accused of being a traitor to whites, Houston countered that "I received balls and arrows in this body in defense of suffering humanity, particularly women and children, against the Indians . . ."[19]

Texas was the fastest-growing state in the Union during the 1850s, swelling from 212,592 in 1850 to 604,215 a decade later. Slavery grew even more rapidly, more than tripling from 58,161 (27.4 percent of the population) to 182,566 (30.2 percent of the population). No state supported the Kansas-Nebraska Act more strongly than Texas, and in 1855 Senator Houston was officially reprimanded by the Texas Legislature for his position on the controversial bill.

By 1856 Houston was recognized as the only prominent Southern politician who stood for Union above sectional concerns. But stubbornly persisting in the belief that presidential candidates still should be drafted by popular movement, Houston refused to court a party nomination. James Buchanan of Pennsylvania won the Democrat nomination, and Houston supported his longtime friend. Buchanan won the Election of 1856, while the new Republican Party impressively generated more than 1.3 million votes behind John C. Fremont. But Buchanan was quickly revealed to be perhaps the weakest president in American history, and the conflict between North and South worsened precipitously.

Members of the Texas Legislature, having condemned Houston's position on the Kansas-Nebraska Act in 1855, in November 1857 nominated a successor to his Senate seat, when his term expired in March 1859. Three times the legislature had voted for Senator Houston, but when his third term ended he would be replaced by Judge John Hemphill. A native of South Carolina, Hemphill came to Texas in 1838. He was a skilled lawyer who served as Chief Justice of the Texas Supreme Court, and during the mid-1850s he became an ardent secessionist. Not only would Hemphill replace Senator Houston in 1859, when the Civil War broke out he was sent to Richmond as a member of the Confederate Congress.

In his sixties Sam Houston still radiated determination and force of personality. He also retained his flair for colorful attire. *Courtesy National Archives.*

Aware that he was a lame duck after the legislative reprimand of 1855, Senator Houston nevertheless remained as outspoken as ever. On February 11, 1857, for example, he spoke on the Senate floor about the deterioration of decorum in both houses of Congress. He described the Senate when he first had seen it as a young congressman decades earlier. "Then it was a majestic body indeed. There was something awful indeed. The solemn stillness, the gravity of Senators, the propriety of conduct, the silent auditory—all impressed the spectator with a solemn awe when he entered this Chamber or came into its galleries or lobbies . . ." Perhaps Houston spoke out of nostalgia for a more stable time in America. "There was grandeur about legislation then; there was impressive awe."[20]

Houston had been in the Senate for more than a decade, and the anticlimactic expiration of his senatorial term was two long years away. Houston's temperament called for solutions, but rancor in Washington rendered the efforts of a single senator largely ineffective. Perhaps if he were chief executive of the Lone Star State he could lead his beloved Texas to safer ground. Congress adjourned early in March, and soon after reaching Texas he decided to run for governor.

*I have heard all the great orators
of the Republic and State of Texas,
except Lamar and the Whartons.
Houston . . . before a frontier audience
excelled them all.*

Judge A. W. Terrell

Chapter Fourteen

Governor Houston

"The people want excitement and I had as well give it as any one."[1] In the summer of 1857, Sam Houston conducted the most exciting political campaign Texans had ever seen. Early in May Texas Democrats gathered in Waco to conduct the first party convention ever held in the state. Hardin R. Runnels, a wealthy slaveholder and staunch states' rights advocate, was nominated to run for governor. The Waco convention pointedly condemned Senator Houston, who took pleasure in repeatedly calling it the "Wacko Convention."

Within days Houston announced he was a candidate for governor. He wrote to Thomas Rusk that the Democrats "make the issue as they declare 'Houston' or 'anti-Houston'," then promised that he would provide excitement for Texans.[2] Houston's letter to Rusk was written on May 12, 1857, and that same day a traveling salesman named Ed Sharp walked south from downtown Huntsville to Woodland Home, hoping to meet the town's most famous resident. Sharp encountered Houston on the road. When Houston found out that the young man had walked more than a mile just to make his acquaintance, he brought Sharp to the house to meet Margaret.

Houston told Sharp that he needed to walk into town to buy a stagecoach ticket to the growing town of Houston, where he intended to print and publish a schedule of his campaign appearances. The two men walked to the stagecoach station, only to find that the next coach was sold out. Sharp said that he was about to travel to Houston in his own conveyance, and offered a ride. The ride turned into a summer-long adventure.

Houston always had been an eager traveler, and at sixty-four he remained physically powerful with a wellspring of stamina. He would need it. Houston intended to start his campaign in Crockett on May 27, followed by a speech in Alto the next day, Rusk the next day, and Nacogdoches the next day. There would be a day of travel here and there without a campaign stop, but twice there would be five speeches in five days at five different communities. This sweeping tour of northeast Texas scheduled twenty-four towns in thirty-eight days. At the bottom of this printed schedule, Houston included a challenge to his opponent to join him in debate—a challenge which was not accepted. Following a break of a few days around the Fourth of July with his family at Woodland Home, there would be another trek through West and South Texas. San Antonio, Austin, Waco—eighteen towns in twenty-five days, July 8 through August 1.

Salesman Ed Sharp drove a bright red buggy which advertised, in big gold letters, "Warwick's Patent Plow." Houston was delighted with the eye-catching vehicle, and at the start of the journey he stopped in Madisonville to make the first of several unscheduled speeches. During the summer of 1857 Houston appeared in over fifty towns while traveling more than 1,500 miles. Although Houston occasionally stayed at the home of a friend, on most nights he and Sharp camped beside a road. Sharp enjoyed countless conversations with Sam Houston, while his buggy advertised Warwick's Patent Plow across the state.

The summer junket energized Houston, despite temperatures that often reached 100 degrees. Audiences frequently included San Jacinto veterans and old friends. When Houston spotted a political opponent in the crowd he went on the offensive, usually with sarcasm and ridicule. Most Texas newspapers sympathized with Democrats, and when one called Houston a traitor to Texas he read the editorial to a crowd while wearing gloves. "What! I a traitor to Texas! I who in defense of her soil moistened it with my blood!" His limp became pronounced and a wave of sympathy swept through the audience.

"I had never before heard him speak," reminisced Judge A. W. Terrell, who witnessed this performance in Lockhart, ". . . but his erect bearing, the majesty of his appearance, his deep-toned, commanding voice, impressive gestures, and perfect composure made a lasting impression on me."

Judge Terrell remembered that Houston wore a long linen duster, and an open collar which revealed "grizzled" chest hair "as thick as a buffalo mop." Even though Terrell was one of the objects of Houston's sarcasm, the Judge appreciated what he had witnessed. "I have heard all the great orators of the Republic and State of Texas, except Lamar and the Whartons. Houston . . . before a frontier audience excelled them all."[3]

Runnels was not in Houston's class as an orator, although a trio of Democrats who were capable speakers followed Houston's trail and tried to refute his positions. Runnels enjoyed the support of an organized political party and of Texas newspapers, and on August 3, two days after Houston closed his campaign in Victoria, Runnels won the election as governor. The final vote totals were 32,552 to 28,678.

For the only time in his long political career, Sam Houston lost an election. But he immediately shrugged off the defeat. For one thing, he had not resigned his seat in the U.S. Senate, and would continue to be employed in a prominent if increasingly ineffective position. Houston had found his campaign through Texas invigorating, and it was not long before he began thinking about taking on Runnels again in two years.

Meanwhile, Houston had accumulated considerable debt during the campaign, staging barbeques and other events, and incurring large printing costs. Houston's close friend, Henderson Yoakum, had died of tuberculosis late in 1856 at the age of forty-six. In addition to Houston's personal loss, Yoakum apparently owed him $4,000. Houston suffered another painful loss toward the end of his campaign when his longtime friend and ally, Thomas J. Rusk committed suicide over a medical condition and the death of his wife. When next in the Senate, Houston delivered a moving tribute to Senator Rusk.

Houston made a large dent in his indebtedness by selling Woodland Home, a regrettable necessity. The Houstons still owned Cedar Point, as well as a farm near Independence, where a family home soon would be established. Senator Houston returned to Washington, but as a lame duck he was scorned by Southern senators still resentful over his opposition to the Kansas-Nebraska Act, as well as his general anti-secession position.

An inveterate whittler, Houston had plenty of time to whittle during the last period of his senatorial tenure. He engaged in a tiff with Senator Jefferson Davis about the artistic values of statuary during the remodeling of the Capitol building. He introduced a resolution that the United States establish a protectorate over Mexico, which he felt would benefit that ill-governed nation —and which might unite North and South in a common goal. His proposal went nowhere.

As the nation lurched toward civil war, Houston expressed regret to Margaret that "I cannot control the destiny of this country. Were I its ruler, I could rule it well." Houston, of course, harbored no belief in monarchy, and he reflected upon the difficulties of democratic governance. "To govern well is a great science, but no country is ever impressed by too much governing. Govern wisely and as little as possible."[4]

Senator Houston refused to give his political enemies in the Texas Legislature the satisfaction of an early resignation. The Legislature appointed J. P. Henderson to replace Thomas Rusk in the Senate. But Senator Henderson died in June 1858, and in the Senate Houston provided his old enemy a respectful tribute.

On February 28, 1859, Houston delivered his farewell address to the Senate. Recently a New York minister, who had lived in revolutionary Texas, spouted from his pulpit calumnies against General Houston's role at San Jacinto. Houston's final Senate address recounted for the record the Runaway Scrape and San Jacinto. Houston's closing words to the Senate were met with applause from the galleries. He stated that his prayers for members of the Senate will be "that light, knowledge, wisdom, and patriotism may guide them, and that their efforts will be perpetually employed for blessings to our country; that under their influence and their exertions the nation will be blessed, the people happy, and the perpetuity of the Union secured to the latest posterity."[5]

Houston's term expired on March 3, 1859. His farewell visits included dinner at the White House with President James Buchanan. Gazing at the Capitol, he may have recalled first seeing it more than four decades earlier, as an injured lieutenant. On the night before his departure for Texas, his rooms were filled with friends making a final call. Sam Houston left Washington—for the last time—on March 10, 1859.

Now Houston could travel by rail most of the way to Texas. The trip from Washington to Texas took barely more than a week. And once in Texas, Houston was urged by friends to run against Governor Runnels. Runnels had proved to be a weak governor. He was an ardent secessionist, but for Texans there were more immediate problems: Comanche raiders were mauling the frontier counties, and on the border with Mexico Juan Cortina, also known as "Cheno" and the "Red Robber of the Rio Grande," terrorized the Lower Rio Grande Valley with an army of 400 men.

Houston was not hard to persuade. Of course he wanted to defeat Runnels, the only man who ever had beaten him in a political race. And as chief executive of his beloved Texas he must have hoped he could exert a strong hand in guiding the Lone Star State away from the disaster that awaited secession and civil war.

But there would be no hard-charging, colorful, exhausting summer of travel and speeches like the campaign of 1857. Houston went into debt in 1857 and he lost the election. So in 1859 he delivered only one major speech, in Nacogdoches to a large crowd. "I am a Democrat of the old school. In politics I am an old fogy," he announced. "An old fogy because I cling devotedly to those primitive principles upon which our government was founded . . . I have no modern improvements to make on the principles of our fathers."

Candidate Houston made a chilling—and all too accurate—prediction. "Mark me, the day that produces a dissolution of this Confederacy will be written in history in the blood of humanity." Indeed, in a North and South that totaled 31,000,000 in population (merely one-tenth of today's U.S. population), 620,000 soldiers would die. "Preserve Union and you preserve liberty. They are one and the same . . ."[6]

Houston defeated Governor Runnels, carrying eighty-five of 120 Texas counties, and winning the statewide vote, 33,375 to 27,500. Sam Houston became the first—and to date the only —American to win election as governor of two states, Tennessee and Texas. During a quarter of a century beginning in 1835, Houston was appointed Major General of the Texas Army, twice was elected President of the Texas Republic, served thirteen years as U.S. Senator from Texas, and won election as Governor of the Lone Star State. Despite unrelenting criticism from his enemies, despite unpopular stands on political issues, Sam Houston was entrusted by Texans with the most prominent leadership positions Texas could offer.

Governor Houston was inaugurated on December 21, 1859. Hostile Democrat legislators opposed appropriations for furnishing the Governor's Mansion and to providing the House chamber for Houston's inauguration. Ignoring these and other insults,

When Houston became Governor of Texas, there was a new State Capitol, which had opened in 1853. Governor Houston's office was on the ground floor. *Courtesy Texas State Capitol.*

This illustration, which depicts Houston holding a map labeled "Texas," was from a brief campaign book, *Sam Houston, A Short Autobiography.*

Houston characteristically organized the inauguration himself. He took the oath of office and delivered his inauguration address from the columned entrance portico of the State Capitol. A large crowd gathered on the rolling lawn below, and Margaret, who had moved the family into the Governor's Mansion, also made a rare appearance at one of her husband's political events.

Governor and Mrs. Houston brought a large family to the Executive Mansion, which had opened only three years earlier, in 1856 for Governor Elisha Pease. It was a classic Greek Revival brick residence, with a broad central hallway flanked by two rooms on both sides, downstairs and upstairs. There were six columns across the front gallery, while a kitchen/pantry wing off the rear gallery had two more bed chambers above. The most striking feature was a curved stairway to the second floor, a handsome stairway style which Sam Houston had admired many times at The Hermitage. Houston, a large man, had a six-foot long bathtub installed, although water had to be heated and carried.

The Houstons were the largest family ever to reside in the Texas Executive Mansion. They brought seven children to Austin: Sam, Jr., Nancy, Margaret, and, born in the 1850s, Mary (1850), Antoinette (1852), Andrew Jackson (1854), and William (1858). Sixteen-year-old Sam enrolled at Bastrop Military Institute, and Bastrop was only thirty miles from Austin. The First

The Greek Revival Governor's Mansion was only three years old when Governor Houston moved in with his large family. On August 12, 1860, Margaret gave birth to the first baby born in the Governor's Mansion, Temple Lea Houston. *Courtesy Ed and Charlene Eakin.*

Lady already was pregnant again, and Temple Lea Houston was born on August 12, 1860. Temple was the first baby born in the Governor's Mansion. Governor Houston was sixty-seven when his eighth and final child was born. During the last four years of his life, 1859-1863, Houston was no longer an absentee father but —finally—a daily presence in their lives. The little children chased each other around the big house, while friends of the older girls added to the juvenile crowd.

To young Sam at school in Bastrop, Houston sent a blizzard of correspondence, offering instruction on what to read and how to hold a pen and how to fold his letters. Houston constantly urged his son to write more often, and he opened one letter with a gentle reproof that was ignored: "My Dear Son, I know I have spoiled you by writing so often to you, for I write two letters to your one."[7]

Working from his first-floor office in the State Capitol, Governor Houston efficiently dealt with office-seekers and he improved conditions at the State Penitentiary in Huntsville. Houston sent Texas Rangers against Comanche raiding parties, and he called for the organization of small, mounted militia companies in the frontier counties. Governor Houston wrote to Secretary of War John B. Floyd requesting that the federal government provide Texas 2,000 rifles, 1,000 Sharps breech loaders, 3,000 Colt revolvers, and equipage for 1,000 cavalrymen. When Col. Robert E. Lee returned to Texas for a second duty assignment on the Lone Star frontier, he stopped in Austin to confer with Governor Houston, an old acquaintance.

Many of Governor Houston's activities, along with other evidence, convinced historian Walter P. Webb that he still hoped to establish a protectorate over Mexico, working now as chief executive of Texas, rather than from the U.S. Senate, where his initial proposal had been ignored. Webb realized that Houston sincerely hoped that an expansionist enterprise against Mexico would avert civil war, which would make him "the savior of the Union" and perhaps even bring him the presidency. Webb felt that Houston's effort came too late to succeed.

"Rich in wisdom, wise, cautious, and crafty, Houston played at last with plans he could not execute, with dreams he could not make come true." Webb felt that Houston hoped the protectorate would achieve grand goals: "For Mexico peace, for the United States unity, for Sam Houston fame and glory . . . Had the opportunity come to Houston ten years earlier, he might have carried his plan through with success."[8]

Governor Houston's apparent efforts toward a protectorate in the early months of 1860 went nowhere. By this time national events were spiraling out of control. During the two presidential elections of the 1850s, Southern Democrats found Northern candidates—Franklin Pierce of New Hampshire in 1852 and James Buchanan of Pennsylvania in 1856—who were willing to cooperate with the South. Pierce and Buchanan thus won Southern as well as Northern votes, but were subject to the Southerners who dominated the Democrat Party during the decade.

With the utter failure of President Buchanan's administration, the most promising Northern Democrat for 1860 was Sen. Stephen A. Douglas of Illinois. But the Democrat Convention met in April 1860 in Charleston, South Carolina, the hotbed of secessionist sentiment. Senator Douglas was the leading candidate, but delegates from eight states of the Deep South—including Texas—walked out of the convention. With this split of Democrats, a "party" of Northern Democrats later nominated Douglas, while the Southern Democrat "Party" nominated Vice President John C. Breckenridge of Kentucky, a slave state. Meanwhile, in May Republicans convened in Chicago, where the nomination went to Illinois favorite son Abraham Lincoln.

A fourth splinter-group party, calling themselves the Constitutional Unionists, also entered the race. Before the Constitutional Union Party held its convention in Baltimore, two mass meetings in Texas passed resolutions promoting Sam Houston for president. One meeting was in Austin on March 20, and the other was at the San Jacinto battlefield on April 21. In early May the new party convened in Baltimore. Members were trying to avoid secession, and their favorite candidates were John Bell from Tennessee and Governor Sam Houston. Houston was not far behind Bell on the first ballot, but Bell pulled away on the second ballot.

Houston disliked the party nominating system. "If my name should be used in connection with the Presidency, the movement must originate with the people themselves, as well as end with them. I will not consent to have my name submitted to any convention, nor would I accept a nomination if it were tendered me and procured by contrivance, trick, or management."[9]

In the political trend to nominating conventions, Houston had become an "old fogy," as previously quoted. Indeed, many political leaders of the time, including Tennessean Andrew Johnson, who became Lincoln's vice president, believed that if Houston had secured a party nomination he would have won the presidency in 1860. "Thus," concluded Houston biographer James Haley, "Sam Houston was denied the chance to face what would have been the supreme test of both his vision and his political skills."[10]

Abraham Lincoln was elected president in November 1860.

Lincoln amassed 180 electoral votes but barely 1,900,000 popular votes. The other three party candidates totaled 2,700,000 popular votes but only 123 electoral votes. If Sam Houston had been the nominee of an organized political party, with his remarkable background and oratorical gifts and fervent message of Union, he might well have won the Election of 1860.

But Lincoln won the electoral vote, and in just their second presidential election the Republicans had triumphed, controlling Congress as well as the White House. With sweeping victory by the Northern-based, anti-slavery Republicans, Southern secessionists garnered a flood of support. At a convention on December 20, South Carolina adopted an Ordinance of Secession, 169-0. During the next six weeks Mississippi, Florida, Alabama, Louisiana, and Georgia seceded. Delegates from these six states met in Montgomery, Alabama, on February 4, 1861, and organized the Confederate States of America, with Jefferson Davis elected as president. The C.S.A. urged the other nine slave states, including Texas, to join them.

Governor Houston conducted a strategic retreat from Texas secessionists, delaying for possible advantage. "So long as the Constitution is maintained by the 'Federal authority,' and Texas is not made victim of 'federal wrong,' I am for the Union as it is," counseled Houston. "Let us pause and ponder well before we take action outside of the Constitution."[11]

A formidable array of Texas political leaders worked diligently to excite public opinion in favor of secession. Such men as Associate Justice of the Texas Supreme Court Oran M. Roberts, Col. John S. Ford, former Governor Hardin R. Runnels, Attorney General George Flournoy, and Congressman John H. Reagan wrote letters to other prominent Texans throughout the state. Secessionists delivered public addresses and published articles in newspapers, while conducting planning meetings in Austin. In December a call for a convention to consider secession was issued, endorsed by state officials and other influential men. Election of delegates was scheduled for January 8, 1861, and these delegates would meet in Austin on January 28.

Governor Houston called a special session of the Legislature to meet on January 21, hoping to persuade legislators to avert the convention. Instead, the Legislature sanctioned the Secession Convention, and offered the hall of the House of Representatives for the meeting. The Convention drew up an ordinance of secession to be voted on statewide on February 23. Convention approval of the ordinance was scheduled for a vote on February 1, and all state officials were invited. Governor Houston was escorted into the hall and was given a cordial welcome by Oran M. Roberts, the presiding officer. But when the roll was called, the seven delegates who courageously voted against it were booed and hissed. The ordinance passed, 167-7, and the statewide referendum was scheduled for February 23.

Houston spoke in several towns and worked behind the scenes, but the stampede to secession could not be restrained. On February 23 the secession ordinance passed statewide by a three to one margin, 46,129 to 14,697. The convention reassembled to announce the results on March 2, the twenty-fifth anniversary of Texas Independence—and Sam Houston's sixty-eighth birthday.

Three days later, on March 5, the Secession Convention voted, 109 to 2, to join the Confederate States of America. An oath of loyalty to the C.S.A. was to be sworn by all state officials, and those who refused would be automatically deposed from office. At noon on Saturday, March 16, in the State Capitol, all state officials were expected to sign the ordinances.

During these events, Governor Houston received at least one letter from Abraham Lincoln, offering to send a large invasion force to Texas and to commission Houston as major general, all in an effort to keep Texas in the Union. Houston called four trusted friends together, read the letters, and asked their opinion. Three of the four thought such an effort foolhardy and likely to trigger a civil war among Texans. Houston tossed the letter into the fireplace, probably having heard confirmation of his own inclinations. "Gentlemen, I have asked your advice and will take it, but if I were ten years younger I would not."[12]

On Friday night, March 15, Houston retired to his upstairs bedroom. Removing his coat, vest, and shoes, he began pacing, deep in thought about the oath-taking ceremony at noon the next day. In the still of night, sporadically he could be heard praying aloud. By morning he had determined his course of action, and he marched up the hill to the Governor's Office on the first floor of the Capitol.

Governor Houston remained in his office as the Secession Convention opened the oath ceremony. The secretary called out, "Sam Houston." When there was no answer, the call grew louder. "Sam Houston! Sam Houston!"[13] When there was no answer to three summons, the office was declared vacant, and Lieutenant Governor Edward Clark was sworn in as Governor.

Houston and many supporters held that his removal as Governor was unconstitutional. When he reported for duty the next week, the frail, sickly Edward Clark was sitting in his office chair. Houston made a couple of sarcastic remarks, then began placing personal effects into his lunch basket. When he reached the washstand, he passed over a bar of soap. "I will leave this bar of soap," he announced pointedly, "a Governor should have clean hands."[14]

Friends came to the Governor's Mansion to help with packing and to say farewell. On Tuesday, March 19, as the family was almost ready to set out, early Texas settler Noah Smithwick rode up, armed to the teeth. He told Houston there were 100 men ready to seize the Capitol and place Houston back in office. Houston expressed gratitude to his old friend, but repeated his resolve not to pit Texan against Texan.

Finally the Houstons headed east. Driven by his faithful slave, Jeff, Houston led the way in a top buggy. Margaret and the seven children followed in a yellow coach, driven by another loyal slave, and the other servants brought up the rear in a wagon. In one town after another Houston was asked to speak and, as he had before his ouster, he pointed out the hard realities of war and the possibility that the North might be able to overwhelm the South.

With a large family to feed, Houston arranged to have firewood cut at Cedar Point and sold at Galveston. He had no pension, although after his death Margaret, in severe financial straits, was voted $1,700 by the Legislature, a sum which paid the remainder of his governor's salary.

The Houstons soon decided they wanted to live in Huntsville again. Sam could not persuade the new owner to sell Woodland Home, but he managed to rent the "Steamboat House," which stood on a hill a few blocks south of the town square and a short distance east of Oakwood Cemetery. The sturdy structure was built with thick beams and heavy timbers. The home was erected in 1858 by Dr. Rufus Bailey, president of Austin College (where Houston had been a trustee). Dr. Bailey built the house to resemble a Mississippi River steamboat and to present as a wedding gift to his son and new wife. But the young couple hated the eccentric house and refused to live in it. Therefore, the Steamboat House was available when the Houston family returned to Huntsville.

Houston repeatedly had warned the public that Civil War would bring bloodshed and ruin to the South, and his predictions of heavy casualties struck close to home. Sam, Jr., turned eighteen shortly after the Civil War broke out at Fort Sumter. For young men the war seemed the great adventure of the age. Sam Houston repeatedly counseled his namesake to "attend to busi-

The Steamboat House was built in 1858 to resemble a Mississippi riverboat. When the Houston family returned to Huntsville in 1861, Sam rented the Steamboat House. Two years later he died in the downstairs front room. *Photo by the author.*

ness . . . We are not wanted or needed out of Texas, and we may soon be wanted or needed in Texas. Until then, my son, be content."[15] But young Sam could not be content. Caught up by the excitement—like his father during the War of 1812—young Sam enlisted in the company being raised by family friend, Capt. Ashbel Smith. Smith's "Bayland Guards" Company was part of the Second Texas Infantry Regiment, which assembled and drilled in Houston.

When General Houston visited Pvt. Sam Houston, Jr., he was invited to drill the troops. He donned much of the attire he wore at San Jacinto, tucking his dark tan pants into worn riding boots. General Houston pinned one side of his broad-brimmed hat into a jaunty military look, and wore his San Jacinto sword. As he put the young soldiers through their paces, the old drillmaster ordered, "Eyes right," and asked if the command saw _____, _____, or _____, prominent men who were slackers. After receiving negative answers, General Houston commanded: "Eyes left! Do you see anything of young Sam Houston here?"

"Yes!" came the shouted reply.

"Eyes front! Do you see anything of old Sam Houston here?" The regiment and the audience spontaneously roared out cheers and applause. General Houston—with his bearing, his impressive size, his battlefield exploits—still commanded admiration and respect in a military setting.[16]

The Second Texas Infantry became part of the Army of the Mississippi, commanded by Gen. Albert Sidney Johnston of Texas. On April 6, 1862, General Johnston attacked Gen. Ulysses S. Grant at Shiloh's Landing in western Tennessee. The two-day Battle of Shiloh produced more than 1,700 deaths and 8,000 wounded on each side. General Johnston was killed. Capt. Ashbel Smith was wounded, and so was Pvt. Sam Houston. One doctor thought he was fatally injured, and the young soldier lay helpless on the battlefield—as his father had at Horseshoe Bend. But like his father young Sam survived, one of 959 Confederates captured by Union soldiers. His recovery was slow, but he became part of a prisoner exchange and finally returned to his home.

A month before Private Houston was wounded, Eliza Allen

Houston Douglass died at the age of fifty-two. After she was divorced by Sam Houston, Eliza married Dr. Elmore Douglass, a widower with ten children. Eliza bore Douglass more children, two of whom preceded her in death. She was buried among family members at Gallatin, but she insisted that her grave remain unmarked. Eliza also destroyed all painted and photographic images of herself. Eliza remains as much of a mystery as the reason—or reasons—she rejected marriage to Gov. Sam Houston.

After leaving Austin, Houston continued to make an occasional speech, trying to project an optimism that he usually tempered with a touch of realism. "The South, chivalric, brave, and impetuous as it is," he stated to a crowd in Independence, "must add to these attributes of success through discipline, or disaster will come upon the country."[17] Early in 1863 to an audience in Houston, he tried to raise spirits: "The success of our cause depends alone upon the ardent and devoted hearts and the strong arms of our people."[18]

In Huntsville Houston visited around the neighborhood, and was as courtly as ever in the company of ladies. Houston maintained a busy correspondence, although he had to use homemade ink because of the tightening Union blockade. However, friends in the North—he had friends everywhere—kept him supplied with coffee and sugar. Texas friends approached him about running for governor in 1863. Texas was suffering from the blockade; unprotected frontier counties were being hammered by Comanche and Kiowa raids; tax money was flowing to the Confederate government; schools were closing; roads were not maintained; with men away from plantations and farms, slaves were harder to control. Texas needed strong leadership, and many Texans understood that Sam Houston was an extraordinary leader.

But by 1863 Houston was in failing health. He developed a persistent cough. His voice, always a powerful, resonant instrument, became noticeably weaker. He lost weight, and his great frame took on a skeletal appearance. "This is the second day that I have risen from a spell of sickness that lasted me a week," he wrote to his oldest daughter. "I am quite lean, but hope soon to mend again." The next day, before sending the letter, he penned an addendum. "Today I am afraid I have taken a relapse."[19]

On April 2, 1863, Houston wrote a will. At one point he was so ill that the attending physician called the family to his bedside. Houston gave final instructions and asked for a Bible passage to be read. But he rallied and went off to Sour Creek to take the waters. After four weeks he returned to Huntsville, but his condition deteriorated rapidly. Ashbel Smith took leave from his military duties for a few days at the Steamboat House, but there was nothing this old friend and skilled physician could do.

Sam Houston spent his last days in the front downstairs bedroom of the Steamboat House. The bandages on his wounds from Horseshoe Bend still had to be changed daily, and the summer heat was oppressive. On July 25 he began to fall in and out of consciousness. At Houston's request Rev. Samuel McKinney was summoned. Reverend McKinney, a Presbyterian who had served as president of Austin College, spoke quietly with Houston, who assured him that, "All is well." McKinney conducted a prayer and departed for the night.

On the morning of July 26 Margaret read Bible passages and the seven youngest children gathered around their father. Houston regained consciousness for a moment. Fifteen-year-old Maggie distinctly heard and recorded his final words.

"Texas – Texas – Margaret."[20]

Margaret removed the thin gold ring with the word "Honor" inscribed on the underside. Houston's body was prepared by members of the Huntsville Masonic Lodge and placed in a coffin in the upstairs parlor, where the funeral was held. There was a sermon, and Judge Joab Banton, a member of the Legislature who had visited Houston almost daily, delivered a eulogy. Houston was buried with Masonic rites at nearby Oakwood Cemetery. Houston was interred at the southwestern edge of the graveyard, only a short distance from his devoted friend, Henderson Yoakum.

Houston's grave is marked with monument stones and historical markers. The largest stone boasts an equestrian relief statue of Houston. On the backside of this handsome monument is inscribed a tribute list which sums up the qualities which made

Sam Houston a great man.

A Brave Soldier. A Fearless Statesman.

A Great Orator – A Pure Patriot.

A Faithful Friend, A Loyal Citizen.

A Devoted Husband and Father.

A Consistent Christian – An Honest Man.

The world will take care of Houston's fame.
Andrew Jackson

Chapter Fifteen

Remembering a Leader

The reservoir of public memory about Sam Houston features a rich collection of statues, paintings, and biographies. One of the nation's largest cities is named after Houston, along with counties in three states, a national forest, a military base, a nuclear submarine, a memorial museum, parks, a university, and numerous schools. Sam Houston has been honored and commemorated and memorialized in a manner worthy of an historic icon.

No commemoration better captures the larger-than-life aura of Sam Houston than *A Tribute to Courage*, the towering, sixty-seven-foot statue located on the east side of Interstate 45 a few miles south of Huntsville. David Adickes, a Huntsville native who graduated from Huntsville High School, created an enormous memorial from 60,000 pounds of concrete (the sculptor also utilized concrete and steel to erect a sixty-foot statue of Stephen F. Austin in Angleton). Nicknamed "Big Sam," the statue is mounted atop a ten-foot base, and can be seen for six miles from the south. For a number of years a student favorite of my Traveling Texas History Course itinerary was "Big Sam." They looked in awe at it from sides and front, climbed up on the base, photographed it (and had me photograph them lined up on the base). Suggesting grandeur and nobility, "Big Sam" is enjoyed by legions of travelers from I-45, and by thousands who stop at the visitor center.

There are other Sam Houston sculptures that are seen by great numbers of people. A pioneer of the art of sculpture in Texas was Elisabet Ney. Born in Germany in 1833, she became the first female student accepted into the Munich Art Academy. When she was thirty she married physician and scientist Edmund Montgomery, and in 1871 they migrated to the United States. Elisabet, Edmund, and their two little sons moved to Texas in 1872,

purchasing the Liendo Plantation near Hempstead. While her husband devoted himself to scientific pursuits, Elisabet managed the plantation for two decades.

Encouraged by Gov. O. M. Roberts, she decided to resume her career in art. In 1892 she opened a studio in Austin, and among her early commissions were Italian marble statues of Sam Houston and Stephen F. Austin. These impressive works were displayed at the Chicago's World Fair in 1893. Now they stand at the entrance to the rotunda in the Texas State Capitol.

In 1864 Congress authorized the President to invite each state to provide, for display in the National Capitol, two statues of distinguished citizens. The old House of Representatives chamber would become Statuary Hall. In 1905 Texas sent copies of Elisabet Ney's statues of Houston

Perhaps the most representative image of the larger-then-life Texas icon, Sam Houston, is the sixty-seven-foot statue which overlooks I-45 south of Huntsville. Made of 60,000 pounds of concrete and mounted atop a ten-foot granite base, it is visible for more than six miles. *Photo by the author.*

and Austin to Statuary Hall—where Sam Houston was the first seated as a freshman congressman in 1823.

In the Virginia State Capitol a bust of native son Sam Houston is displayed in the northwest corner of the old Hall of the House of Delegates. A magnificent equestrian statue of Sam Houston stands prominently in Hermann Park in the city of Houston. A statue of Houston stands at the west entrance of the Lorenzo de Zavala State Archives and Library Building, which is across the east lawn from the State Capitol. Just north of the State Archives and Library Building is the Sam Houston State Office Building. On the second floor of the State Capitol Building, atop a bookshelf in the Legislative Reference Library, is a bust of Sam Houston by an unknown artist.

Elisabet Ney's statue of Sam Houston stands in the main entrance to the State Capitol, after first being on display at the Chicago World's Fair of 1893. A copy of this work represents Texas in Statuary Hall in the U.S. Capitol building. *Photo by the author.*

Inside the front (south) entrance to the State Capitol, and within a few steps of the statue of Sam Houston, is the historic painting, *Surrender of Santa Anna.* Artist William Henry Huddle completed the seven-foot by nine

Hanging the in State Capitol entrance near the statue of Sam Houston is William Huddle's epic painting, *Surrender of Santa Anna*. *Photo by the author.*

and one-half foot painting in 1890. Thirty-five historical characters are depicted in the work, centering upon Sam Houston, lying on his pallet and accepting the surrender of Santa Anna. Huddle was a Confederate veteran from Virginia who studied painting in New York and Europe. He moved his family to Texas during the 1870s and established a studio in Austin. Huddle obtained a commission from the state to create portraits of the four presidents of the Republic of Texas and the first seventeen governors of the State of Texas. Huddle produced his portrait of Houston in 1890, and it is displayed behind the speaker's rostrum in the State House of Representatives. Houston's portrait hangs beside the only textile in the Capitol art collection—the flag of the Texas Army during the Battle of San Jacinto.

During his lifetime Houston seemed to enjoy posing for portraits—watercolors and oils, later progressive methods of photography. Perhaps he realized that as a man of achievement and importance he should leave an image record. Images reveal that as a young man he enjoyed dazzling good looks, including a dimpled chin and piercing eyes and dark curly hair. As he aged

The magnificent equestrian statue of Sam Houston points the way into Hermann Park. *Photo by Dr. Berri O'Neal.*

his features remained strong and handsome. He dressed with individual style and flair and a sense of costume. Houston wore a hat well, and mutton chop sideburns became a well-remembered feature. There are ample portrait images which permit a search for character indications, and which record the physical development of a fascinating individual. The largest collection of photographs and illustrations of Houston is at the Sam Houston Regional Library and Museum, located three miles north of Liberty.

The intriguing character and dramatic life of Sam Houston was a story worth telling, and biographers began to tell it to the public even before his death. In 1846 *Sam Houston and His Republic* was published anonymously, although Houston apparently collaborated on the brief book with Charles Edwards Lester. An almost identical book was published nine years later as *The Life of Sam Houston, The only Authentic memoir of Him Ever Published*. This slender volume was intended to support an 1856 campaign for the presidency by Houston, but the campaign did not materialize. In 1855 Henderson Yoakum, a friend and admirer of Sam Houston, published *A History of Texas*, covering the years 1685 to 1846. There was considerable material about Houston, including a number of documents, and again Houston lent his assistance.

More than sixty biographies have been written about Sam Houston. *The Raven*, published in 1929, won a Pulitzer Prize for Marquis James (who claimed another Pulitzer Prize less than a

Behind the Speaker's rostrum in the Texas House of Representatives is displayed the only textile in the Capitol art collection, the San Jacinto Battle Flag. Flanking the flag, at right, is William Huddle's portrait of Sam Houston, and at left a portrait of Governor James Hogg. *Photo by the author.*

decade later for his biography of Andrew Jackson). James enjoyed assistance from Houston family members, and wrote compelling prose. In 1954 a brilliant political biography appeared, *Sam Houston: The Great Designer*, by Llerena B. Friend. Other reliable, informative biographies include M. K. Wisehart's *Sam Houston: American Giant* (1962), Marshall De Bruhl's *Sword of San Jacinto: A Life of Sam Houston* (1993), and Randolph Campbell's *Sam Houston and the American Southwest* (2006). Of special usefulness is *Sam Houston's Texas* (1964), a photographic history of Houston's years in Texas by Sue Flanagan. Most notable of all is James Haley's *Sam Houston* (2004). Haley spent fifteen years on this masterful book, combing resources that previously had been unavailable.

Houston's magnificent life inspired far more biographers than novelists. A fine historical novelist, Paul Wellman, wrote *Magnificent Destiny* (1962), focusing upon high points of the career of Andrew Jackson. But Sam Houston also is featured in the book, from Horseshoe Bend through San Jacinto. Lucia St. Clair Robson wrote of the relationship between Sam Houston and Tiana Rogers in *Walk in My Soul* (1985). *Empire of Bones: A Novel of Sam Houston and the Texas Revolution* (1993) was penned by Jeff Long.

For a man with such a complex character and dramatic life, Sam Houston has attracted only modest attention from film makers. Silent movie star William Farnum played Houston in the title role of *The Conqueror* in 1917. Richard Dix, a big, sturdy headliner of Western movies, portrayed Houston in *Man of Conquest*, a minor film of 1939. In *Lone Star* (1952), veteran character actor Moroni Olsen played a white-haired, bearded Houston in a supporting role to Clark

This bust of Sam Houston is placed just inside the entrance of the Sam Houston Regional Library and Research Center north of Liberty. Photo by the author.

Gable, Broderick Crawford, and Ava Gardner. Both Gable and Crawford loomed physically larger than Olsen's Houston on the silver screen. *Lone Star* is a slow-moving film with scant historic background. Lionel Barrymore was crusty and loud as Andrew Jackson, but Olsen was unconvincing as Old Sam Jacinto.

A year later Glenn Ford starred as *The Man From the Alamo* (1953), while little-known Howard J. Negley played Houston in a minor role. *The Last Command* (1955) starred Sterling Hayden as Jim Bowie in a good version of the Alamo story. Arthur Hunnicutt was the best Davy Crockett until Billy Bob Thornton's portrayal in *The Alamo* (2004), but once again Sam Houston, as played by Hugh Sanders, was a minor character. Tall, stalwart Joel McCrea starred as Sam Houston in *The First Texan* (1956). But the script calls for Houston to resist the role of Texas savior that others try —and eventually succeed—in thrusting upon him. McCrea was serious and convincing as a reluctant hero, but in real life Houston embraced leadership opportunities.

Sam Houston was honored with a United States postal stamp in 1964. *Courtesy U.S. Postal Service*

An epic production of 1960 was John Wayne's *The Alamo.* The movie focused on the superb Alamo and San Antonio sets, and the massive battle scenes. But the stellar cast included Richard Boone as Sam Houston. Although Boone had just two scenes, one early and one late in the film, the rugged actor captured Houston as no one else has ever on screen. Boone's Houston radiated power. He was a large, strong man, and his costume included a beaded belt and other Indian touches. Richard Boone fills the screen with the Sam Houston of the spring of 1836.

A made for television movie, *Houston: The Legend of Texas,* aired in 1986, the year of the Texas Sesquicentennial, and starred Sam Elliott as Sam Houston. Aside from Elliott's wife, Katherine Ross in a brief portrayal as Susannah Dickinson, the supporting cast is weak. The "acting" consists of everyone shouting at each other. Elliott wears his trademark bushy moustache, although Houston rarely cultivated one. Elliott has a trim physique, and the other actors appear physically larger than Houston on-screen. Houston, of course, towered over most men in real life. This film, now known as *Gone to Texas,* appears often on cable-TV, and those familiar with Houston's story will enjoy the many accurate details

Fort Sam Houston's most famous landmark is the Watch Tower, built in 1876 in the center of the Quadrangle. *Courtesy Fort Sam Houston.*

that were worked into the script. *Gone to Texas* was filmed to good effect in the Lone Star state, but budget limitations make the opposing armies seem more like opposing platoons.

The most recent portrayal of Sam Houston was by Dennis Quaid in *The Alamo* (2004). Like Sam Elliott, Quaid has the deep, powerful voice of Houston. Quaid even wears the tricorn hat that Houston sometimes wore during the Revolution, although his slender build does not suggest Houston's physicality. But the Battle of San Jacinto is superbly staged, the best depiction ever lensed of this momentous battle.

Another TV movie, *Two for Texas* (1998) starred Kris Kristofferson as an adventurer and friend of Jim Bowie (played by Peter Coyote). Kristofferson and a young companion arrive in Texas in 1836, just in time to join Houston's army at the beginning of the Runaway Scrape. Houston is portrayed by Tom Skerritt, who is convincingly costumed in cape, vest, and a good hat, although a set of chin whiskers somewhat spoils the image. Skerritt's Houston is strong, and his "Remember the Alamo" speech is especially rousing. The Battle of San Jacinto is well-staged. While dramatic license is taken with several events, *Two for Texas* is worth viewing, especially for an effective screen version of Sam Houston.

Sam Houston never enjoyed the musical benefit of a best-selling TV series theme song such as *The Ballad of Davy Crockett* ("Born on a mountaintop in Tennessee . . . ") or a catchy song about Andrew Jackson's most famous exploit. *The Battle of New Orleans* won two Grammys in 1959: Song of the Year, for composer Jimmy Driftwood, and Best Country and Western Performance, by Johnny Horton. But in the early 1850s a ballad was composed to support a Houston presidential candidacy during the Election of 1852. Sung to the tune of *Oh! Susannah!*, the campaign song did little to promote Houston's candidacy, which failed to develop outside Texas. Houston's campaign ballad was nearly forgotten, but Texas writer Mike Cox discovered and reproduced it:[1]

Come, all ye good Republicans [Citizens]
Come join the song with me.
Who want a man for President
To rule the brave and free.

Old Sam Houston, he's the boy for me,
He lives away in Texas, and a good old man is he.
Old Sam Houston, he's the boy for me,
He lives away in Texas, and a good old man is he.

He's of the Andrew Jackson school,
As true and tried as steel,
And he loves the land of Freedom well,
Its glory and its weal.

Just listen to his sturdy voice,
Within the Nation's hall [the capitol],
Proclaiming loudly to the world
The Union shall not fall.

At San Jacinto's bloody field,
Our Hero met the foe,

And Santa Anna there was fixed
For traveling very slow.

A statesman true and hero bold,
In him are both combined;
And with him we can whip the world,
'And the rest of (Whig) mankind.'

We'll bring him out in fifty-two
And on our banners high,
His name shall float for President,
So, Whiggies, don't you cry.

And when we've placed him in the chair,
Where brave Old Hick-ry sat,
We'll say good-bye, old Uncle Sam,
Hang up that wide-brimmed hat!

Old Sam Houston, he's the boy for me,
He does not live in Texas, for the President is he.
Old Sam Houston, a good old man is he;
The White House is his residence, Whiggies call and see.

In recent years, Scott Miller, a native of Virginia and a singer-songwriter, has performed his composition about Sam Houston, the *Say Ho* song. "He was born in Virginia / In the Shenandoah Valley / Right about the time that this country got free." The ballad moves on to Horseshoe Bend. "Took an arrow in the hip / A ball in the shoulder but he never quit." After "Reading Homer to some Cherokee maidens" Houston managed to become governor of Tennessee. "Partied hard and ran the state / Found a girl to take his name / And they still don't know why he up and left it all." Later Houston made it to Texas. "San Jacinto was the place / That destiny was ready to be seized." After more than forty lines, Miller ends with a statement: "In Texas anywhere that you may wander / Sam Houston was the man that kept his word."[2]

The nation's seventh-largest city features Houston's name on one of its best-known institutions. In 1890 the U.S. Army Quartermaster Depot in San Antonio was named Fort Sam Houston. When Texas became a state the army established a base in San Antonio, and with a proliferation of frontier and border forts pri-

The Main Building of Sam Houston Normal Institute, established in Huntsville in 1879. *Courtesy Sam Houston State University.*

or to the Civil War, a vast amount of supplies and equipment was handled, first in an around the Alamo, and finally at a base simply called the Quartermaster Depot, located in the east part of town. When it was decided to assign the name to the Quartermaster Depot, there was no more suitable label than the name of the leading Texas hero of the nineteenth century.

The U.S. Navy also has used the name of Sam Houston. Four warships have borne the name *U.S.S. Houston*: A World War I cargo ship; two World War II cruisers (the first was sunk in 1942); and an attack submarine launched in 1981. But these vessels were named after the city of Houston (which, of course, was named for "Old Sam Jacinto"). In 1959 the keel was laid down for the *U.S.S. Sam Houston*, the U. S. Navy's seventh ballistic missile submarine. Launched in 1961, the *U.S.S. Sam Houston* was on duty around the world for thirty years before being decommissioned in 1991.

In addition to Houston, Texas, now the fourth-largest city in the United States, Houston, Missouri, (population 2,000) is the seat of Texas County. There are Houston counties in Texas, Tennessee, and Minnesota, each named in honor of Sam Houston.

Four National Forests were established by the Texas State Legislature in 1933, and one was named for Sam Houston. Located just south of Huntsville, the Sam Houston National Forest has 161,508 acres in San Jacinto, Montgomery, and Walker counties. Visitors enjoy camping, hiking, bicycling, hunting, and fishing in a beautiful woodland setting that Sam Houston would recognize.

The site of Houston's birthplace and childhood home is marked by the Sam Houston Wayside, a roadside park eight miles northeast of Lexington, Virginia, on Highway 11. The Wayside features a marker made of a 38,000-pound piece of Texas granite. The hilly, heavily wooded countryside is reminiscent of the wilderness neighborhood when the Houstons lived there. After the family moved to east Tennessee, the site of their home was established at another hilly wilderness. There is an historical marker beside the rural road, and a short distance away, on a hillside, are three flagpoles designating the location of the house, several miles south of Maryville. A few miles north of Maryville, on Sam Houston Lane, is the Sam Houston Schoolhouse, operated as a Tennessee Historic Site. The one-room log school was built in 1794 and is the oldest school building in Tennessee. As a young man Sam Houston taught in this school, and there is a good museum on the grounds.

I attended the fourth and fifth grades at Sam Houston Elementary School in Corsicana. Elementary schools also were proudly named after Sam Houston in Huntsville (of course!), Dallas, Port Arthur, Odessa, Bryan, Grand Prairie, La Feria, Corpus Christi, Harlingen, Galena Park, Conroe. San Antonio boasts Fort Sam Houston Elementary School. In Tennessee there are Sam Houston elementary schools in Maryville, where Houston enlisted in the U.S. Army, and in Lebanon, where he opened his first law office.

Sam Houston middle schools are in Amarillo, Marshall, Garland and Irving. There is a Sam Houston High School, appropriately, in the Houston Independent School District, as well as in San Antonio and Arlington. In Lake Charles, Louisiana, the Sam Houston High School football team is supported by the "Big Sam

In 1936 the Texas Centennial Commission authorized $25,000 for construction of a museum on the grounds of Sam Houston's Woodland Home. The original rotunda, pictured above, has been expanded with two large wings. *Courtesy Sam Houston Memorial Museum.*

Boosters." Sam Houston would appreciate the nickname of the booster club.

Legislation creating the Sam Houston Normal Institute was named by Gov. Oran M. Roberts on San Jacinto Day, April 21, 1879. The state-supported Institute was formed to provide Texas with sorely-needed school teachers. Sam Houston Normal Institute, located on a hill east of Houston's beloved Huntsville home, was the first teacher-training school in Texas, and served as a model for other schools around the Lone Star State. The Institute became Sam Houston State Teachers College in 1923. SHSTC was elevated to Sam Houston State University in 1969, and today more than 18,000 students attend this fine university.

In 1889 students of Sam Houston Normal Institute began walking to Houston's grave, located about a mile north of the institution, each year on his birthday. This traditional march was expanded by the Walker County Historical Commission in 1981, and the history department of SHSU has encouraged students to join "The March to the Grave," which is led by the university's ROTC company. In recent years the Walker County Historical Commission, the Sam Houston Memorial Museum, and the Sam Houston Statue and Visitor's Center have combined efforts to provide an annual celebration of Texas Independence Day and Gen. Sam Houston's Birthday.

On Sunday, March 2, 2014, I was privileged as State Historian to deliver an address on "Sam Houston as a Leader" in Huntsville. The previous day, a Saturday, featured an afternoon panel discussion at the museum on the "Cherokee Tennessee-Texas Connection," followed by a wine and cheese reception at the Sam Houston Statue and Visitor Center. Sunday activities began at the education center of the Sam Houston Memorial Museum. There was a buffet luncheon, climaxed by a traditional "Toast to Texas" and the cutting of the beautifully-decorated Sam Houston Birthday Cake. After relocating to the gravesite, the crowd watched the ROTC march up. The program of the Texas State Historian was delivered to a receptive audience, and the ROTC fired a salute over Houston's grave.

The gravesite is dominated by an impressive equestrian relief statue of Texas gray granite. Created by Italian sculptor Pompeo Coppini, the statue was unveiled on the seventy-fifth anniversary of the Battle of San Jacinto, April 21, 1911. General Houston is mounted and flanked by symbolic figures of Liberty and History. A quote from Andrew Jackson's tribute to the victory is inscribed below Houston's image: "The World Will Take Care of Houston's Fame."

Immediately following the ROTC gravesite salute was the "Baptized Texan Ceremony," during which the genial James Patton of the Walker County Historical Commission "baptized" as new Texans about a score of non-native Texans. Patton sprinkled the candidates for "baptism" with water taken from Rocky Creek, where Houston was baptized.

In Huntsville, just west of the main campus of Sam Houston State University, a complex of buildings comprise the Sam Houston Memorial Museum. In 1905 faculty and students headed a

On Sam Houston's gravestone is the prescient prediction by Andrew Jackson: "The world will take care of Houston's fame." As seen in this photo from March 2, 2014, on the night before his birthday a plate of food is anonymously placed in front of the gravestone. *Photo by the author.*

movement to purchase eighteen acres of Houston's old farm. Six years later Woodland Home and the log law office were moved back to the site, and in 1929 the museum was dedicated. In 1936 the state legislature appropriated funds to erect a rotunda museum building, which since has been expanded. The Steamboat House, where Houston died, has been moved onto the site, along with other structures. Permanent exhibits present the largest collection of Houston artifacts and memorabilia on display anywhere. A scenic artificial pond is named "Lake Oolooteka," after the Cherokee chief who adopted young Sam Houston.

To paraphrase Andrew Jackson, Huntsville has taken care of Sam Houston's fame. So have many historians and photographers, sculptors and painters, and miscellaneous admirers of a man who achieved greatness as a military and political leader.

Rest in Peace
Passing of Persons Close to Sam Houston

1806 Maj. Samuel Houston, 62: soldier, father

1824 Joseph McMinn, 66; Tennessee governor, early mentor

1831 Elizabeth Paxton Houston, 74: mother

1838 Chief Oolooteka: adoptive father of "The Raven"

1838 Tiana Rogers, ca. 40: Cherokee wife of Houston

1845 Andrew Jackson, 78: general, president – and mentor

1849 James K. Polk, 53: congressman, Tennessee governor, president

1850 John C. Calhoun, 68: sec. of war, vice president – and longtime enemy

1852 Henry Clay, 75: senator, speaker of the house, orator

1852 Daniel Webster, 70: senator and orator

1856 Henderson K. Yoakum, 46: Tennessee senator, Texas historian, friend

1857 Thomas J. Rusk, 53: attorney, soldier, senator, friend

1858 Thomas Hart Benton, 66: soldier, senator, early mentor

1862 Eliza Allen Houston Douglass, 52: troubled bride

1863 Sam Houston, 70

1867 Margaret Lea Houston, 48: wife, helpmate, mother of eight

Leadership Principles That Shaped Sam Houston

- As a boy Sam Houston was influenced by his father, a militia officer and a veteran of the American Revolution. From Major Houston, young Sam acquired military ardor and a sense of leadership.

- Sam also observed and learned leadership skills from his adoptive father, Chief Oolooteka of the Cherokee. Houston referring to Oolooteka: "He had the most courtly carriage in the world, and never prince sat on a throne with more peerless grace than he presided at the council fire of his people."

- Young Sam disliked school and attended class for only about a year. But like another backwoods boy fourteen years his junior, Abraham Lincoln, Sam Houston became a voracious reader. He soaked up a large fund of knowledge, acquired a deep feel for words, and committed a great number of passages to memory.

- Despite his lack of formal schooling, Houston successfully taught a term of school, which reinforced his confidence that he could achieve virtually anything. Houston: "I experienced a higher feeling of dignity and self-satisfaction than from any office or honor which I later held."

- During the War of 1812, twenty-year-old Sam Houston enlisted in the U.S. Army as a private. Private Houston almost immediately was promoted to sergeant, thanks to the support of Lt. Col. Thomas Hart Benton. By the time he engaged in combat, Houston had advanced to lieutenant. His leadership abilities were obvious in a military setting.

- At the Battle of Horseshoe Bend, Lieutenant Houston suffered three wounds while leading charges with ferocious courage. Gen. Andrew Jackson noted Houston's valor, and would become his most important mentor.

- Houston served in the U.S. Army for five years, distinguishing himself in combat and maturing as a leader of men.

- Following his discharge, Houston read for the law for a time. With his powers of memorization he learned enough to practice sporadically during the rest of his life. An attorney commanded a level of prestige in American society, and Houston's knowledge of the law proved useful during the succession of political positions he held.

- Houston grew to be a tall man with a strong frame. His imposing physique was an asset as a military leader, especially in an age of hand-to-hand combat. Houston's impressive size inspired confidence in men who followed him into battle, as a strapping lieutenant and, two decades later, as a general.

- In addition to an impressive physique, Houston possessed handsome features and a rich, powerful voice. He developed a flair for dramatic and colorful attire. His appearance often was striking, appealing to both men and women.

- Houston was sociable and gregarious. He was a convivial companion to men, and a courtly, charming gentleman among women. He had a gift for making friends, and he kept friendships alive with correspondence and personal visits, both local and during his far-ranging travels.

- Houston asked his friends for loans and favors, both political and personal. But he faithfully paid his debts, and in turn he extended loans and favors.

- Houston kept careful financial records to avoid accusations of impropriety with public funds.

- When Houston entered politics, he advanced rapidly, with the assistance of highly-placed mentors. He embraced each new position with full confidence that he could successfully perform greater responsibilities.

- Houston knew every president from Thomas Jefferson to Abraham Lincoln, fourteen in all, plus the president of the C.S.A., Jefferson Davis. He also knew and interacted with other prominent national leaders such as Henry Clay, Daniel Webster, and John C. Calhoun. From these men he emulated techniques of leadership, oratorical skills, and the manners of a cultivated gentleman.
  Houston: "The General [Jackson] is calm, dignified, and

makes as polished a bow as any man I have seen at court."

- Houston's long relationship with John C. Calhoun—vice-president, cabinet member and senator—was abrasive. But from Calhoun, Houston had a negative learning experience—what not to do, how not to lead men.
  Houston: "I will remember your personal bad treatment . . . I will remember as a man."

- Houston's most powerful mentor was President Andrew Jackson, whose name labeled the era—the Age of Jackson, Jacksonian Democracy. Houston became a Jacksonian intimate, on the closest terms with the most influential man in the nation.
  Houston: "To you, General, I find myself vastly indebted for many principles which I have never abandoned through life."

- When his marriage to Eliza Allen collapsed, Houston resigned the governorship of Tennessee rather than offer a public explanation that probably would have reflected badly on his troubled bride.
  Houston: "If my character cannot stand the shock, then let me lose it."

- With his political career seemingly in ruins, Houston sought refuge among the Cherokee in the wilderness of Indian Territory. But immediately various tribes implored the Raven to work on their behalf through his friend, President Jackson, in Washington, D.C. Houston soon reawakened to the call of public service.
  Houston: "It is hard for an old Trooper to forget the note of the Bugle!"

- In 1832 Houston was drawn to Texas, where Anglo settlers were clashing with the government of Mexico. With his political and military experience—and his connections in high places—Houston willingly assumed a prominent role in revolutionary events. Houston: "The work of liberty has begun . . . The morning of glory is dawning among us."

- During the Texas Revolution, all of Houston's leadership qualities—courage, decisiveness, powers of persuasion, physical stamina, military experience, willingness to shoulder vast responsibilities – were mined to their fullest extent.

- During the long strategic retreat and the desperate Runaway Scrape, General Houston kept the Texas Army together while paying for time, while waiting for the invading Mexican Army to make a mistake.
  Houston: "Remember one Maxim: it is better to do well late than never."

. General Houston kept a careful eye on his men during the campaign of 1836. He was readily accessible to his soldiers, responding to inquiries courteously while offering steady encouragement.

- Many of Houston's officers disagreed with his strategy, some to the point of open defiance. He ignored them, and refused to take them into his confidence, while shouldering full responsibility.
  Houston: "I consulted none—I held no councils-of-war. If I err, the blame is mine."

- At midday of April 21, 1836, with a superior force of Mexicans camped nearby, General Houston finally agreed to a council-of-war with his senior officers. All but two of the officers voted not to fight until the next day, but Houston remained noncommittal. After riding among the soldiers, he ordered an attack at mid-afternoon.
  Houston: "We go to conquer."

- As he had at Horseshoe Bend, Houston led from the front at San Jacinto. He had two horses shot out from under him, and his ankle was shattered by a copper ball. But General Houston led his men to a spectacular victory.

. President Houston practiced strict economies during his two terms. Leading by example, President Houston reduced his own salary. Forced to operate the government with almost no money, he endured long periods without being paid.

. President Houston appointed able men to his cabinet and to other government positions. Many were longtime friends, while others were promising young men whom he mentored, as he himself once had been mentored by men of influence.

. President Houston, who traveled widely around Texas, at a time when travel was difficult and there were few amenities, connected with Texans—at barbeques and political rallies and

holiday events – though his power of oratory.
Judge A.W. Terrell: I have heard all the great orators of the
Republic and State of Texas, except Lamar and the Whartons.
Houston . . . before a frontier audience excelled them all."

- President Houston demonstrated superlative leadership skills
  in crushing the long-lasting Regulator-Moderator War of
  East Texas. By 1844 thirty-one men were dead and 300 armed
  and mounted men were at battle. But Houston raised and
  organized 600 militia volunteers and scattered the feudists.

- Houston married Margaret Lea of Alabama in 1840, when he
  was forty-seven and she was twenty-one. Margaret curbed
  his drinking, inclined him to practice religion, and bore him
  eight children.
  Houston: "I love you `veerie much'."

- Margaret Houston was a gifted homemaker, but she made
  it clear from the first that she had no interest in politics.
  Houston was free to spend as much time as necessary in
  Washington or at the Texas capital city, while his wife stayed
  with the children, maintaining a warm home environment for
  his return.

- President Houston worked diligently for the annexation of
  Texas by the United States. After Texas achieved statehood
  in 1846, the new state legislature selected Sam Houston and
  Thomas J. Rusk as U.S. Senators.

- When Senator Houston returned to Congress, he was a
  national hero with political experience as congressman and
  governor of Tennessee and as president of the Republic
  of Texas. Asserting himself immediately, he ignored the
  tradition of silence for freshmen senators and promptly began
  delivering major addresses to the Senate.

- Sam Houston became the only prominent Southern politician
  who stood for union above sectionalism. In 1850—eight years
  before Abraham Lincoln's famous "house divided" speech—
  Houston delivered a powerful message to the U.S. Senate
  based upon the same Bible passage. Houston: "For a nation
  divided against itself cannot stand."

- Houston's benevolent policies toward Native Americans were
  disliked by Texans, and so was his anti-sectionalism stance.

But Houston had the courage of his convictions, even though his outspoken calls for Union cost him his Senate seat and the governorship of Texas.

Houston: "Preserve Union and you preserve liberty. They are one and the same."

- Denied reappointment after thirteen years in the U.S. Senate, Houston won election as governor in 1859. He had earned the highest offices Texas could offer: General of the Texas Army; President of the Texas Republic; U.S. Senator; Governor of Texas.

  Houston: "To govern well is a great science, but no country is ever improved by too much governing. Govern wisely and as little as possible."

- Governor Houston strongly opposed secession, repeatedly predicting civil war that would be disastrous for the South and for Texas.

  Houston: "Mark me, the day that produces a dissolution of this Confederacy will be written in history in the blood of humanity."

- After Texas seceded from the Union and joined the Confederate States of America—against the steady opposition of Governor Houston —he refused to take an oath of office to the C.S.A. Houston declined all offers from Texas supporters and from Pres. Abraham Lincoln to maintain him as governor —he would not consider being the focal point of a civil war in Texas.

  Houston: "The people want excitement and I had as well give it as any one."

End Notes

Notes to Chapter 1

1. Houston, *Life of General Sam Houston*, 1.
2. Houston, Day, Ullom, *Autobiography of Sam Houston*, 3-4.
3. Houston, Day, Ullom, *Autobiography*, 4.
4. Houston, Day, Ullom, *Autobiography*, 4.
5. Houston, *Life of General Sam Houston*, 1.
6. Houston, *Life of General Sam Houston*, 1; Houston, Day, Ullom, *Autobiography of Sam Houston*, 3-4.
7. Houston, *Life of General Sam Houston*, 1.
8. Houston, Life of *General Sam Houston*, 1.
9. Houston, Day, Ullom, *Autobiography*, 5.
10. Houston, *Life of General Sam Houston*, 1.
11. Houston, *Life of General Sam Houston*, 1.
12. Houston, *Life of General Sam Houston*, 1.
13. Houston, Day, Ullom, *Autobiography*, 5-6.
14. Houston, Day, Ullom, *Autobiography*, 6.
15. Houston, Day, Ullom, *Autobiography*, 6.
16. Houston, Day, Ullom, *Autobiography*, 8.
17. Houston, Day, Ullom, *Autobiography*, 8.
18. Houston, Day, Ullom, *Autobiography*, 8.
19. Houston, Day, Ullom, *Autobiography*, 8.
20. Houston, Day, Ullom, *Autobiography*, 8.

Notes to Chapter 2

1. Houston, Day, Ullom, *Autobiography*, 9.
2. Houston, Day, Ullom, *Autobiography*, 9.
3. Houston, Day, Ullom, *Autobiography*, 9.
4. Houston, *Life of General Sam Houston*, 2; Heitman (comp.), *Historical Register of the U.S. Army*, I, 545.
5. Houston, *Life of General Sam Houston*, 2; Heitman (comp.), *Historical Register of the U.S. Army*, I, 545.
6. Houston, *Life of General Sam Houston*, 2.
7. Houston, *Life of General Sam Houston*, 2.
8. Houston, *Life of General Sam Houston*, 2; Houston, Day, Ullom, *Autobiography*, 11-12.
9. Houston, *Life of General Sam Houston*, 2.
10. Houston, *Life of General Sam Houston*, 2.
11. Houston, Day, Ullom, *Autobiography*, 14; Houston, *Life of General Sam Houston*, 3.

12. Houston, Day, Ullom, *Autobiography*, 14; Houston, *Life of General Sam Houston*, 3.
13. Houston, Day, Ullom, *Autobiography*, 14; Houston, *Life of General Sam Houston*, 3.
14. Houston, Day, Ullom, *Autobiography*, 14.
15. Houston, Day, Ullom, *Autobiography*, 15.
16. Houston, Day, Ullom, *Autobiography*, 15-16.
17. Yoakum, *History of Texas*, I, 305; Heitman (comp.), *Historical Register of the U.S. Army*, I, 545.
18. Houston, *Life of General Sam Houston*, 3; Houston, Day, Ullom, *Autobiography*, 17.
19. Houston, Day, Ullom, *Autobiography*, 17.
20. Houston, Day, Ullom, *Autobiography*, 18-19; Houston, *Life of General Sam Houston*, 3.
21. Houston, Day, Ullom, *Autobiography*, 19; Houston, *Life of General Sam Houston*, 3; Yoakum, *History of Texas*, I, 305; Heitman (comp.), *Historical Register of the U.S. Army*, I, 545.
22. Houston, Day, Ullom, *Autobiography*, 9; Houston, *Life of General Sam Houston*, 3; Heitman (comp.), *Historical Register of the U.S. Army*, I, 545.
23. Houston, *Life of General Sam Houston*, 2, 3.

Notes to Chapter 3
1. Houston, Day, Ullom, *Autobiography*, 20.
2. Letter from Houston to Capt. Alexander Campbell (April 25, 1815), in Houston, Day, Ullom, *Autobiography*, 20-21.
3. Houston, Day, Ullom, *Autobiography*, 20-21.
4. Houston, Day, Ullom, *Autobiography*, 21.
5. Houston, *Life of General Sam Houston*, 3.
6. Quoted in Haley, *Sam Houston*, 33.
7. Quoted in Haley, *Sam Houston*, 33.
8. Houston, *Life of General Sam Houston*, 3.
9. Houston, Day, Ullom, *Autobiography*, 22.
10. Houston to Calhoun, June 4, 1822, in *Autobiography*, 22-23.
11. Houston to Calhoun, July 6, 1822, in *Autobiography*, 23-24.
12. Houston to Calhoun, April 15, 1824, in *Autobiography*, 27-28.
13. Houston to McMinn, February 15, 1823, and March 30, 1823, in *Autobiography*, 25-26.
14 Houston, Day, Ullom, *Autobiography*, 26.
15. Houston to Jackson, August 3, 1822, in *Autobiography*, 24-25.
16. Houston to Abram Maury, December 13, 1823, in *Autobiography*, 27.

Notes to Chapter 4
1. Houston, *Life of General Sam Houston*, 1.
2. Houston to Andrew Jackson, May 11, 1829, in *Autobiography*, 50.

3. Quote in Haley, *Sam Houston*, 3.

4. Houston to John Hancock, July 1, 1856, in *Autobiography*, 243-244.

5. Houston to Andrew Jackson, January 31, 1843, in *Autobiography*, 188-190.

6. Quote in Haley, *Sam Houston*, 32.

7. Houston to Mrs. Houston, May 19, 1858, in *Autobiography*, 255.

8. Quote in Haley, *Sam Houston*, 42..

Notes to Chapter 5

1. Houston mentioned "the Dear Girls" in a letter to Captain Alexander Campbell, April 25, 1815. In *Autobiography*, 16. Houston recalled strolling through the woods "by the side of some Indian maiden" in *Autobiography*, 6. The New Orleans promenade incident was related by Marquis James, *The Raven*, 37.

2. James, *The Raven*, 39-40, and Haley, *Sam Houston*, 19-20.

3. Houston to A.M. Hughes, January 22, 1825, in Autobiography, 29.

4. Houston to John H. Houston, April 20, 1825, in *Autobiography*, 31.

5. Houston to William J. Worth, January 24, 1826, in *Autobiography*, 32.

6. Houston to Dr. John Marable, Dceember 4, 1828, in *Autobiography*, 43.

7. Houston to William J. Worth, January 24, 1826, in *Autobiography*, 32.

8. Quote in Haley, *Sam Houston*, 51.

9. Martin, Mary L., "A Noted Talk." *Franklin Review and Journal*, September 1, 1881.

10. Houston to John Allen, April 9, 1829, in *Autobiography*, 45-46.

11. Houston, Day, Ullom, *Autobiography*, 46.

12. Houston, *Life of General Sam Houston*, 4.

13. Haley, *Sam Houston*, 59.

14. Houston, *Life of General Sam Houston*, 4.

15. Houston, Day, Ullom, *Autobiography*, 48.

16. De Bruhl, *Sword of San Jacinto*, 107.

17. Houston, Day, Ullom, *Autobiography*, 47.

18. Houston, Day, Ullom, *Autobiography*, 48.

19. Houston, *Life of General Sam Houston*, 4.

20. Houston, Day, Ullom, *Autobiography*, 51.

Notes to Chapter 6

1. Houston, Day, Ullom, *Autobiography*, 51.

2. Houston, *Life of General Sam Houston*, 4.

3. Houston to Eaton, July 22, 1829, in *Autobiography*, 52.

4. Haley, *Sam Houston*, 70.

5. Houston to Jackson, September 19, 1829, in *Autobiography*, 51-55.

6. De Bruhl, *Sword of San Jacinto*, 112.

7. Houston to John Overton, December 28, 1829, in *Autobiography*, 57-58.

8. Houston to John Van Fossen, April 4, 1830, in *Autobiography*, 58-59.

9. Houston, Day, Ullom, *Autobiography*, 59.

10. Houston to Andrew Jackson, May 18, 1830; and Houston to Major

William B. Lewis, in *Autobiography*, 59-60, and 60-61.
11. *Arkansas Gazette*, July 7, 1830. Barker and Williams. eds., I, 155-163.
12. *Niles' Weekly Register*, August 27, 181.
13. Haley, *Sam Houston*, 78-80.
14. Houston, Day, Ullom, *Autobiography*, 66.
15. Houston, Day, Ullom, *Autobiography*, 67.
16. Barker and Williams, eds., Writings, I, 207-224.
17. Houston, Day, Ullom, *Autobiography*, 67-68.
18. Houston, defense on Stanbery case, May 7, 1882, in *Autobiography*, 68-70.
19. Houston, Day, Ullom, *Autobiography*, 71.
20. To the Public, July 9, 182, in Barker and Williams, eds., Writings, I, 250-257.
21. Houston, Day, Ullom, *Autobiography*, 71.

Notes to Chapter 7
1. Houston, Day, Ullom, *Autobiography*, 76-77.
2. Houston to John H. Houston, December 2, 1832, in *Autobiography*, 77.
3. James, *The Raven*, 186. Rector's memory of the encounter with the future president of Texas may have been convenient.
4. Houston to Andrew Jackson, February, 13, 1833, in *Autobiography*, 78-79. Houston mentioned "the late commotions in Texas" and his "regrets that I was not there" in a letter to James Prentiss, August 18, 1832, in *Autobiography*, 75.
5. Houston to John H. Houston, July 31, 1833, in *Autobiography*, 80-81.
6. Houston to James Prentiss, June 27, 1832, in *Autobiography*, 75.
7. James, *The Raven*, 201-202.
8. Houston to James Prentiss, April 20 and April 24, 1834, in *Autobiography*, 82-83.
9. Haley, Sam Houston, 78-80; James, *The Raven*, 206.
10. Pope, *Early Days in Arkansas*, 153.
11. Featherstonhaugh, *Excursion trough the Slave States*, 119.
12. Houston, *Life of General Sam Houston*, 8.

Notes to Chapter 8
1. Houston, *Life of General Sam Houston*, 6.
2. Perry quoted in Clark, *Land of Promise*, 181.
3. Austin's speech is reprinted in Clark, *Land of Promise*, 182.
4. Barker and Williams, eds., Writings, I, 304-305.
5. James, *The Raven*, 213.
6. Barker and Williams, eds., Writings, I, 302.
7. Houston, *Life of General Sam Houston*, 6.
8. Borden's letter quoted in Friend, *Sam Houston, The Great Designer*, 63.
9. Houston to Fannin, November 13, 1835, in *Autobiography*, 85.
10. Houston, *Life of General Sam Houston*, 6.
11. Houston, *Life of General Sam Houston*, 6, and Proclamation of December 12, 1835, in *Autobiography*, 91.

12. Houston to Colonel Barrett, January 2, 1836, in *Autobiography*, 91.
13. Houston to Governor Smith, January 6, 1836, in *Autobiography*, 91-92.
14. Houston, *Life of General Sam Houston*, 7.
15. Letter quoted in Tinkle, *Thirteen Days to Glory*, 44-45.
16. Barker and Williams, eds., *Writings of Sam Houston*, VI,7.
17. Houston, Day, Ullom, *Autobiography*, 90.
18. Houston, Day, Ullom, *Autobiography*, 93.

Notes to Chapter 9

1. Gray's account of Houston in his diary is quoted from James, *The Raven*, 226.
2. Gray's diary, quoted in James, *The Raven*, 224.
3. Houston proclamation, March 2, 1836, in *Autobiography*, 99.
4. Houston, Day, Ullom, *Autobiography*, 100-101.
5. Quote in Gilbert, *Churchill, A Life*, 645.
6. Houston, *Life of General Sam Houston*, 7.
7. Houston, Day, Ullom, *Autobiography*, 101-102.
8. Yoakum, *History of Texas*, II, 105-106.
9. Houston, Day, Ullom, *Autobiography*, 104-105.
10. Houston, Day, Ullom, *Autobiography*, 104-105.
11. Houston, Day, Ullom, *Autobiography*, 104-105.
12. Houston to the chairman of the Military Committee, March 15, 1836, in *Autobiography*, 106; and Hockley to Secretary of War Rusk, March 21, 1836, in Yoakum, *History of Texas*, II, 478.
13. Houston to the chairman of the Military Committee, March 15, 1836, in *Autobiography*, 106;
14. Zuber, *My Eighty Years in Texas*, 63-64.
15. Zuber, *My Eighty Years in Texas*, 64, 71.
16. Zuber, *My Eighty Years in Texas*, 71.
17. Houston to Rusk, March 29, 1836, in Yoakum, *History of Texas*, II, 485-486.
18. Quote in Haley, *Sam Houston*, 117.
19. Houston to Rusk, March 29, 1836, in Yoakum, *History of Texas*, II, 480-482.
20. Quote in Haley, *Sam Houston*, 129.
21. Houston to Secretary of War Rusk, March 29, 1836, in Yoakum, *History of Texas*, II, 485-486.
22. Houston to Baker, April 5, 1836, in Yoakum, *History of Texas*, II, 492.
23. Hockley to Rusk, April 1, 1836, in Yoakum, *History of Texas*, II, 488-489.
24. Houston to Rusk, April 4, 1836, in Yoakum, History of Texas, II, 491.
25. Burnet to Houston, April 7, 1836. *Telegraph and Texas Register*, June 9, 1841.
26. Houston to David Thomas, Acting Secretary of War, April 13, 1836, in Yoakum, *History of Texas*, II, 496-497.

Notes to Chapter 10

1. Houston to David Thomas, Acting Secretary of War, April 13, 1836, in Yoakum, *History of Texas*, II, 496-497.

2. Houston to Citizens of Texas, April 13, 1836, in Yoakum, *History of Texas*, II, 495.
3. Houston, Day, Ullom, *Autobiography*, 117.
4. To the People of Texas, April 19, 1836, in *Autobiography*, 118.
5. Houston to Raguet, April 19, 1836, in Yoakum, *History of Texas*, II, 408.
6. Zuber, *My Eighty Years in Texas*, 85-87.
7. Houston, Day, Ullom, *Autobiography*, 121; and Labadie, "San Jacinto Campaign," in Day, ed., *Texas Almanac 1857-1873*, 155.
8. Houston, Day, Ullom, *Autobiography*, 119.
9. Houston, *Life of General Sam Houston*, 9.
10. Houston, *Life of General Sam Houston*, 9.
11. Houston, *Life of General Sam Houston*, 9.
12. Houston, *Life of General Sam Houston*, 9.
13. Houston to David G. Burnet, April 25, 1836, in Yoakum, *History of Texas*, II, 500.
14. McCullough in *Writings of Sam Houston*, VII, 25-326.
15. Houston to David G. Burnet, April 25, 1836, in Yoakum, *History of Texas*, II, 501.
16. Houston, *Life of General Sam Houston*, 10-11.
17. Houston, *Life of General Sam Houston*, 11; Zuber, *My Eighty Years in Texas*, 98.
18. Houston to the Army, May 5, 1836, in *Autobiography*, 124.
19. Houston, Day, Ullom, *Autobiography*, 122.

Notes to Chapter 11

1. Houston, *Life of General Sam Houston*, 12; Rusk to Houston, August 9, 1836, quoted in James, *The Raven*, 266.
2. Houston, Day, Ullom, *Autobiography*, 131; quoted in James, *The Raven*, 266; Houston, *Life of General Sam Houston*, 12.
3. Houston, *Life of General Sam Houston*, 12.
4. Houston, Day, Ullom, *Autobiography*, 132.
5. Houston, Day, Ullom, *Autobiography*, 132.
6. Houston, Day, Ullom, *Autobiography*, 132-133; Houston, *Life of General Sam Houston*, 12.
7. Houston, Day, Ullom, *Autobiography*, 138.
8. Houston to Jackson, September 20, 1836, in *Autobiography*, 134-135.
9. Houston, *Life of General Sam Houston*, 12.
10. Houston, Day, Ullom, *Autobiography*, 144-145.
11. Lubbock, *Six Decades in Texas*, 59-60.
12. Houston to Anna Raguet, January 29, 1837, in *Autobiography*, 139-140.
13. McKinney to S.M. Williams, November 3, 1838, quoted in James, *The Raven*, 302.
14. Houston to Texas Congress, June 6, 1837, in *Autobiography*, 147-148.
15. Houston to Ashbel Smith, May 31, 1838, in *Autobiography*, 157.
16. Houston to Andrew Jackson, August 11, 1838, in *Autobiography*, 158-159.
17. Houston, Day, Ullom, *Autobiography*, 160.

18. Houston, *Life of General Sam Houston*, 13.
19. Houston, *Life of General Sam Houston*, 13.
20. Margaret's poem is quoted in full in DeBruhl, *Sword of San Jacinto*, 265.
21. Houston to Anna Raguet, January 29, 1837, and Houston to Robert Irion, March 19, in *Autobiography*, 139-140, 141-142.
22. Margaret to Houston, July 17, 1839, in Roberts, ed., *The Personal Correspondence of Sam Houston*, I, 2-3.
23. Houston to Anna Raguet, December 10, 1839, in *Autobiography*, 163-164.
24. Roberts, ed., *The Personal Correspondence of Sam Houston*, I, 8.
25. Houston to Margaret, June 30, 1840, in Roberts, ed., *The Personal Correspondence of Sam Houston*, I, 4-5.
26. Margaret to Houston, August 1, 1839, in Roberts, ed., *The Personal Correspondence of Sam Houston*, I, 8.
27. Houston, Day, Ullom, *Autobiography*, 166-167.
28. Houston to Margaret, December 13, 1841, in Roberts, ed., *The Personal Correspondence of Sam Houston*, I, 134-136.
29. Houston, *Life of General Sam Houston*, 14.
30. Houston, Day, Ullom, *Autobiography*, 211.
31. Haley, *Sam Houston*, 250.

Notes to Chapter 12

1. For a narrative account of the Regulator-Moderator War, see O'Neal, *War in East Texas: Regulators vs. Moderators*.
2. Ashcroft, *The History of the War Between the Regulators and Moderators*, unpublished ms, 92-94, 100-101, 117; Daggett, *Recollections of the War of the Moderators and Regulators*, unpublished ms, 23-24.
3. Roberts, "The Shelby War," *Texas Magazine*, 13-14.
4. Ashcroft ms, 95.
5. *San Augustine Redlander*, August 17, 1844; Roberts, "The Shelby War," *Texas Magazine*, 16-17.
6. This proclamation may be found in Ashcroft ms, 121-122; and Crockett, *Two Centuries in East Texas*, 199-200.
7. Ashcroft, ms, 121-122; Bradley, ed., *A. Horton*, 38.
8. Daggett ms, 34.
9. Daggett ms, 34; Middleton, *Regulators and Moderators*, 26; Ashcroft ms, 122.
10. Williams and Barker eds. *Writings of Sam Houston*, IV, 361-362.
11. Williams and Barker, eds. *Writings of Sam Houston*, IV, 361-367. The correspondence cited in the text is within these pages in chronological order.
12. Middleton, *Regulators and Moderators*, 26; Ashcroft ms, 122.
13. Ashcroft ms, 123-16; Daggett ms, 34-35; Middleton, *Regulators and Moderators*, 26.
14. Houston to Smith, August 23, 1844. Williams and Barker, eds. *Writings of Sam Houston*, IV, 365-366.
15. Houston to Smith, August 23, 1844, 9 o'clock p.m.; Houston to Smith,

August 26, 1844. Williams and Barker, eds. *Writings of Sam Houston*, IV, 365-366. Williams and Barker, eds. *Writings of Sam Houston*, IV, 366-367.

16. Roberts, "The Shelby War," *Texas Magazine*, 18; Ashcroft ms, 134; Crockett, *Two Centuries in East Texas*, 224.

17. Malone, ed. A. Horton, 38; Roberts, "The Shelby War," *Texas Magazine*, 18; Ashcroft ms, 127. Local lore in Shelbyville relates that Sam Houston addressed the Regulator-Moderator prisoners in an oak grove just east of the courthouse square. But all contemporary accounts place the prisoners and Houston and his address in San Augustine. It is also believed locally that Houston made a political speech in Shelbyville during one of his many campaigns for office, an appearance which may have become confused with his Regulator-Moderator address.

Notes to Chapter 13

1. James, *The Raven*, 357.
2. Dyer quoted in James, *The Raven*, 359.
3. Houston, Day, Ullom, *Autobiography*, 218-219.
4. Houston, Day, Ullom, *Autobiography*, 218.
5. Houston, *Life of General Sam Houston*, 15.
6. Houston to Nicolas Dean, May 8, 1851, in *Autobiography*, 233.
7. Houston to Margaret, December 3, 1848, in *Autobiography*, 220.
8. Houston to Margaret, December 22, 1840, Correspondence, I, 51-53.
9. Houston to Margaret, December 31, 1840; September 25, 1840; December 25, 1840. Correspondence, I, 56-58; 27-28; 55-56.
10. Houston to John R. Burke, July 19, 1851; and response to ministers, July 1, 1853. Both in *Autobiography*, 233 and 238-240.
11. Houston, Day, Ullom, *Autobiography*, 224.
12. Houston to Yoakum, January 31, 1849, *Autobiography*, 221.
13. Houston, Day, Ullom, *Autobiography*, 224-226.
14. Henderson to Ashbel Smith, February 25, 1850.
15. Writings, V, 211-212.
16. Houston to Margaret, April 18, 1856, *Autobiography*, 243.
17. Houston to president-elect Pierce, January 28, 1853; and Houston to D. Miller, June 30, 1853. Both in *Autobiography*, 236-237 and 237-238.
18. Houston, Day, Ullom, *Autobiography*, 240-241.
19. Houston, Day, Ullom, *Autobiography*, 241-242.
20. Houston, Day, Ullom, *Autobiography*, 246-247.

Notes to Chapter 14

1. Houston to Thomas Rusk, May 12, 1857, *Autobiography*, 249.
2. Houston to Thomas Rusk, May 12, 1857, *Autobiography*, 249.
3. Terrell, "Recollections of General Sam Houston," SWHQ, XVI, October 1912.
4. Houston to Margaret, April 22, 1858, *Autobiography*, 254.

5. Barker and Williams, *Writings*, VII, 336-339.
6. Barker and Williams, *Writings*, VII, 343-367.
7. Houston to Sam, Jr., April 16, 1860, Roberts, ed., *The Personal Correspondence of Sam Houston*, IV, 362-363.
8. Webb, *Texas Rangers*, 197-216. Quotes on pp. 197 and 216.
9. Houston, Day, Ullom, *Autobiography*, 262.
10. Haley, *Sam Houston*, 373.
11. Houston to Texas citizens, November 20, 1860, in *Autobiography*, 268-269.
12. Houston, Day, Ullom, *Autobiography*, 270.
13. Houston, Day, Ullom, *Autobiography*, 271.
14. Clark, *Land of Promise*, 238.
15. Houston, to Am, Jr., May 22, 1861, in *Autobiography*, 274-275.
16. Related in James, *The Raven*, 418-419, and Haley, *Sam Houston*, 402.
17. Houston, speech at Independence, May 10, 1861, in *Autobiography*, 274.
18. Houston, speech at Houston, March 18, 1863, in *Autobiography*, 277.
19. Houston to Nancy "Nannie" Elizabeth, April 14 and 15, 1863, *Autobiography*, 279.
20. Houston, Day, Ullom, *Autobiography*, 282.

Notes to Chapter 15

1. Cox, "Old Sam Houston Song," *Texas Escapes Online Magazine*, (July 2006).
2. "Say Ho Lyrics." Songmeanings.com

Selected Bibliography

Ashcroft, Dr. Levi Henderson. "The History of the War Between the Regulator and Moderators of Shelby County." Unpublished manuscript, ca. 1953. Fondren Library, Southern Methodist University, Dallas.

Campbell, Randolph B. *Sam Houston and the American Southwest*. New York: Library of American Biography, 1993.

Clark, Joseph L. *A History of Texas, Land of Promise*. Boston: D.C. Heath and Company, 1939.

Cox, Mike. "Old Sam Houston Song." *Texas Escapes Online Magazine*, July 2006.

Crockett, G. L. *Two Centuries in East Texas*. Dallas: The Southwest Press, 1932.

Davis, Robert E., ed. *The Diary of William Barrett Travis, August 30, 1833-June 26, 1834*. Waco: Texian Press, 1966.

Daggett, Eph M. "Recollections of the War of the Moderators and Regulators." Unpublished manuscript available at the Shelby County Historical Museum, Center.

Day, James M., comp. *The Texas Almanac, 1857-1873: A Compendium of Texas History*. Waco: Texian Press, 1967.

De Bruhl, Marshall. *Sword of an Jacinto: A Life of Sam Houston*. New York: Random House, 1993.

Featherstonhaugh, G. W. *Excursion through the Slave States, from Washington on the Potomac to the Frontier Mexico*. 2 vols. London: John Murray, 1844.

Fehrenbach, T. R. *Lone Star, A History of Texas and the Texans*. New York: The Macmillan Company, 1968.

Flanagan, Sue. *Sam Houston's Texas*. Austin: University of Texas Press, 1964.

Ford, John Salmon. *Rip Ford's Texas*. Austin: University of Texas Press, 1963.

Friend, Llerena B. *Sam Houston, The Great Designer*. Austin: University of Texas Press, 1954.

Gilbert, Martin. *Churchill, A Life*. New York: Henry Holt and Company, 1991.

Haley, James L. *Sam Houston*. Norman: University of Oklahoma Press, 2002.

Hamilton, Jeff, as told to Lenoir Hunt. *My Master, The Inside Story of Sam Houston and His Times*, by His Former Slave. Austin: State House Press, 1992.

Hardin, Stephen L. *Texan Iliad, A Military History of the Texas Revolution, 1835-1836*. Austin: University of Texas Press, 1994.

Heitman, Francis B., comp. *Historical Register and Dictionary of the United States Army*. 2 vols. Washington, D.C.: Government Printing Office, 1903.

Hopewell, Clifford. *Sam Houston, Man of Destiny*. Austin: Eakin Press, 1987.

Houston, Sam. *The Life of General Sam Houston: A Short Biography*. Austin: The Pemberton Press, 1964 [1858].

Houston, Sam and Donald Day and Harry Herbert Ullom, eds. *The Autobiography of Sam Houston*. Norman: University of Oklahoma Press, 1954.

Hughes, W. J. *Rebellious Ranger: Rip Ford and the Old Southwest*. Norman: University of Oklahoma Press, 1964.

James, Marquis. *A Biography of Sam Houston*. Garden City, N.Y. Blue Ribbon Books, 1929.

Jones, Anson. *Memoranda and Official Correspondence Relating to the Republic of Texas, Its History and Annexation, 1836 to 1846*. A Rio Grande Classic, First published in 1859.

Linn, John J. *Reminiscences of Fifty Years in Texas*. New York: D.& J. Sadlier & Co., 1883.

Lubbock, Francis R. *Six Decades in Texas, or Memoirs of Francis R. Lubbock*. Austin Ben C. Jones, 1900.

McDonald, Archie P., ed. *Hurrah for Texas: The Diary of Aldolphus Sterne, 1838-1851*. Waco: Texian Press, 1969.

Martin, Mary L. "A Noted Talk." *Franklin Review and Journal*, September 1, 1881.

Middleton, John W. *History of the Regulators and Moderators and the Shelby County War in 1841 and 1842, in the Republic of Texas*. Fort Worth: Loving Publishing Company, 1883.

Niles' Weekly Register, 1831.

O'Neal, Bill. *War in East Texas: Regulators vs. Moderators*. Lufkin: Best of East Texas Publishers, 2006.

Pope, William F. *Early Days in Arkansas, Being for the Most Part the Personal Recollections of an Old Settler*. Little Rock: Frederick W. Allsopp, Publisher, 1895.

Roberts, Madge Thornall, ed. *The Personal Correspondence of Sam Houston*. 4 vols. Denton: University of North Texas Press, 1998-2001.

Roberts, O. M. "The Shelby County War, or the Regulators and Moderators." *Texas Magazine*, August 1897.

"Say Ho Lyrics." Songmeanings.com

Seale, William. *Sam Houston's Wife: A Biography of Margret Lea Houston*. Norman: University of Oklahoma Press, 1970.

Silverthorne, Elizabeth. *Ashbel Smith of Texas: Pioneer, Patriot, Statesman, 1805-1886*. College Station: Texas A&M Press, 1982.

Smith, Ashbel. "Reminiscences of the Texas Republic." *Historical Society of Galveston Series*, No. 1, 1876.

Smithwick, Noah. *The Evolution of a State: Or, Recollections of Old Texas Days*. Compiled by Nanna Smithwick Donaldson, Austin: Gamel Books, 1900.

Tinkle, Lon. *13 Days to Glory, The Siege of the Alamo*. New York: McGraw-Hill Book Company, Inc., 1958.

Webb, Walter Prescott. *The Texas Rangers, A Century of Frontier Defense*. Austin: University of Texas Press, 1935.

Williams, Amelia W., & Eugene C. Barker, eds. *The Writings of Sam Houston*, 6 vols. Austin: University of Texas Press, 1938-1843.

Wisehart, M. K. *Sam Houston, American Giant*. Washington: Robert B. Luce, Inc., 1962.

Yoakum, H. *History of Texas, From Its First Settlement in 1685 to Its Annexation to the United States in 1846*, 2 vols. New York: Redfield, 1855. Facsimile Reproduction of the Original by the Stock Company of Austin, 1935.

Zuber, William Physick. Janis Boyle Mayfield, ed. with notes and an introduction by Llerena Friend. *My Eighty Years in Texas*. Austin: University of Texas Press, 1971.

Index

Author Bio

Bill O'Neal currently is serving his second term as State Historian of Texas. As an ambassador for Texas history, Bill travels constantly across the Lone Star State, providing programs at schools and universities and a variety of historical events. His appearances have included several oc-casions honoring Sam Houston and the Battle of San Jacinto. He is a past pres-ident and fellow of the East Texas His-torical Association, and immediate past president of the West Texas Historical Association.

Bill is the author of more than 40 books, as well as 300 articles and book reviews. His most recent writing award, the A. C. Greene Literary Award, was presented at the 2015 West Texas Book Festival in Abilene. In 2012 Bill received the Lifetime Achievement Award of the Wild West Historical Association, and in 2007 he was named *True West Magazine's* Best Living Non-Fiction Writer.

Bill has appeared on TV documentaries on TBS, The History Chan-nel, The Learning Channel, CMT, A&E, and, currently,The American Heroes Channel Series, *Gunslingers*. During a long career at Panola College at Carthage, his most prestigious teaching award was a Piper Professorship, presented in 2000. In 2013 Panola's new dormitory was named Bill O'Neal Hall, and in that same year he received an honorary Doctor of Letters degree from his alma mater, Texas A&M University at Commerce.

Bill's four daughters all have entered the field of education, and he is the proud grandfather of seven grandchildren. His wife Karon teaches math at Panola College. She works closely with Bill on his books, and after his appointment as State Historian she cheerfully agreed to be his Chief of Staff.

CPSIA information can be obtained at www.ICGtesting.com
Printed in the USA
BVOW02s1214290416

445799BV00012B/158/P

9 781681 790374